Little White Lies

Paul Thomas Anderson

ADAM NAYMAN

Masterworks

Abrams, New York

PTA
MASTERWORKS

As a gift to Homo Sapiens,
Adam Nayman
M.O.C., PhD, MD

CONTENTS

Foreword
Josh and Benny Safdie

"I'm really drunk . . . really, I am. I'm out of my head. I'm so wasted—I'm really wasted. . . . Really Dirk, I'm really just wasted. I'm crazy right now. I'm really crazy. You know?"

Dirk rushes back inside—hoping to catch the clock strike midnight as it marks the end of a year he owned—leaving Scotty alone with his Dirk Diggler—wannabe car still sticky from a crummy paint job. Scotty gets inside (I don't believe he's half as drunk as he claims to be) and sobs to himself, "I'm a fuckin idiot! . . I'm a fuckin' idiot . . . Fuckin' idiot! Fuckin' idiot! Fuckin' idiot! Fuckin' idiot!" The Watts 103rd Street Rhythm Band kicks in and its cool laissez-faire vibe represses your own loneliness deep down to a place you know will come back to haunt you.

I was fourteen or so when I saw *Boogie Nights* for the first time. It was our first film by Paul Thomas Anderson. Our introduction to his work coincided with the beginning of a life-long journey and obsession with Al Goldstein and his late-night public-access show *Midnight Blue* (which a few years later would host Anderson's subversive Frank T.J. Mackey's 900-number commercial). *Boogie Nights* is a movie that wears its fascinations and obsessions on its sleeve. Suffice it to say: There was a lot of overlap on the Venn diagram.

Don't know what it says about us, but as much as we relate to Dirk's quest for "real imported Italian leather," it was the Scotty, the Rollergirl, the Buck Swope, or even the Kurt Longjohn wanting to talk about lighting with Little Bill while his wife has an "ass in her cock" that cut us deep. Anderson fills his movies with peripheral Characters that feel like the center of their own films.

I remember being a young teen watching the "Fuckin' idiot" scene (as it would become dubbed) with Philip Seymour Hoffman. I remember rewatching it . . . Rewinding it . . . rewatching just that scene, trying to 'understand' it. Here we had a moment of cosmic humanity in the midst of a film told in the "Hollywood-style". It was so lived-in. Bravura filmmaking by a twenty-six-year-old.

When *Punch-Drunk Love* came out, I was eighteen. We had grown up with Adam Sandler. In particular, we had grown up with and obsessed over his first two comedy records. The jewel cases were monuments. Then came his movies, which were always perfect. As kids we loved comedies. Comedies were "the movies." The serious stuff that our dad showed us to help us better understand life is simply that: "Life."

They were not even called movies. They were the things that weren't out to make us laugh, but to rescue answers from the wholly ambiguous. These films moved us, but Sandler's were our first religion: Absurdist tales about pulling through in your own weird way despite everyone and everything conspiring against you.

As we grew older, the type of movies that our dad obsessed over eventually became part of our own personal wanderings. Some of those films were by Paul Thomas Anderson. Movies like *Boogie Nights* unlocked a gateway to a trove of other films by filmmakers of the seventies like Robert Altman . . . *Boogie Nights* was a manhole to our own sewers, a passageway for ourselves away from the ones our dad forged. Of course, we still watched Sandler films, but they started to mean something else. They were, and will always remain, "pure" to us. Remember our dad was the one who turned us onto Sandler to begin with. So you could imagine the inner psychic whirlpool when *Punch-Drunk Love* came out. It was a "Sandler" film, but through this realist formalist lens. Happy learned how to putt.

Of course, everyone points to the explosive rage in the scene where Barry smashes those panes of glass, but it's the first-date dinner scene that blew and continues to blow our minds. It's the intricate yet loud micro-performing—like the way Hoffman put his hand on Wahlberg's back when he leans forward to check his ride, Sandler's instinctual wrist flick when Lena brings up the hammer story from his youth . . . or the leg bouncing while the manager confronts him about destroying the bathroom . . . or the bathroom destruction itself!

Sandler's rage and inner madness was being filtered through Anderson's subtle microscope and, yes, it was still funny and entertaining. But now it was also begging us to ask ourselves about our own repressions. . . . It forced us to recall Sandler's previous films through a new lens. The worlds were no longer mutually exclusive . . . they could co-exist.

For that, we owe Anderson everything. . . .

For his documentary-style blocking. . . . For his deft, warm allegories of impossible people. . . . For his repertoire of actors shuffling around playing different characters from film to film—like a big book of stories—like the films of Fassbinder, Cassavetes, Altman, or Sandler. . . . For recording hundreds of firecrackers hoping to find that "one" that CRACKS. . . .

For the performances zapped-alive in a composed frame like controlled experiments. . . . For the formalism that feels perfectly in tune with the subject matter. . . . For the realism found in that formalism. . . . For the shared obsessions. . . . For reflecting the psychic creative god-complex conundrum that IS filmmaking in masterpieces like *Phantom Thread, There Will Be Blood* and *The Master.* . . . For each and every event a film of his becomes. . . .

. . . For being **vanguard** always. 🍒

Introduction

"Maybe he is the most demanding man," says Alma (Vicky Krieps) in the opening scene of *Phantom Thread* (2017). The "he" in question is Reynolds Woodcock (Daniel Day-Lewis), a celebrated designer of high-end women's fashion, whose imprimatur is an aspirational status symbol for those who can only dream of affording it. Alma's introduction not only ensures that Reynolds's reputation precedes him, it also cues us to see the man's demandingness as his defining trait. In tandem with the subsequent, fetishistically detailed sequence depicting the great dressmaker's daily ablutions—a straight razor shave, vigorous shoe polishing, gangly legs sheathed in purple stockings— the phrasing generates an expectation of gold-plated standards, and that the film to follow will be a portrait of the artist as an emissary of rigorous discipline.

THE MOST DEMANDING

It would do a disservice to the complexity of _Phantom Thread_ to describe it as a film that begins and ends with Reynolds in the bathroom—from primping to purging. But if there's one thing that this most sardonically scatological of romantic comedies requires—one thing that, like its self-monogramming (anti-)hero, it demands—it's an unclenched perspective. For all its forbidding, foreboding atmosphere, _Phantom Thread_ is a surpassingly funny movie, and the satisfaction of seeing a figure as singularly fastidious as Reynolds come progressively unruffled has a component of pure, ecstatic schadenfreude.

Few directors are as fascinated by the spectacle of carefully maintained facades crumbling as Paul Thomas Anderson. Think of the alpha machismo of Tom Cruise's Frank T.J. Mackey ebbing away during a calamitous night in the San Fernando Valley in _Magnolia_ (1999). Or of cult leader Lancaster Dodd (Philip Seymour Hoffman) inadvertently undercutting his own grandiloquent psychobabble with an angry epithet in _The Master_ (2012). Or of Day-Lewis's tight-lipped oilman Daniel Plainview coming unglued during a church service in _There Will Be Blood_ (2007), crying out "I've abandoned my child" in abject, guilty humiliation, knee bent in resentful deference towards a higher power. Breakdowns are Anderson's specialty; in light of his fixation with physical and psychological deterioration, it's no wonder he eventually made a film called _Inherent Vice_ (2014).

Phantom Thread imagines a scenario where the journey from hubris to humiliation results not only in a leveling effect, but a kind of liberation as well. As a piece of filmmaking, it is a tour-de-force of artistic control, matching the formal assurance of his other films without relying on or succumbing to their wild tonal and rhythmic shifts. Yet buried at the center of _Phantom_

Thread—or, to take up its script's various embroidery metaphors, stitched into its lining—is an insistence on the necessity, for Reynolds as well as the martinet-ish mindset he represents, of embracing helplessness and, with it, release: Of recognizing that purity and Puritanism are not natural conditions.

The author of this revelation will turn out to be Alma, who is initially willing to humor her husband's control-freak tendencies. "I have given him what he desires most," she says towards the end of the film's prologue: "Every piece of me." Her dreamy appraisal of her relationship with Reynolds paints married life less as a blessed union than an ultimatum met, yet she also insists on finessing the terms of her submission. Her resourcefulness gives *Phantom Thread* its shape as both a domestic farce and a meditation on balance and equilibrium, with both qualities embodied in a final two-shot that transforms the widescreen frame into a frieze of complicity and collaboration. If Reynolds is the "most demanding man," then it is Alma who is at once his enabler and his equal, not to mention the person best-suited to teach him a lesson in humility.

The degree to which *Phantom Thread* asks—or demands—to be understood as an especially personal film for its creator is debatable. The media narrative around its release seemed to conclude that, both on its own terms and in contrast to the more historically oriented and/ or literary derived narratives of *There Will Be Blood* (a loose adaptation of Upton Sinclair's 1927 novel *Oil!*), *The Master* (a veiled account of the history of Scientology) and *Inherent Vice* (a largely faithful transposition of Thomas Pynchon's 2009 novel), the prism of self-portraiture was the most apt entry point. "It hardly seems an accident that Paul Thomas Anderson has inscribed his monogram in the title of his eighth feature," wrote A.O. Scott in the *New York Times*; "this is a profoundly, intensely, extravagantly personal film . . . [that] almost offhandedly lays out intriguing analogies between Reynolds's metier and [Anderson's]."

In an interview with *Collider*, Anderson addressed both the genesis of the project and the idea of Reynolds as an exacting workaholic who has to be manipulated into relaxing his professional drives:

> *When I get sick, I deal with it in a few different ways. First, I get very cranky and I pretend that I'm not sick because I don't want to be slowed down. I don't want to miss anything. Usually, that can work. But if that doesn't work, and you get really sick and you're flat on your back, you need help and you become vulnerable. I remember that I was very sick, just with the flu, and I looked up and my wife [Maya Rudolph] looked at me with tenderness that made me think, "I wonder if she wants to keep me this way, maybe for a week or two." I was watching the wrong movies when I was in bed, during this illness. I was watching* Rebecca, The Story of Adele H., *and* Beauty and the Beast, *and I really started to think that maybe she was poisoning me. So, that kernel of an idea, I had in my mind when I started working on writing something.*

Unsurprisingly for a filmmaker who by 2017 was entering his third decade of parrying press requests—his career having been, since the splashy premiere of his debut feature *Hard Eight* (1996) in the Un Certain Regard section of the Cannes Film Festival, a going and high-priority concern for film journalists in the United States and beyond—Anderson's anecdote makes for good copy, perhaps even to the point of doing critics' work for them. The conflation of the director's own marital dynamic with Rudolph (a star comedian whom he met while she was part of the cast of *Saturday Night Live* in the late nineties) with the characters of Reynolds and Alma is provocative, endearing, and coyly self-deprecating in line with a contemporary celebrity culture proffering the private lives of stars as a public concern. The citation of three well-known older films as subconscious touchstones fulfills the similarly established conceit of Anderson as a conscientious and encyclopedic cinephile who wears his inspirations proudly and flamboyantly on his sleeve.

NEW NEW HOLLYWOOD

The auteurist turn in film criticism in the 1950s has had enduring consequences in terms of how cinema is categorized and canonized. "In order to criticize a movie, you have to make another one," quipped Jean-Luc Godard, and the praxis of JLG and his fellow critics-turned-filmmakers yielded a series of New Waves with comparably insurrectionist

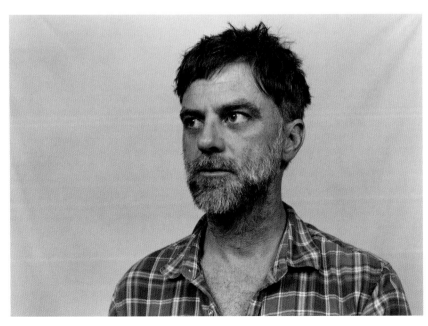

aims. It also unleashed a tendency in reviewers to emphasize the primacy and temperament of the director like never before. This practice was then taken up so widely that auteurism's original purpose of sussing out individual signatures within a highly standardized studio system—of, we might say, untangling phantom threads—was revised. Its new direction: Inventorying and, more crucially, enshrining easily visible idiosyncrasies and (often) ostentatious directorial displays, frequently, if not necessarily, at the expense of acknowledging other collaborators.

Of all the myriad industrial subplots and mythologies connected to this shift, the valorization of the leading figures of the New Hollywood casts the longest shadow. *How the Sex-Drugs-and-Rock-N'-Roll-Generation Saved Hollywood* is the subtitle of Peter Biskind's dishily definitive *Easy Riders, Raging Bulls* (1998); the book's Icarus-tinged narrative, which breathlessly chronicles the cohort's meteoric rise and collective fall from grace (the latter condition embodied by Michael Cimino's *Heaven's Gate* (1980)) is irresistible. Which is why it keeps getting told, over and over; ironically, given Biskind's implicit skepticism towards the franchise mentality inaugurated at the end of the decade by *Star Wars*, other authors have more or less sequelized his argument. James Mottram's 2006 book *The Sundance Kids: How the Mavericks Took Back Hollywood* proposes that the loose grouping of Alexander Payne, Sofia Coppola, David O. Russell, and the Andersons (Wes and P.T.), were hard-charging inheritors, or maybe keepers of a wavering flame. Meet the New New Hollywood, same as the Old New Hollywood.

By this postmodern calculus, it was Paul Thomas Anderson whose dutifully annotated, avowedly seventies-inflected, and, above all, personally assertive films—ones that served more effectively as star turns for their director even as, by the time of *Magnolia*, they could countenance the participation of a present-tense megastar like Tom Cruise—mounted the most compelling case on two fronts: To be granted entry directly to the old canon or placed at the epicenter of a new one. It's not just that the eight features Anderson has made since 1996 have been well-reviewed, with the Oscar-winning *There Will Be Blood* ensconced as a proverbial modern classic upon release, its reputation shored up via numerous "best of the decade" polls. With Anderson, what has often been at stake in the reception of his films, positive and negative, is nothing less than the status of a heroic—indeed, mythic—auteurism, bridging past and present, personal and populist. In 2012, the *Guardian* called him "the most devout filmmaker of his generation," a designation flipped on its head in 2019 by *Variety*'s Owen Gleiberman, who disparagingly referred to "the cult of PTA" in an attempt to leverage the filmmaker's critical reverence against itself—as a sign of too-worshipful groupthink. "Anderson enjoys unearned good will among today's film nerds," wrote Armond White in 2007; "[he's] the small white hope for Gen-Xers wishing that there was a Griffith, Stroheim, Ford, Wyler, Vidor, or Stevens among them."

Hyerbole begets hyperbole, and for all the extreme rhetoric surrounding Anderson and his work it's undeniable that both lend themselves to auteurist analysis. Such is the tack taken by critics who've mapped a vast yet familiar constellation of themes and character types onto each new film: Dysfunctional families; wayward fathers and disconsolate sons; social and cultural alienation; shysters and salesmen; the passage of time and the reinvention of the self. There has also been ample discussion of recurring stylistic traits: Assertive, mobile camerawork; elliptical editing; heavy reliance on both orchestral and pop scores. And there's the idea of Anderson as an "actor's director," evinced both by the consistently high quality of performance in his films (with Day-Lewis copping an Oscar for *There Will Be Blood*) and the tendency of certain actors (John C. Reilly, Luis Guzmán, Julianne Moore, Philip Baker Hall, William H. Macy, Joaquin Phoenix, Philip Seymour Hoffman) to work with him on multiple occasions. That none of Anderson's films have been box-office champions doesn't weaken the case for deconstruction. In the context of the seventies myth, where *Star Wars* infantilized studios and audiences in one fell swoop and ushered in an age of Empire, the understanding that ambitious, challenging American films are now mostly for a self-selecting (read: Elite) audience increases the urgency for auteurist approbation—the urge to assert that these are films that will stand up in the midst of a disposable movie culture.

ANYTHING FOR A SHOT

Paul Thomas Anderson was born in Studio City, Los Angeles, in June of 1970, the seventh of nine children. His childhood neighborhood, located deep in the San Fernando Valley, was also submerged figuratively within show business at what would later become the intersection of Radford Avenue and Ventura Park. In Thom Andersen's 2003 essay film *Los Angeles Plays Itself*, the filmmaker notes that the city's name is too often used interchangeably with "Hollywood," reducing a real place to a "metonym for the motion picture industry," but Studio City's name is distinctly nonmetaphorical, referring to the production complex erected in 1927 by Mack Sennett; if not quite ground zero for the city's cinematic legacy then close enough.

He also grew up in a show-business family. Anderson's father, Ernie, had been a minor celebrity as a presenter for the Cleveland television station Channel 8; his character, Ghoulardi, was a postmodern creation, a living riff on the mad scientists populating vintage sci-fi movies who also happened to act and talk like a beatnik-homage, and send-up in one self-reflexive package. By openly mocking the genre films he presented during a late-night slot, Ghoulardi prefigured the modus operandi of *Mystery Science Theater 3000*. His was a multidirectional sarcasm, with one-liners directed at unhip cultural figures (Lawrence Welk, Mike Douglas) and even the show's implied midwestern audience, although the winking hostility was part of the joke.

In time, Paul Thomas Anderson would come to name his production company after his father, and Ernie's shadow looms over his son's career in ways that have been both explicitly acknowledged and presumptuously intuited by critics. A 2008 *Esquire* profile pointed out that for a director whose films are suffused with autobiographical and familial details—the frantic gaggle of siblings in *Punch-Drunk Love* (2002); the local-TV station backdrop of *Magnolia*; the Navy sequences in *The Master*, which correspond to the time of Ernie's enlistment—Anderson has been hesitant to talk about his past. "Most stories about [him] offer some variation on 'very little is known about his early years,'" wrote John H. Richardson, who nevertheless pieced together a portrait of a kid who grew up in joint thrall to his outsized icon of a father—who, after relocating to Los Angeles, became the voice of ABC and a fixture on the neighborhood party circuit—and the television industry itself. Paul attended an elite private school, styling himself as a fast-talking cutup; at age twelve, he was gifted a Betamax camera and began making short movies starring his dad and his TV star friends.

The "movie brat" narrative is a well-worn one, with Steven Spielberg as its most celebrated archetype: The suburban kid chasing glory with a hand-cranked camera (J.J. Abrams's Spielberg homage from 2011, *Super 8*, turns the myth into an actual sci-fi blockbuster). In Anderson's case, the vignettes don't sound particularly innocent: "Instead of taking drugs," recalled one childhood friend, "we'd try to fuck with people and film it." By the time Anderson was in high school—and after being enrolled in a series of other schools—he was carrying himself like a full-fledged filmmaker, cranking out juvenile parodies, some of which proved more disposable than others. It was during this period that Anderson made *The Dirk Diggler Story*, an affectionate tribute to the porn star John Holmes that, just over a decade later, provided the raw material for his mainstream breakthrough *Boogie Nights* (1997).

By the time Anderson started actual film school at NYU, he carried himself like a young old-pro, famously dropping out after passing off a David Mamet script as his own writing sample (the C+ grade he received served as a justification for quitting). He found work in production, including as an assistant on a game show (an experience that would inform the writing of *Magnolia*) and on a PBS drama starring the character actor Philip Baker Hall, whom Anderson had admired in a supporting role in Martin Brest's action-comedy *Midnight Run* (1988). Anderson was such a fan, in fact, that he wrote a script specifically for Hall, a short entitled *Cigarettes & Coffee*, which he made in 1993 with a borrowed Panaflex camera and private financing. What was supposed to be a quick shoot ballooned to three weeks as Anderson, then twenty-three, displayed an unwillingness to compromise despite his lack of experience. He was, as Richardson writes, "still living by his teenage motto—'anything for a shot.'" But the results spoke for themselves: *Cigarettes & Coffee* played at Sundance, garnering acclaim and earning Anderson a spot in the festival's filmmaking lab the following summer, where he developed the feature screenplay that would become *Hard Eight*.

Generally, the prevalence of literal and figurative father-son relationships in Anderson's cinema, starting with *Hard Eight*'s surrogate dad narrative and finding their fullest flower in *Magnolia*'s paternal pathos plays, has been suggested by critics as a Rosetta Stone for his body of work. Another approach would be to trace a correlation between Anderson and his protagonists, beginning with John C. Reilly's hard-luck *Hard Eight* hero—a fast learner in search of a tutor—and culminating in the aforementioned Anderson-as-Reynolds Woodcock proposition. Directorial doppelgängers abound in his films; at one point in *Phantom Thread*, Reynolds tells Alma about his tendency to sew personal items into the linings of his creations, "things that I always knew were there." *Boogie Nights* also demands such a reading, with Anderson figured in both the emergent, in-demand male ingenue Eddie Adams/Dirk Diggler (Mark Wahlberg) and the crafty, demanding artiste Jack Horner (Burt Reynolds). While *Magnolia* doesn't contain a comparable stand-in, its unrestrained millennial anxiety can be interpreted as an expression of a then-thirty-year-old writer/director trying to make a masterwork before the clock runs out on his creative freedom.

From there—following the strange screwball detour of *Punch-Drunk Love*—the rerouting of Anderson's cinema towards obsessive, individual character studies set against historical backdrops—the oil fields of *There Will Be Blood*; the midcentury psychodrama of *The Master*; the Summer of Love simulacrum of *Inherent Vice*—has been used to support other auteurist readings: Anderson as what Nick Pinkerton calls "the historian and chronicler of driftless individuals and the sad secret life of the United States." Most extended studies of Anderson's career propose a straightforward evolution, or perhaps a series of them, all predicated on the perception of artistic growth along a horizontal axis. There is a convincing argument to make for Anderson moving from the callow bravado of youth, of films kitted out in naked ambition and received technique, to a middle age marked by a more advanced and original personal style—from promise to fulfillment, apprenticeship to mastery.

By this logic, *Phantom Thread* is Anderson's "mature" masterwork. Yet the film's wry self-reflexivity also hints that we should proceed with caution as far as auteurism goes. "Mastery" is a central, fragile concept here, with the imperious, revered Reynolds ultimately unveiled as a commitment-phobic fuddy-duddy with mommy issues: He is, finally, a joke, albeit, as viewed through the prism of Alma's dedication, a loveable one. In the same way that Anderson's anecdote about his wife's predatory bedside manner demystifies some of *Phantom Thread*'s carefully brocaded inscrutability, the filmmaker's confession during the same interview cycle that the name of the film's main character was the result of a giddy months-long correspondence between director and star indicates that jokes are a big part of the film's makeup. "[Day-Lewis and I] were texting back and forth trying to come up with names, and he came up with that one, and I fucking choked on my cornflakes," Anderson told *GQ*, elaborating further in an interview with *Vulture*:

> We were making each other laugh, texting each other back and forth like teenagers, trying to come up with names . . . it was lingering around but not quite right, and then the text from Daniel came through: "Reynolds Woodcock." And on two simultaneous coasts, we both started laughing so deeply and so hard that I suddenly had tears pouring down my face. I thought, "We can't do that, right? Of course we can't. But . . . we have to do that!" I remember calling him, and he was laughing as much as I was, and I said, "We've got to do this. Let me write it into the script and we'll live with it. We'll try it on for size."

Size matters in the films of Paul Thomas Anderson—and so does
innuendo. The title of *Hard Eight* refers to a dice roll in a craps game,
but it also has unmistakable phallic connotations. Strip away *Boogie Nights*'s
layers of historical and cinematic allusion and it's the story of a penis so
large and remarkable that its owner is reduced to an attachment (or else
obliged to wield it as his weapon of choice). In *Magnolia*, Cruise's self-help
guru—a character who has found his cultural context twenty years later in
a moment where male-grievance grifting has migrated online—uses
"respect the cock!" as an overcompensatory battle cry. The protagonists
of *Punch-Drunk Love*, *There Will Be Blood*, *Inherent Vice,* and especially *The
Master* can be read as either cosmically or microscopically cock-blocked:
"Stick it back in, it fell out," laughs Freddie Quell (Joaquin Phoenix) at the
close of the latter, a throbbing psychosexual odyssey that also proffers, as
its proxy for L. Ron Hubbard's *Excalibur*, an epic tome called *The Split Saber*.
This title's implied castration anxiety ranks as the finest dick joke in the
veritable House of Woodcock that comprises Anderson's filmography.

The intersection of penis worship and auteurism—increasingly
problematized and called out by a popular and academic film culture bent
on revising the implicit imbalances fostered by the veneration of straight,
white male filmmakers—is obvious enough. It is also completely inescapable
in Anderson's case. To pretend that the cult around a filmmaker whose
gifts and cinephilic fixations are to a large extent bound up in his privilege,
and whose early-career outlawry (i.e., dropping out of film school) speaks
similarly to an insulated and elevated position, is entirely about what's
on-screen, is disingenuous. So is ignoring the fact that what actually is
on-screen, in terms of subject matter, setting, and politics (class and
otherwise), lines up with that same comparatively front-running, white
demographic. While it's not quite true to say that Anderson's films are
fully whitewashed—*Hard Eight*, *Boogie Nights*, *Magnolia,* and *Inherent
Vice* all feature significant African-American characters—there has been
commentary about the relative deracination of his Los Angeles; that the
only excised subplot from *Magnolia* foregrounded black characters doesn't
help his case. Similarly, Anderson has been pilloried by some critics for
perceived misogyny, a charge that doesn't so much cancel out the fine,
acclaimed work by female actors in his films as prompt an examination
of how the characters they portray function—often more perfunctorily
than his male protagonists, with less depth and shading past what the
performers bring to their roles.

One consequence of auteurist criticism divorced from the cultural
context that generated it in the first place is writing that becomes
tantamount to cheerleading—the stroking, in prose, of already tumescent
reputations. With this in mind, I will attempt to follow my subject's own
lead in not taking the House of Woodcock and its implied self-importance
all too seriously, while also prodding its conceptual foundations—both in
Anderson's films and my own impulse to study them. The search for potency
is present as much in the films' reception as it is on screen; in the same way
that Anderson's characters search for salvation and fulfillment—and, in the
mirrored rom-com parodies of *Punch-Drunk Love* and *The Master*, for the
relief of orgasm—critics in the Biskind-Mottram mold who see Hollywood
as perpetually in need of "saving" have anointed Anderson as their white
knight (the heroic iteration of White's sarcastically invoked and rhetorically
neutered "small white hope").

It is in the interest of scrambling that romantic narrative that I've opted
to look at Anderson's films not in the order that they were released but
rather—with one important and, I think, justifiable exception—in the order
in which they are set. Besides preventing the umpteenth reiteration of the
boy-to-man-to-master monomyth (let's leave the Joseph Campbellisms
to Lancaster Dodd), one goal of this arrangement is to let each film exist
on its own terms rather than as stops on a retrospectively determined

auteur-pilgrim's progress. Another goal is to try, both in my own analysis and via the inclusion of interviews with Anderson's collaborators, to stress the extent to which other people are responsible for what is sometimes understood (or sold) as a purely individual virtuosity. Again, *Phantom Thread* gestures persuasively in this direction by showing how the House of Woodcock stands primarily through the anonymous but expert labor of its seamstresses. When a badly damaged dress is rescued by an all-night sewing session, Reynolds is off retching in the next room; after it's been rescued, we understand that he's still going to get all the credit anyway. The artists I spoke to for this book were all wonderfully forthcoming about their contributions to Anderson's films, and if there was generally agreement among them about his qualities as a director, it had less to do with his embodiment of artistic authority than his entreaty to let them create on their own terms. What is the lovely, sub-feature-length documentary *Junun* [2015] but an expression of Anderson's curiosity in Jonny Greenwood's music-making process?

Finally, by placing Anderson's films in this order, I want to take another critical commonplace about his work—the extent to which the city of Los Angeles, and more specifically, the San Fernando Valley, exists as another character in these stories—and expand it to the same epic proportions quested after in his "historical" films. *There Will Be Blood* unfolds in an unsettled, forbiddingly flat California in the 1890s and spans three decades as its blank stone canvas gets filled in and built up. Daniel Plainview's oil derrick thrusting upwards against the sky is as much a symbol of modernity as male potency; the film is, at its molten core, a drama about a man remaking a state in his own image.

There Will Be Blood ends in 1927, with both its protagonist and the country around him mired in a Great Depression; *The Master* picks up a couple of decades later to focus on a character struggling to find his bearings amidst post-World War II prosperity. Keep moving forward through *Inherent Vice*'s Vietnam-era mystery tour and foreshocks of global corporate capitalism and *Boogie Nights*'s allegory of the cultural and cinematic transition between the 1970s and eighties, and you arrive in the 1990s—and at the beginning of Anderson's filmmaking story—with *Hard Eight*. From there, *Magnolia* looms as a millennial monolith and *Punch-Drunk Love* as a happy ending, although the real endpoint is *Phantom Thread*, a film whose play with time places it outside the rest of Anderson's work even as it subsumes and refines the qualities of its predecessors.

The result of this shuffling, respecting fictional chronology rather than a production timeline, is risky in the context of an auteurist study, but yields something of value beyond replicating the subject's own playfully postmodernist gaze. What emerges is a largely localized yet hugely allusive and expansive cinematic century, a social, economic, architectural and psychogeographic history in which LA—the epicenter of Anderson's cinematic universe—not only plays itself but comes of age, one era at a time.

If one hallmark of auteurism is consistency, Anderson's insistence on staging his films on home turf fits the bill while also generating a dialectic between the perceived boldness of his approach and a possible in-built timidity about wandering too far afield. "Write what you know," goes the old writer's-workshop chestnut, and what Anderson knows—and loves, wholly if ambivalently, and in his own way despite so many others having gotten there first—is the San Fernando Valley: Its flat horizontal topography and winding side streets; its proximity to showbiz; its transient menagerie of wanderers who've headed west in the spirit of manifest destiny, getting as far as the final paving stone before hitting the beach. For all his other sundry accomplishments, Anderson's ability to mingle fidelity and imagination in the representation of his hometown may be his defining trait, or at the very least a sign of how deeply he has been defined by his surroundings.

Writing in *Grantland* in 2014, Molly Lambert examined the relationship between the Valley's spatial layout and Anderson's fondness for complex lateral storytelling:

Paul Thomas Anderson, like his LA forefather Robert Altman, embraces the sprawl. Why not tell several different stories with loose threads? Why limit yourself to one great performance in a movie if you can get 20? Why pick one genre when you can pull from everything and make movies that push the whole idea of genre to its city limits?

The minor exceptions to this rule are the short films, music videos, and side projects that Anderson has produced at odd intervals over the last twenty-five years, some of which are included here. The major exception is *Phantom Thread*, which is set in England in the early 1950s, and which I will return to towards the end of this book in the kind of detail warranted by its exquisite realization. For what it's worth, it is my personal favorite of Anderson's films, perhaps because above and beyond the themes and tropes more commonly attributed to his oeuvre—all those bad, sad dads and fateful cruises through the Valley—it's a movie about time, offering an attenuated, exquisite elaboration on the sublime moment in *There Will Be Blood* where the passage of fifteen years is delineated in the space of a single match cut.

There, a pair of children hopping off a porch gives way to a wedding ring slipping onto a woman's finger, collapsing youth and adulthood into one intimate, upward movement. *Phantom Thread* contains a comparably fleeting sequence that, in its own way, complicates *There Will Be Blood's* breathless, beautiful evocation of matrimony as forward progress; I'll get there eventually. Its overall treatment of time is as a transient field to be inhabited rather than conquered—a reality that exists in pitiless, indifferent contrast to both Reynolds's fear and Alma's desire as they edge perilously towards commitment. This seems to me to be *Phantom Thread's* most affecting and unsettling aspect, rendering as it does the demands being made by the characters, of each other and of themselves, simultaneously more pressing and more futile.

"Nobody can stand for as long as I can," remarks Alma of her chosen fate as Reynolds's muse. While her endurance is impressive, it cannot staunch the flow of time. The eruptive side of Anderson's films—their eccentric outbursts and erratic ellipses, their wild detours and leaps of faith—can plausibly be celebrated (or dismissed) as showmanship, but it also expresses a fundamental understanding of inherent vice: That the center cannot hold. If in the longview, his films stand up—whether as examples of ingenious and enduring engineering, glittering edifices to artistic self-regard, or markers of both their actual and imagined time and place—it is paradoxically because of their acknowledgement, so achingly direct in places or else lurking in the corners of the frame (and the back of our minds) that nothing is ever built to last. 🐦

here's gold in them thar hills," exclaims Colonel Mulberry Sellers in Mark Twain's 1892 novel *The American Claimant*, a galumphing picaresque about an eccentric midwesterner trying to infiltrate the British aristocracy. First introduced as a supporting character in Twain's 1873 book *The Gilded Age: A Tale of Today*, Sellers reflects Twain's satirical vision of a young republic driven by grift. As a confidence man, the colonel is his own best client: Eternally optimistic despite his dire financial straits, he's a portrait of an American daydreamer who tries to sweep up those around him into a similar delirium.

The story goes that Twain derived the expression "there's gold in them thar hills" from a speech given by a metallurgist, Dr. Matthew Fleming Stephenson, who was attempting to halt the exodus of local miners westward in 1849. "Why go to California?" Stephenson queried the employees of Georgia's mighty Dahlonega Mint. "In that ridge lies more gold than man ever dreamt of. There's millions in it." That latter line also ended up in *The American Claimant*, but Stephenson's provincialist rhetoric proved unpersuasive to its target audience. Over the next decade, some 300,000 Americans decamped to California to chase their fortune in a massive and mercenary migration that would reshape the social and economic topography of the state, especially after the revelation that other, more liquid riches were buried in the soil.

In 1931, the guitar-slinger Frankie Marvin recorded a tribute to the Gold Rushers that transformed Twain's catchphrase into a folk-Utopian sing-along:

> *I could go to China, for China's full of tea*
> *But I'm off for California, that's the place for me*
> *For there's gold in them thar hills*

There's gold in them thar hills
I'm off to California
For there's gold in them thar hills.

Paul Thomas Anderson opens *There Will Be Blood* with a view of them thar hills, preceded by a stark title card. In this arrangement, the phrase "There Will Be Blood" scans as a sinister twin to Mulberry's rallying cry, similarly promissory but drenched in consequence. The location is New Mexico circa 1898, not California, and the man who is introduced in the film's second shot is prospecting for silver rather than gold. Yet he's still recognizable as a cousin to Frankie Marvin's striver, or else an expatriate of Twain's "Gilded Age:" An American claimant, trying to will all that glittering, sardonic promise into material reality.

For the first seven minutes of *There Will Be Blood*, we watch as this shadowy interloper repeatedly negotiates the perilously narrow confines of the mine shaft that he's carved, seemingly by himself and over a long period of time, into the gray expanse of rock. Emerging and descending at his own methodical pace, he's an infernal figure moving in a Sisyphean rhythm, and the trajectory of his movements—grueling ascents and sudden, punishing drops along a vertical axis, punctuating an otherwise steady horizontal forward progress—establishes the visual and narrative patterning of the film to come. The image of the miner's signature on an assayer's claim document, scrawled after a successful silver strike and significantly superimposed on an establishing shot of his next work site—an oil well outside of Los Angeles, with the timeline shifted forward to 1902—juxtaposes ink and crude: A controlled scribble versus a burbling spill. It also inscribes a deeper theme: The branding of the landscape and its inhabitants in the name of the individual.

"Daniel Plainview" is the baldly symbolic moniker given to this character: The juxtaposition therein is between biblical kingship and unencumbered perception. *There Will Be Blood* actually features two scenes in which the name is written out in full: The second comes exactly two hours later into the movie's running time, as Daniel, now long since ensconced as a titan of industry, signs a cheque in the spacious kitchen of his Tudor Revival mansion. In a movie that plays consistently and obsessively with doubling motifs, these two close-ups are a matched set. They render Daniel the author of his own circumstances at either end of his mercurial career.

There are other signifiers of recurrence: The limp that Daniel acquired during that first tumble down the mine shaft has grown more pronounced, while the stooped posture adopted for the purposes of working underground

has deepened. Despite being fabulously wealthy, Daniel still sleeps on the ground rather than in a bed, the habits of a man who has not known the comforts of home and may never adjust. His physical gestures resemble those of his youth; in the film's final moments, he will repeat his earlier hammering, with the pickaxe swapped out for a bowling pin. *There Will Be Blood* is a profoundly linear story about a man moving in a straight line, externalizing his one-track desire in the form of an oil pipeline extending from the desert to the sea. But it's also got the contours of a loop: Manifest destiny as a vicious cycle.

There are multiple entry points into the massively scaled and incredibly dense cinematic object that is *There Will Be*

Blood, beginning with its status as its director's first literary adaptation—specifically of Upton Sinclair's novel *Oil!*. Sinclair, whose Chicago-set novel *The Jungle* established him as one of the early twentieth century's great realists, applied the same terse, unvarnished style to his follow-up about a California wildcatter. "This very long novel is at once a love story and a tract for the times," opined the unnamed critic for the *Spectator*; "Mr. Sinclair writes primarily with the purpose of exposing modern civilization in general and Big Business in particular ... there is no questioning the sincerity with which he castigates the greed and corruption of our material age."

The movie rights to *Oil!* had originally been purchased in 2005 by *Fast Food Nation* author Eric Schlosser, whose admiration was mainly for Sinclair's muckraking verisimilitude. The writer deliberately styled his main

The myriad possibilities of a seemingly endless, untapped landscape are displayed as Daniel moves slowly but with purpose towards a horizon line whose ultimate unreachability suggests his own insatiable appetites for expansion and control.

Intrigued by the cover imagery of derricks and heavy industry, Anderson purchased a copy of Upton Sinclair's 1927 novel *Oil!* while writing in London and ended up adapting its narrative into *There Will Be Blood*; while the screenplay deviates sharply from Sinclair's plot and characters, the setting and theme are transposed faithfully.

character, the self-made millionaire James Arnold Ross, after Edward L. Doheny, the founder of the Pan American Petroleum and Transport Company, who was eventually disgraced for his participation in the Teapot Dome scandal of 1921–1923. A key plot turn involving congressional subpoenas was more or less ripped from the headlines; when Orson Welles engineered *Citizen Kane* as a barely veiled biopic of William Randolph Hearst, he was following Sinclair's template.

"I was immediately struck by the idea that [*Oil!*] would make a great film," Schlosser said in 2008. "It had a great setting and characters and set of issue—the corruption of government by oil money, the rise of the car culture, the birth of Los Angeles—which seemed fascinating and cinematic." By coincidence, Anderson, then in the midst of writing a different screenplay about two feuding families, picked the book up from a bookstore in London, drawn to the cover illustration of a California oil field. He then contacted Schlosser about taking over the project.

It's fascinating that the qualities that drew Schlosser to *Oil!* are things that Anderson largely elides in his adaptation. Sinclair's novel is set mostly during the 1920s and observes the growth of Los Angeles as a city of industry and an epicenter of entertainment; the oil industry is but one institution depicted among many, although its subterranean tendrils have a broad reach, whether as a literal source of fuel for the booming automobile business or fodder for ideological debate. "We were really unfaithful to the book," Anderson admitted in 2008. "That's not to say I didn't really like the book; I loved it. But there were so many other things floating around."

There Will Be Blood veers from Sinclair's reportage, and doesn't really deal with the 1920s at all. It also reimagines the book's central father-son pairing via Daniel's relationships with two surrogates: His adopted son, H.W. (Dillon Freasier) and an evangelical preacher, Eli Sunday (Paul Dano), the latter loosely based on one of Sinclair's minor characters. In *Oil!*, the reader is confronted with the collision of capitalist and socialist values, with the latter serving as a site of resistance in a complex political analysis. In *There Will Be Blood*, the battle is between business and religion, each framed as the other's (barely) distorted mirror image, a reduction that also inflates the battle to the arena of moral transcendence. *Oil!* features a vast and diverse ensemble of characters, while *There Will Be Blood* is, despite its intermittent emphasis on H.W and Eli, essentially a one-man show.

As for the "other things" Anderson refers to, they include, in no particular order, a series of intertextual references to several monumental midcentury American movies (John Huston's *The Treasure of the Sierra Madre* (1948), George Stevens's *Giant* (1956), and, more abstractly, Stanley Kubrick's *2001: A Space Odyssey* (1968); visual and tonal elements drawn from ostensibly incongruous genres like Gothic horror; deftly interlaced critiques of capitalism and masculinity; and a set of anachronistically twenty-first-century subtexts (i.e., the less-than-cryptic mingling, in several passages, of blood and oil as a reference to the Iraq Wars of 1991 and 2003).

↑ *Top* The Church of the
Third Revelation emerges as
an institutional partner and
rival to Daniel's empire, with
Eli Sunday coming into focus
as a distorted mirror image.

↑ *Bottom* The friendship
between Daniel's adopted
son H.W. and Eli's younger
sister Mary ends up blending
the story's two families, while
Daniel's paternal protectiveness
towards Mary tempers and
complicates his contempt
for her father and brother.

↑ **Top** The opening and closing sequences both nod to Stanley Kubrick's science-fiction classic *2001: A Space Odyssey*, evoking the lonely, windswept aesthetic of "The Dawn of Man" prologue as well as its lurking undercurrent of violence (embodied by the ape-man pounding a skeleton with his bone-club, a gesture replicated by Daniel).

↑ **Bottom** In interviews, Anderson cited *The Treasure of the Sierra Madre* as a major influence, both in terms of its bleak, dusty visual style and its underlying themes of vicious, masculine greed.

← **Opposite** The intermittent oil gushers from Daniel's wells help to structure *There Will Be Blood* as a film of eruptive rhythms, as well as consolidating its phallic imagery—the derricks stand as towering monuments to their maker's masculine potency even as they're ultimately damaged or destroyed in the process.

↓ **Below** In the early passages of the film, Daniel's outsider status is signaled by his isolation within the frame, but he's not dwarfed by his surroundings; crouching by a fire at the top of a silver mine, he looms as large as the mountain ranges in the distance.

If it's possible for a film to be spacious and compartmentalized at the same time—to impart a sense of open-endedness even as it keeps rigorously fixing its meanings into place—*There Will Be Blood* fits the bill. In terms of critical reception, *There Will Be Blood* achieved instant canonization, topping a plethora of critics' polls and earning raves from nearly every prominent American byline. "An enthralling and powerfully eccentric American epic," was the verdict of *The New Yorker*'s David Denby. "With *There Will Be Blood*," wrote *LA Weekly*'s Scott Foundas, "Paul Thomas Anderson has taken a stab at making the Great American Movie—and I dare say he's made one of them." Such extravagant praise can be seen, in part, as symptomatic of *There Will Be Blood*'s own overweening ambitions. Foundas's assessment touches on how Anderson's simultaneous reduction and inflation of his source material, paring away its journalistic basis and tilting it towards the mythic, all but demanded an equally hyperbolic response.

There Will Be Blood was not Anderson's first epic, but its imaginative scope was new. Where in *Hard Eight*, *Magnolia* and *Punch-Drunk Love*, the director had worked to capture aspects of an actually existing Los Angeles, *There Will Be Blood*'s turn-of-the-century setting—a bygone time and place well beyond the fond, formative nostalgia of *Boogie Nights*—required research and reconstruction. Working in tandem with the estimable production designer Jack Fisk, who had so indelibly rendered the Panhandle in Terrence Malick's *Days of Heaven* (1978), Anderson had to create the fictional township of New Boston on a ranch in Marfa, Texas, whose dusty expanse of 50,000 acres offered a fair approximation of California.

Before shooting, Anderson sent Fisk a cache of 150 black-and-white, period-specific photographs to aid his designs, but *There Will Be Blood*'s aesthetic reflects a mix of fidelity and stark, audacious stylization. In an interview with the *A.V. Club*, Anderson used the example of Day-Lewis's experimentation with the tone and timbre of Plainview's speaking voice as an example of the film's play with authenticity. "A great benefit of what we were doing," he said, "was that there were no voice recordings from 1911 that we could draw from . . . we could really do what we wanted."

Considering the primacy of Daniel Plainview's voice in *There Will Be Blood*, his inimitable elocution is as good a place as any to start examining the heady mix of anachronism, allusion, and invention at play in the film as a whole. In an interview with *Time Out London*, Day-Lewis dispelled the idea that he modeled his cadences on John Huston, although he acknowledged that "there was something about the vigour of [his] language that appealed to me." Deliberate or not, the honeyed hoarseness of Daniel's voice evokes Huston strongly enough that the comparison became *de rigueur* for critics, who could in turn connect the apparent impersonation to Anderson's fondness for *Treasure of the Sierra Madre*, as well as Huston's acting role in Roman Polanski's *Chinatown* (1974), itself a period epic steeped in California lore.

The massive oil fire that causes
H.W. to lose his hearing serves
as a mid-film climax and provides
a vivid, abstract illustration of
Daniel's burning interior life;
gazing transfixed at the flaming
column, he could be staring into
his own incandescent abyss.

"[Day-Lewis] gives Plainview the insinuating growl of [Huston's] Noah Cross in *Chinatown*," writes Armond White, "[and] the way Plainview shames his son by calling him an "Ooorphan" combines cruelty and self-dramatization in a way that recalls the hammy grandeur of [Laurence] Olivier and Charles Laughton at their best." White's observation that Day-Lewis's performance is a "postmodern comic turn," is incisive in drawing a bead on Anderson's overall strategy. In *Oil!*, Sinclair was extrapolating, in real time, on Edward L. Doheny's exploits through the character of James Arnold Ross; in *There Will Be Blood*, Anderson and Day-Lewis have the distance and wherewithal to enfold Ross—and by extension, Doheny—into a character informed by other, subsequent, real-life and fictional inspirations. As such they have no true responsibility to history, and can operate instead in the arena of archetype. Because Daniel Plainview has no sole referent, he is able to contain multitudes in the manner of a truly self-invented man ("I like them all" he says when asked what Church he belongs to). Because of Day-Lewis's typically stringent, Method-ical approach to the performance, the character's patchwork background is still sharply particularized.

There is a compelling parallel between Day-Lewis's vocal daring and the stark, emotive musical score by Jonny Greenwood, whose buzzing, clustered micropolyphonies—inspired as much by Györgi Ligeti as his work with Radiohead—serve as an aural analogue for the pent-up animosity of Daniel's character. Speaking in a town hall meeting in a town where he hopes to dig a well, he adopts a relaxed grandiloquence that barely belies a seething contempt. "I like to think of myself as an oilman, and an oilman, I hope that you'll forgive just good old-fashioned plain-speaking." Another one of Mark Twain's aphorisms springs to mind: "A mine is a hole in the ground with a liar at the top." Except that Daniel isn't a liar, exactly. He may operate out of self-interest, but he is also largely a man of his word. It is that same intractable honesty—set against the myriad deceptions of Eli Sunday—that gives him the moral high-ground even when he is waist deep in the muck.

Gregory Alan Phipps has written about the different connotations of Daniel's claim that he's an "oilman" and how they connect to the character's essentially Darwinian thrust. The opening passages are styled as an evolution, as Daniel progresses from "scratching around in the dirt" into a man of means who can pay others to do his dirty work. "Daniel is a character invested in processes of production and transformation, not only because he works to turn crude oil into money, but also because he uses the money to remake his self-definition as an oilman . . . over time, he excavates himself from manual labor, donning elegant clothes, adopting H.W. and becoming an orator."

There is, perhaps, an element of self-deception in Daniel's physical and behavioural gentrification, but it's leveraged against his tangible accomplishments—the way that his words are always translated into action. The massive wooden structures that pop up in New Boston following his arrival—first and foremost the giant oil derrick positioned on the Sunday family ranch—are three-dimensional iterations of his written signature, outsized stakes marking a successful claim.

Early in the film, we see Daniel sketching the derrick, an insert that confirms its pride of place among *There Will Be Blood*'s myriad physical symbols. The terrifying oil fire that provides the film with its most visually spectacular passage has crucial narrative fallout, but it is as a self-contained aesthetic event that the fire has its greatest power. Whether glowing bright orange against a blue sky or simmering a demonic red as day gives way to night, it visualizes Daniel's blazing psychic landscape. An indelible image: Daniel, his face caked in ash and crude—an "oilman" once again, indistinguishable from his workmen—staring, hypnotized, at the flaming column as it ascends into the sky like Jacob's Ladder.

The derrick will be rebuilt: Just as Daniel keeps rising up—out of adversity, beyond his station—so do the monuments to his potency. The phallic aspects of this structure are so obvious as to almost override the need for comment, but sometimes the lack of subtlety can be misunderstood as easily as its abundance. "There are no women in *There Will Be Blood*," wrote *Salon*'s Stephanie Zacharek. "Plainview is apparently so fixated on oil that he has zero interest in sex—and that's fine . . . but their absence is never addressed." Zacharek is half-right when she suggests that Daniel's fixation on oil should be viewed in tandem with his sex drive, but misses the second part of the equation. For Daniel, oil isn't more important than sex—it's a substitutional fetish. It's not that *There Will Be Blood* lacks women so much as they exist beyond Daniel's purview, either as casualties of his general misanthropy or as a source of fear.

Daniel's indifference in this area should not be conflated with Anderson's. The movie is sexualized around the edges in ways that recontextualize Daniel's chastity and lack of attachments. During Daniel's public humiliation at the Church of the Third Revelation, Eli cites Daniel's "[lusting] after women," a charge with no evidence. While it might be risky to force a queer reading onto *There Will Be Blood*, there is an impression that the two men co-exist on a continuum of strenuous celibacy, with plenty space for insinuation. "The Devil [grabbed] hold of me in ways I'd never imagined," Eli confesses vaguely late in the film, a decidedly wink-nudge bit of phrasing given both mens' monkish comportment.

Anderson has described *There Will Be Blood* as a "boxing match," an analogy that works if one can accept the prospect of a title fight between contenders in different weight classes. Anderson parallels the construction of Daniel's towering derrick with that of Eli's comparatively low-rise church—dueling yet disproportionate edifices. So many of the film's effects are dependent on the idea, developed primarily through the somewhat fortuitous casting and performance of Paul Dano, who stepped in for Kel O'Neill after two weeks of shooting, that Daniel and Eli are not naturally evenly matched opponents. This feeling is partially extra-textual, rooted in the audience's recognition of Day-Lewis as a master actor and Dano as a relative newcomer. "I'm older than you and I'm smarter than you" Daniel bellows during their climactic confrontation, a declaration that's

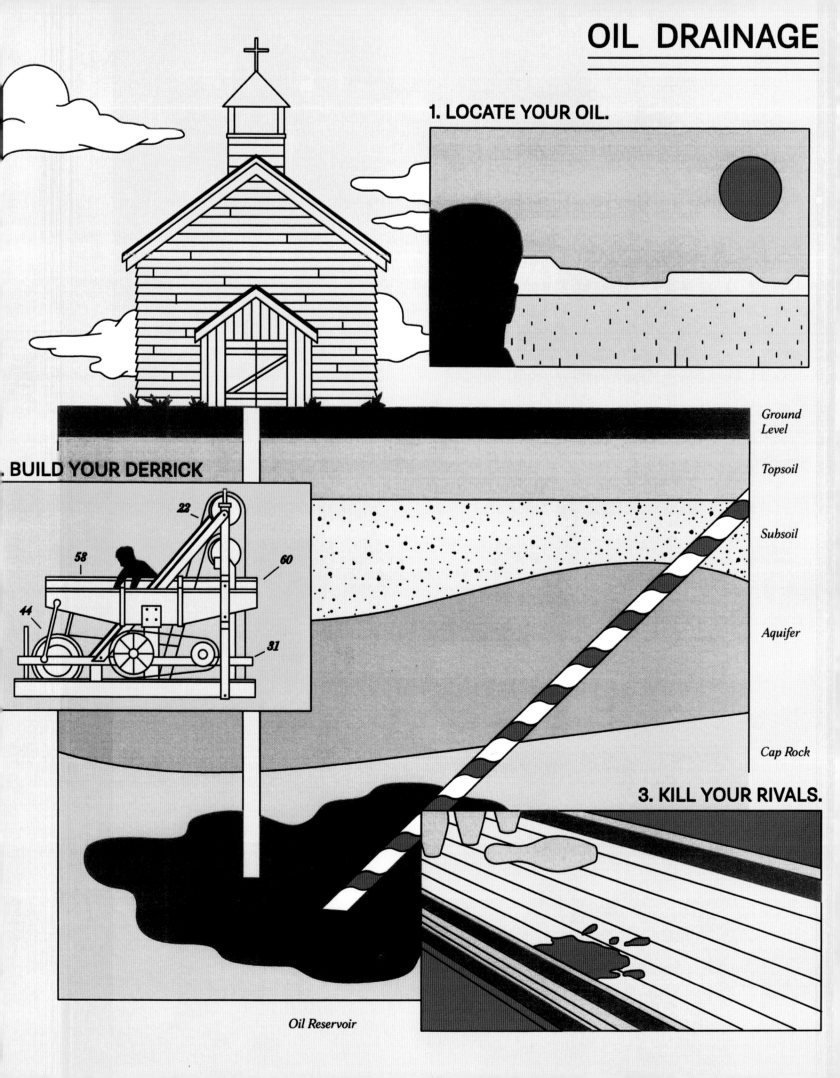

↑ **Above** Kneeling beneath a lighted cross—a religious symbol that mocks and mirrors the fiery oil derrick—Daniel is publically humiliated by Eli, adopting a servile posture as a means to an end; even though he's being physically dominated, it's in keeping with a larger plan to complete his pipeline.

← **Opposite** Heaven is a place on Earth: Walking to meet Daniel to discuss renumeration for his church, Eli is figured as part of a topsy-turvy visual metaphor.

funny partially because it's redundant—he's not saying anything that either man (or the audience) doesn't know. But in this particular time and circumstance—i.e. in a small community of mostly upright, God-fearing Christians—Eli is able to gain a partial foothold in the contest to control New Boston.

Daniel's accomplishments are tangible: He drills into the earth and extracts its raw materials. Eli, by contrast, is associated with sleight of hand and faulty perceptions. In one of the film's most beautiful shots, he's shown crossing a pool of oil turned resplendently blue by the reflection of an afternoon sky. Heaven is a place on Earth, but it's also an illusion. When Eli performs an exorcism on one of his parishioners, the scene is constructed simultaneously as a complement to Daniel's "I am an oilman" speech, with the showmanship keyed up even higher (Eli's keening whine is the opposite of Daniel's gravitas) away from "good, old-fashioned plain-speaking" to Old Testament declamations. Crucially, Eli is shown "extracting" a demon from Mrs. Hunter and casting it out of the church through the open front door, a pantomime both sanctified and satirized by Elswit's camera, which hovers as an observer before seemingly adopting the phantom's place mid-exorcism. It's a bravura bit of filmmaking that links Eli's showmanship with Anderson's while indicating that the former isn't to be taken seriously. "One goddamn hell of a show," smirks Daniel, who has been watching from the back pew and has chosen the sacrilegious terms of his praise judiciously.

That Daniel eventually becomes part of that goddamn hell of a show is a function of *There Will Be Blood*'s pugilistic progression, the "boxing match" alluded to by Anderson in three punishing rounds. In the first, Eli makes the mistake of approaching Daniel in the aftermath of the derrick fire—when he is distracted and devastated by H.W.'s hearing loss—to ask for funds for the Church and is beaten down and dragged through the mud in a brutal mock baptism (a scene with some distinctly S&M connotations). The second offers a reversal, as Eli, capitalizing on Daniel's sudden need to purchase

Hippolyte Flandrin's 1836 painting "Young Male Nude Seated Beside the Sea" (*right*) describes a lonely, enigmatic figure lost in thought by the edge of the ocean; contemplating his dubious bond with Daniel (or perhaps the dire consequences of its possible dissolution), Henry adopts a conspicuously similar posture (*above*).

a tract of land owned by one of his flock ("the Bandy tract") in order to complete his pipeline to the Pacific, entreats him to be "born again" in the Church of the Third Revelation. Here, Eli's screeching mania is directed not at a hypothetical demon but at Daniel, who absorbs insults and blows with calculated patience—as a means to an end.

There is one remarkably acted moment of rupture when, instructed by Eli to admit that he has "abandoned his child" (referring to the decision to send H.W. to San Francisco to seek treatment for his hearing loss), Daniel's guardedly rote recitation of his sins gives way to an outpouring of emotion. The guilty, breathless inflection when he changes from saying "I've abandoned my child" to "I've abandoned my *boy*" transubstantiates the physical reality of an oil strike into spoken language: The words "my boy" dredge up feelings of paternal love and, perhaps, a God-fearing humility that Daniel would rather keep buried.

Eli's "victory" is extremely provisional: Given that Daniel ends up securing the Bandy tract and building his pipeline, it's probably truer to call it a draw, setting up the fatally decisive final bout at Daniel's mansion. The perverse pleasure of seeing Eli definitely outmatched, forced to confront and confess his own status as a "false prophet" in the same manner as he had badgered Daniel for his abandonment of H.W. is undeniable, while the staging provides another opportunity to consider Anderson's uncanny mingling of fidelity and imagination. The bowling alley where Daniel receives Eli and beats him to death is located in Doheny's actual former residence, while the much-quoted line "I drink your milkshake!", with its intimations of vampirism, allegedly dates back to testimony given during the Teapot Dome scandal that Anderson happened upon in his research.

The murder scene is pure Anderson, with slow-burn comedy giving way to shocking, appalling slapstick: It's drawn-out and abrupt, shapely and overwrought, unlikely and fully inevitable. In a movie filled with relentless penetration, it's a gusher. But the true, molten emotional core of *There Will Be Blood* lies elsewhere, in the second of Anderson's variations on Sinclair's father-son story. If the "boxing match" between Daniel and Eli is a "hell of a good show"—a vivid illustration of Anderson's grand-entertainer side—the far less satisfying (and yet even more poetically realized) outcome of Daniel's relationship with H.W. manifests a more elusive mastery—the difference between eruption and ellipsis.

George Toles has written about the function of ellipsis in *There Will Be Blood*—the way that the film has been written and edited (by Dylan Tichenor) to omit chunks of time and exposition. There are precedents for this hurtling rhythm: Specifically *2001: A Space Odyssey*, which is also evoked visually in several sequences. But Toles notes that beyond homage, ellipsis is also Daniel's defining characteristic, that "the compression that editing ellipsis strives for that which seems to operate in his own nature: A rigorous sifting out of "extraneous" elements." If Daniel is a mystery, it is because Anderson and Tichenor work to pare away the connective tissue between his various actions and behaviours, and with it any overt indication that the forces of expansion and development he represents should be taken as purely positive.

Ellipsis also defines Daniel's loving, troubled, and tragic journey with H.W. far more than it does his comparatively uncomplicated contest with Eli. With the exception of the deliberately inscrutable depiction of Eli's twin brother Paul (also played by Dano), the Daniel-Eli conflict doesn't seem to be *missing* anything: The boundaries and stakes of their "boxing match," such as it is, are clearly laid out. But Daniel's relationship with H.W. is far harder to grasp, beginning with the identity of the latter's biological father. Referred to in the credits as "Ailman" (a clear play on "oilman") and played by Barry Del Sherman, he has less than two, worldess minutes of screen time during the second "movement" of the prologue in 1902, and yet is one of the film's most significant figures.

Because of the sudden, staccato nature of Ailman's death (he's crushed by a falling support beam while standing next to Daniel in the oil well), we have no way of knowing the nature of their relationship, and no real insight into Daniel's choice to adopt H.W. Its unclear whether it's a matter of guilt or expediency. The shot of Daniel gazing down at the infant in a train compartment does not take us inside his point of view: Indeed, no image in the film ever truly penetrates his interiority. But it does move us for the first time to wonder *what* he might be thinking, at which point another, even more severe ellipsis catapults us nine years into the future with the conjoined professional/paternal/exploitative psychology of his step-fatherhood long since established, yet equally remote.

Daniel's treatment of H.W. as a prop in his business dealings plays on the old saying that "children should be seen and not heard," an aphorism that has a grotesquely ironic payoff when H.W. goes deaf after suffering a fall during the derrick fire and loses the ability to hear or speak. On one hand, H.W.'s condition does not affect his status as Daniel's "silent partner," but it damages the possibility of granting his adopted son more fulsome participation. Daniel's response to the accident is in keeping with the furtive, evasive side of his personality: He sends H.W. out of town, ostensibly for medical treatment but also so that he doesn't have to live with—and see, but not hear—another example of human collateral damage. That H.W.'s departure opens up space for Daniel to get closer to another quasi-familial figure, Henry (Kevin J. O'Connor), who claims to be his lost half-brother but is revealed as a false profiteer, makes sense insofar as there is less competition for his attention. It is telling that Daniel's manias and motivations—as well as his vulnerabilities, as expounded to Henry during the period before the latter's deception has been revealed—come into focus most clearly during H.W.'s absence.

To go back to the lacerating moment in the church where the true depth of Daniel's sorrow over H.W.'s injury and exile bursts forth, the giveaway is his sudden inability to modulate his voice. By taking away H.W.'s voice, Anderson complicates Sinclair's narrative of a son gradually speaking up and defying his father; in a movie where power is bound up in speech and language, H.W.'s strength becomes diminished, or else he attempts to assert himself in wildly undisciplined ways, like when he sets a fire in an attempt to murder Henry. H.W.'s ability to "see through" the usurous intruder Henry mirrors Daniel's skepticism about Eli; it may be connected to H.W.'s own eventually confirmed suspicions that he's not Daniel's "real" son. Conversely, H.W. brings out Daniel's cowardice: He leaves him on the train and then later tries to insult him into oblivion, in both cases eliding the clear, decisive (im)moral certainty guiding his final reckonings with Henry and Eli.

This unknowability of Daniel and H.W.'s relationship is skilfully encoded into Anderson's mise-en-scène. When H.W. returns from San Francisco, their reunion is shot at a distance, framed by the pipeline, a reminder of the forward momentum that Daniel has chosen as a coping mechanism. H.W. swats his kneeling father in the face twice—a precise reenactment of Eli's glancing blows at the Church of the Third Revelation. There, Daniel masochistically absorbed the punishment in the name of "hell of a goddamn show," and perhaps also genuine sorrow for his transgressions. Now, he lets H.W. hit him but then pushes him away, an admission of guilt followed immediately by an attempted return to the status quo.

This equilibrium is short-lived, however. In an extremely strange sequence, Daniel and H.W. have lunch at a restaurant where representatives of the powerful Standard Oil Company are having a drink. Earlier in the film, Daniel had taken exception to H.M. Tilford (David Warshofsky)'s suggestion that selling the New Boston well would let him spend more time "with his family," tapping a reservoir of shame as deeply as Eli's attack in church. Daniel's well-lubricated crowing about closing Standard Oil out of his own dealings and completing the pipeline without their help shows him at his most prideful and bizarre, but he's out of control. During his "oilman" speech, Daniel's use of language was precise and sober; now, rambling and repeating himself, helplessly slurring his vowels, he's less an orator than a figure of sad pathos.

There is a way in which this conversation with Tilford is "the end" for Daniel: It is his final public appearance, presaging his transformation, in the long closing passage, into an addled, Hughesian recluse. But in between the scene at the bar and the shift to the mansion, Anderson deploys his most devastating and visionary ellipsis. Unexpectedly, the film's focus shifts to H.W. as he works with his sign language instructor, their interactions buried in the soundscape; we also see him stealing moments with Mary Sunday (Sydney McCallister), Eli's younger sister. These developments are, in and of themselves, elliptically rendered: The exact nature of H.W.'s therapeutic progress and his level of intimacy with

(continued on page 50)

→ **Opposite** The ellipsis that takes place after H.W. and Mary leap off of the porch together (top) compresses sixteen years into the space of a single edit; Mary drops out of frame and is replaced in a match cut by her adult self on her wedding day (we then see H.W. at the altar). Of all the temporal ruptures, this is the most profound and destabilizing, simultaneously contracting and expanding the narrative beyond expectations.

Despite its daunting scale, George Stevens's 1956 melodrama *Giant* doesn't exactly loom large over American cinema. The film was a box-office hit for Warner Bros. and earned Stevens his second Academy Award for Best Director, but he's better remembered for *A Place in the Sun* (1951) and *Shane* (1953); its star, James Dean, will always be associated first and foremost with *Rebel Without a Cause* (1955). Like so many massive monuments erected via the backbreaking labor of countless hired hands and artisans, *Giant's* reputation is that of a dusty relic; placed side by side with John Ford's smaller-scale yet relentlessly obsessive *The Searchers*, released in the same year, its influence seems comparatively puny.

The exteriors for *Giant* were filmed in the border town of Marfa, Texas, which sits in the high desert of the state's Trans-Pecos region; the arrival of a Hollywood mega-production was unexpected and transformative in the city's trajectory towards becoming a tourist town. Never one to pass up a chance to show off his cinephile credentials, Paul Thomas Anderson made the decision to shoot his own oil-baron melodrama in Marfa fifty years later, in effect turning Stevens's old stomping grounds into his own Monument Valley.

In terms of theme and tone, *There Will Be Blood* is much closer to John Huston's blackly cynical, muscularly masculine *The Treasure of the Sierra Madre* than it is to *Giant*, which unfolds as a stately movie-star romance. Rock Hudson's deep-pocketed tyro Jordan "Bick" Benedict gladly shares his fortune and his spread with Elizabeth Taylor's debutante Leslie Lynnton, whom he regards as his true life's work and enterprise: In the famous final lines, the now-aged rancher smiles affectionately and tells his wife, "If I live to be ninety, I will never figure you out." But as played by Taylor, Leslie isn't all that much of an enigma: She's so steadfast, in fact, that she can resist the thick-tongued charms of James Dean's cattle-hand Jett Rink, whose designs on the ranch's prim and proper mistress dovetail with his desire to coax forth some black gold from the ground beneath her feet.

It's in the depiction of the oil business—its grueling physical process and hard-driving psychology—that Anderson's film connects with its predecessor, with the point of greatest convergence located in Dean's performance. In dramatic terms, the conflict is between Jordan's aristocratic stolidity and Jett's hardscrabble ambition—Bick wants to keep dealing cows and Jett has a yen to go looking for oil on Reatta's 500,000 acres—but it plays out more powerfully in the contrasts between the actors. Hudson's broad-shouldered, lightly milque-toasted star persona is precisely the sort of old-Hollywood monolith that Dean's Method-ology was threatening to topple by the mid-1950s. *Giant* mines this old-money/new-guard dynamic for all it's worth. A poor kid who only gets partial ownership of some land because of his affair with the boss's sister—an end run around the patriarchal ideas of inheritance that Bick holds so dear—Jett is a churning furnace of mixed emotions and competitive impulses. He's willing to get his hands dirty in a way that Bick never would, but only so he can have the same things as his rival.

Viewed from the right angle, *There Will Be Blood* plays out as a West Coast remake of *Giant*, with an established titan pitted against a usurping upstart, and the oil fields themselves as the fertile leading lady lying between them. (It's also a movie that showcases contrasting acting styles to powerful effect.) Except that Daniel Plainview actually has more in common with Jett Rink than he does with Jordan Benedict, whom we never see earning his vast wealth and exalted status: He was born into his own looming shadow.

Daniel, though, is a self-made man, building an empire from the ground up and then refusing to rest on his laurels for even a moment. If Jordan is defined by his commitment to his stately status quo—and finally redeemed in the eyes of his wife and the audience by one small, progressive gesture in protest of his native state's history of racism—Daniel is an agent of change, forever trying to reshape the world in his own image.

As such, he has more in common with Jett, an echo that Anderson exploits smartly. Even after striking it rich, Jett is reduced to a shambling alcoholic, succinctly disparaged and then nobly smacked down by Bick en route to the latter's happy ending; that Dean died before the film was released renders his character's sad fate—and the actor's appearance in some aging makeup—in even more melancholy tones. If Anderson did take anything from *Giant* beyond the location and its sense of grandeur, it's the idea of a man who is fulfilled and diminished by his own success. Daniel's shrunken stature at the end of *There Will Be Blood* recalls Jett's fate; in both films, oil inflames a man's passions only to corrode his soul.

A PICTURE OF PROUD PEOPLE. A LOVE STORY. A CAVALCADE--A CONFLICT OF CREEDS--A PERSONAL DRAMA OF STRONG LONGINGS --A BIG STORY OF BIG THINGS AND BIG FEELINGS. THIS IS GIANT!

The ever-shifting power dynamic between Daniel and Eli is wittily encoded into the choreography and framing of the film's climax, which features Daniel's gradual, profound ascent juxtaposed against Eli's prideful, fatal fall. Delivering the killing blow, Daniel is framed identically to the murderous ape-man wielding a bone club in the prologue for *2001: A Space Odyssey*; splayed out on the floor in the aftermath of the attack, Eli becomes the human equivalent of a "gusher," pouring forth blood that looks as thick and black as oil.

Mary are indeterminate. And then we see H.W. and Mary wander out onto a porch and, one after the other, jump off, at which point Anderson and Tichenor cut to a shot of a woman's arm, clad in white, raising into view and towards her face. This is the adult Mary (Colleen Foy), signing her wedding vows to H.W. (Russell Harvard) in the year 1927—fifteen years compressed into the space of a single edit.

More than any of *There Will Be Blood*'s other ellipses, this cut is surpassingly discombobulating, while also quite beautiful in its equation of youthful romance—and later, matrimony—as a leap of faith, a mutual plunge into the unknown. The elegance of the edit is bound up in its criss-crossing trajectory: The children drop out of frame, while Mary's arm raises up, reversing the film's pattern of hard downward falls and tracing an ecstatic upward arc. In an instant, Anderson completely destabilizes the audience while orienting them, at last, in a more traditional domestic tableaux and, for the first time in the film, a sanguine and relaxed tonal space: Daniel, and the chaos that he cultivates, are conspicuous by their absence.

It is only after the conclusion of the wedding, which unfolds in the space of just three shots, that the implications of this leap become clear. Daniel is now in his house, built not by the sea, as he'd mused to Henry, but deep in a forest. The dim ruinous state of the place corroborates its owner's decline: Daniel has shrunk in inverse proportion to the size of his empire. For H.W. and Mary, we can intuit the "lost time" as a blissful idyll, whereas for Daniel, it corresponds with the severe advance of his alcoholism, as if that drunken encounter with Tilford had instigated a bender lasting a decade and a half.

Certainly, the ravages of drink inform Daniel's final encounter with H.W., who, unlike the son in *Oil!*, is not bent on defying his father: Rather, he wants to be an oilman as well and to strike out on his own, an assertion of independence that may also be an expression of their congenital non-relation. Daniel's defensive response ("this makes you my competitor") ends up severing their bond once and for all, with an undue excess of cruelty: He forces H.W. to use his own damaged speaking voice to confirm his departure. As the younger man retreats, Daniel's taunts ringing in his ears ("you're a bastard in a basket!") Anderson briefly reverses the ellipsis, returning us to 1912 as the pair rough-house near the well site. For a suspended moment, the melancholy of their parting is also reversed, but even as they play, Daniel pushes H.W. away in order to return to work. It's a gesture that functions, painfully, as a synecdoche of their entire relationship and its motif of abandonment.

With H.W. gone, Daniel is free to take out his aggression even more spectacularly on Eli and to bring the film's portrayal of a lonely, linear victory—over the elements, the ephemeral, and the emotional—to a rousing conclusion. "I'm finished," Daniel crows as he crouches next to Eli's corpse, a final line calibrated for maximum sicko-humour. Daniel's triumph is unqualified because he doesn't seem to mind—or comprehend—what has been lost in order to achieve it. Sitting with his back to the camera, spent and elated, he is at once an emblem of success on one's own terms and a figure of ellipsis, defined as much, if not more, by what he's lost—what has been pushed away, buried, forgotten, and repressed—as that which has been gained.

What's also missing at the end of *There Will Be Blood* is the transformative effect of that "lost time" on the city of Los Angeles, a casualty of Anderson's obsessive fixation on a character ruled by obsessive fixations. As a Californian origin myth, though, *There Will Be Blood* is suggestive, generating a sense of retrospective agape at the transformation of the new landscape in the image of its new arrivals, and foreshadowing the physical and psychic upheavals to come—the emergent industries and cults of personality that will be mapped onto its vast expanse as future strivers and misfits head, hellbent for them thar hills—or even beyond the sea.

IE

TER

I n Susan Loesser's 1993 biography of her father, the Tony-winning songwriter Frank Loesser, she parses the etymology of her dad's late-forties pop standard "(I'd Like to Get You on a) Slow Boat to China." Loesser's great gift as a lyricist was the compression of complex emotions into insinuating innuendo; think of the coy, call-and-response seduction of "Baby, It's Cold Outside," in which metaphorical decorum gets stretched to the breaking point.

For "Slow Boat," Loesser borrowed a phrase common to poker players describing somebody unable to extricate themselves from a run of bad luck yet unwilling to fold—a loser whose agony is drawn out. Recognizing the kinship between gambling and romance—and the exquisite ache of a situation with a high-stakes yet indeterminate outcome—he crafted a love song with possessive undertones, whispered in the barely suppressed language of conquest and control:

Out on the briny
With the moon big and shiny
Melting your heart of stone
I'd like to get you
On a slow boat to China
All to myself alone

The first image in *The Master* is of the ocean, of massive waves churning both of their own implacable accord and also in response to the presence of a vessel—an American military transport tracing a slow, steady swath through the water. Given the subsequent revelation of time and place (the Pacific circa 1945) the ship might even be a slow boat to China, subliminally anticipating the deployment of Loesser's song at the film's climax, where its performance by a major character for another stands in plangently for their mutual dependency.

The singer is Lancaster Dodd (Philip Seymour Hoffman), the founder and frontman of a controversial philosophical movement called "The Cause"; the listener is Freddie Quell (Joaquin Phoenix), a World War II veteran who is the Cause's most ardent and yet intractable initiate. For several group insiders, including members of Dodd's family, Freddie's impulsiveness supersedes his loyalty, making him a liability to a fledgling movement already under scrutiny by the authorities. And yet Dodd, for reasons that are strange even to himself, refuses to let him go.

Dodd's serenade has been selected strategically, playing directly on the younger man's past vocation as an "able-bodied seaman" and the circumstances of their initial meeting. Once, Freddie stowed away on the Cause's luxurious flagship, the *Alethia*, while it sat docked in San Francisco Bay; now, newly headquartered in England, Dodd hopes to keep his wayward disciple close at hand. Digging deep into his bag of tricks, he personalizes the song's melancholic desperation, but Freddie, long resigned to being a receptacle for the great man's charisma, resists—to his surprise, and Dodd's as well. The inference is that this reunion is a precursor to a parting. Freddie's emancipation may be provisional, but it opens up the possibility of independence, while Dodd, for all his influence, appears isolated, a transference that throws the very question of mastery into doubt. "[The song] speaks the sad truth of the aspiring mystic," the writer and critic Kent Jones has said. "There can be no such thing as a cult of one."

"I just want to tell you that I don't think that we're dealing with a cult," Paul Thomas Anderson stated during a press conference for *The Master* at the 2012 Toronto International

Film Festival. The director's defensive posture was unfamiliar, if not unexpected. Most of the advance word on Anderson's sixth feature centered on rumors that it was a veiled biopic of L. Ron Hubbard, the notorious founder of the Church of Scientology, an organization whose history and reputation were particularly acute in California and especially Los Angeles, long the site of Scientology's most sustained recruiting drive. "Celebrities are very special people and have a very distinct line of dissemination," Hubbard said in 1973, sounding as much like a studio publicist as a man who had discovered the secret to unleashing human potential. "They have communication lines that others do not have and many medias [sic] to get their dissemination through."

Dissemination was always Hubbard's game, and his resourcefulness in spreading his version of the good word made him a unique modern entrepreneur, successfully annexing and redeveloping psychic rather than geographical space. In *Bare-Faced Messiah: The True Story of L. Ron Hubbard*, author Russell Miller depicts his subject as a pathological liar who parlayed a knack for pumping out dime-store novels into a religious-industrial complex steeped in the trappings of period science-fiction. Initially trained as a military psychiatrist, Hubbard saw an opening in the early 1950s to monetize the encroaching doubt and despair of those who hadn't (or couldn't afford to) buy into the Eisenhower era's fantasies of prosperity. Imploring his

readers to look within, he promised them a cleaner slate, to say nothing of a more goofily entertaining cosmology, than his longer-tenured Judeo-Christian competitors.

The idea that with the right training and care, people could return themselves to a state of primal perfection—purging their souls of a corrupting influence of extra-terrestrial origin—enacted a nifty synthesis of the Book of Genesis and *Invasion of the Body Snatchers*. While it would take nearly fifty years for a Hollywood studio to actually dramatize one of Hubbard's sci-fi narratives—in Roger Christian's abjectly hilarious *Battlefield Earth* (2000)—the innate appeal of his material aligned with Hollywood's gradual shift in the sixties and seventies towards archetypal yet technocratic fantasies à la *Star Wars* (1977). If Scientology never took hold of the popular imagination, it still cultivated a nicely gilded niche in a specific sphere of influence. The combination of the group's elite connections (and robust war chest) had, for citics, kept their spiritual grift an open Hollywood secret since the construction of the Church of Scientology of California in Los Angeles in 1954 (relocated to Sunset Boulevard in 1977).

For any filmmaker to tackle the checkered and secretive history of an organisation now known the world over and, to its many disciples, respected, would be a risk. There was speculation that the church would object to the script and

The sand sculpture embraced by Freddie during *The Master*'s prologue comes to symbolize the outsized presence of women in his inner life; his position next to her conflates sexual urges with a more innocent, infantile need. Throughout the film, this relationship will be reinforced by Freddie's encounters with significant female characters, including his former lover Doris—whose exaggerated size recalls the woman on the beach—and Winn Manchester, a happy-hour conquest referred to affectionately as "the greatest girl I've ever met."

possibly try to get the production cancelled. In the *Vallejo Times Herald* (June, 2011), producer JoAnne Sellar was quoted as denying that there was any connection in the film to Scientology, calling it "a World War II drama." Universal, who greenlit the film in 2011, eventually backed off, leaving Anderson in the lurch. Had it not been for Silicon Valley heiress-turned-producer Megan Ellison contributing an undisclosed but significant sum, the film's fate might have been sealed. "Could the film have been made without [Ellison?]" queried Danny Leigh in the *Guardian*. "Not the movie you saw," answered Sellar.

It's amusing—and reductive—to parallel Ellison's faith in Anderson and his eccentric auteur vision with the suggestible high-society types being sold a bill of goods by Lancaster Dodd, who employs both grandiloquent oratory and *sotto voce* stage hypnotism to shore up the Cause's collateral. Scenes like the one where Dodd and his entourage peddle their wares to the wealthy are derived, like so many aspects of Anderson's film, from Hubbard's personal life; If

its makers are to be believed and *The Master* is not a film *about* Scientology, it's difficult not to believe that it uses the movement's history and core texts as texture, starting with Hoffman's performance. Cast slightly against type, he doesn't quite impersonate Hubbard but draws on the personality of a man who luxuriated in his powers of persuasion, channeling additional charisma from Mercury Theater—era Orson Welles (who might have admired Hubbard's hoaxster hustle and sci-fi fantasies). The performance earned Hoffman the Best Actor prize at Venice (shared with Phoenix) and his fourth Oscar nomination; less than a year after the ceremony, he would be dead at the age of forty-seven.

As portions of *The Master*'s script were reworked from the initial writing sessions for *There Will Be Blood*, it's tempting to compare the films as journeys into the past. Yet their textures as period pieces are distinct: *The Master* is

Even while frolicking on the beach in Hawaii with his fellow servicemen, Freddie is isolated from the group by his unusual appearance and behavior; the composition and blocking in this shot suggest both a sense of wary remove and a fervent curiosity.

rich and shimmering in opposition to *There Will Be Blood*'s purgatorial minimalism. Working with the Romanian-born cinematographer Mihai Malaimare Jr. (who was swapped in when the director's regular DP Robert Elswit became unavailable), Anderson opted to shoot the majority of the film on 65 mm, a format usually used to accommodate the sprawl of massive outdoor locations. The result is a film whose play with scale is at once subtler and more audacious than *There Will Be Blood*'s. The enlarged format, combined with short lenses ensuring a narrow, stylized depth of field, has the effect of transforming even probing close-ups into panoramas, suggesting entire universes lying behind the characters' eyes.

In contrast to the forbidding mountain range that announces *There Will Be Blood* with a stark sense of physical impediment, the opening oceanic view of *The Master* implies a point of entry and immersion, a deep dive into something impossibly vast. In *Senses of Cinema*, Daniel Fairfax noted that "repetitions of the same shot [. . .] punctuate the film on two further occasions," and that their primacy, "may also connote Freddie's 'oceanic consciousness,' [. . .] a state, according to Freud in his works *The Future of an Illusion* and *Civilisation and Its Discontents*, of 'primitive ego-feeling,' in which the pre-subjective individual lacks any concept of a self divorced from the external world." Where Daniel Plainview reaches the sea and then reroutes in the direction of subterranean sanctuary (an ironically elongated lateral move from a mine shaft to a bowling alley), Freddie is, at least for the majority of *The Master*, content to go with the flow. If *There Will Be Blood* is a film about a man transforming the landscape in accordance with some insatiable appetite for forward momentum, *The Master* follows someone whose most fervent wish, only barely acknowledged amid baser urges but yoked to them as surely as lust is to loneliness, is to fit in—to find a place (and perhaps a partner) in a society that's changing rapidly around him.

Change is in the air in *The Master*. "You could say," noted Kent Jones in *Film Comment*, "that [the film] picks up where *There Will Be Blood* leaves off [. . .] by the '40s, long after the great religious revivals and reforms, after the land has been tamed and settled, the railroads and cities built, the gold mined, the oceans of oil tapped . . . a mounting standardization, desperation, and rancidness has set in, and another war has left men shattered." Jones's swift socio-historical survey of America's transition from the 1920s to the 1940s is aware of the developments that Anderson skips over without ever actually filling in, but this is not to say that he's doing the film's work for it. What Jones is responding to is the suggestiveness of Anderson's scene-setting: The resonance of his few scattered expositional details; the uncanny presence of his structuring absences. In the same way that *There Will Be Blood* more or less dispenses with Upton Sinclair's reportorial thrust in favor of a more archetypal milieu, *The Master* trusts—or perhaps challenges—its audience to be cognizant of a social, historical, and political context that exists in the margins of its judiciously chosen images. And even then it mostly eschews the kind of easily digestible period signifiers used by filmmakers to flatter (and flatten) our understanding of the past in the present tense.

→ *Top; bottom* Freddie's job as a department store photographer explicitly aligns the film's point of view with his own; the images he captures of smiling, prosperous Americans hint at his simultaneous distance from and desire for normalcy. His later portrait of Dodd draws on his previous experience while heightening the sense of posed artificiality.

Anderson's willingness to play with time is evident in the sequence that follows that first, piercingly blue oceanic view. We are on an unnamed Hawaiian island where a company of American servicemen celebrating the Allied victory are portrayed as the inhabitants of a primitive, homosocial Paradise—an Eden overrun by Adams. Eve in this equation is a life-size sculpture of a woman splayed out in the surf, with which Freddie immediately and energetically starts simulating sex, first drawing hoots of supportive, good-humoured approval from his comrades before alienating them with the intensity of his charade. The disarming ribaldry of the prologue, which includes, as its first lines of dialogue, a joke about crabs and genital mutilation told by Freddie to a friend ("You take an icepick and you fucking stab every single last one of them") is balanced against its elemental splendor, the bleached whiteness of the sand and the Gauguin tint of the sea. The scene is at once less lonely and even more abject than the opening of *There Will Be Blood*, where Daniel's solitude is a matter of professional discipline. Here, Freddie's attempts to be "one of the boys" leave him stranded somewhere between uneasy inclusion and exile.

Freddie's sense of difference is signaled by Phoenix's odd posture, which generates kinetic energy even while he's standing still. His crooked, asymmetrical comportment—torso hunched, arms akimbo, neck craned by turns in curiosity and recoil—styles him as a kind of human question mark, a figure of the same ellipsis that marks *There Will Be Blood*, transferred now from the level of narrative to that of characterization. *There Will Be Blood* was edited with increasing openness to keep pace with a man rapidly being consumed by his obsessions; *The Master* begins with Freddie already far gone, a twisted history inscribed on and within a broken body.

There is a visual pun linking Freddie to Daniel in terms of their mutual assault on the earth, but where Daniel penetrates solid rock in order to extract what lies within, Freddie seeks a softer sort of communion. As in *There Will Be Blood*, Anderson nods (more overtly this time) to *2001: A Space Odyssey*'s "Dawn of Man" overture, complete with his own version of the monolith in the form of the woman on the beach, a voluptuous, ephemeral avatar for Freddie's compulsions. Lying side by side with the sculpture in the final shot of the film's prologue, Freddie is physically dwarfed, clinging to her in a fetal position; the conjoining of sexual want, romantic attachment, and infantile need. What Freddie wants is to reach out and touch somebody; *The Master* is a chronicle of his grasping.

In an interview with *Le Monde* (translated and excerpted in *The New Yorker* by Richard Brody) Anderson drew a connection between his protagonist's troubled psychological state and "postwar traumas that often went undiscussed but that emerged in other forms." In this formulation, America itself was blameless for any blemishes on its so-called "Greatest Generation"; its fighting men were broken "over there" and had to be fixed in order to better integrate into a burgeoning society (hence the film's use of of Hawaii as a kind of liminal, layover space—it's America, but it's not the home front). The idea that Freddie is meant as a representative of the battlefield-spawned psychoses that filled military hospitals in the wake of World War II is developed by the scenes of him being examined by Army psychiatrists—terse encounters that play as comic, verbal elaborations of his behavior on the beach. "That's a pussy," he snorts upon observing a Rorschach blot. "That one's a cock turned upside down . . . that's a cock going into a pussy."

Coming from the filmmaker behind the two-and-a-half-hour boner joke that is *Boogie Nights*, Freddie's leering deadpan could be taken as a self-reflexive joke. Yet the visual presentation of these interviews—and of the military hospital overall—draws from dead-serious source material: The 1946 documentary *Let There Be Light*, a compassionate work of observational reportage that dared to show America's veterans as fragile, even broken survivors. John Huston's long-suppressed film was commissioned by the Department of War and then withheld from circulation on the grounds that its devastating footage of men deep in the throes of trauma violated the privacy of its subjects. The very opposite of exploitation, Huston's film—which Anderson has acknowledged in interviews as a major source of inspiration—dared to challenge and complicate the visual and rhetorical syntax of propaganda associated with the majority of wartime features and documentaries, ignoring the question of "why we fight" and instead unveiling the aftermath.

There is some documentary-style verisimilitude in the way *The Master* depicts the period's pioneering psycho-therapeutic techniques and an element of respectful re-creation in Phoenix's gestures and mannerisms. But Freddie's compulsions also seemingly predate his combat experiences. He has a Gothic backstory involving incest that hangs over his behavior like a shroud; as several critics have pointed out, he possesses the existentially haunted qualities of a forties noir hero—a hard-drinking cipher connected to nobody and potentially capable of anything. His forbidding affect remains intact for the duration of the film, but Anderson nevertheless collapses the distance between the character and the viewer through the use of point of view. We're compelled to share Freddie's sightlines even as we observe him from the outside, a double consciousness that turns every sequence and exchange into the spectatorial equivalent of contested territory.

With this in mind, the comic episode with the Rorschach test ends up pulling more than its apparent weight in setting up *The Master*'s methodology. Whether or not Freddie is being truthful when he tells the psychiatrist that the blots appear pornographic, we're being cued to consider the way the world might look through his eyes. His subsequent employment as a department store photographer reinforces this idea of point of view, and the portraits he captures of smiling middle-class strivers—symbols of a prosperity beyond his

experience—radiate with a benevolent envy; the camera is both conduit and barrier for a covetous consciousness.

In *There Will Be Blood*, the shots of Daniel gazing through his telescope as he plots the course of his pipeline bespoke a hard, cartographical focus, but Freddie's lens is imbued with something more elusive and hallucinatory. Entering his field of vision as she hawks an expensive coat, a shopgirl (Amy Ferguson) hijacks his attention (and the camera's as well), whirling teasingly past various designer signifiers of femininity—her trajectory through this deceptively subjective tracking shot features displays of lingerie and bridal wear as backdrops. She's like something out of a daydream—not a Rorschach image but a vivid, even fetishistic emblem of Freddie's erotomania. Anderson's song selection is sublime: "Get Thee Behind Me Satan," an anthem of chastity and restraint whose lyrics are rendered satirical by Ella Fitzgerald's sensuous delivery.

"Get Thee Behind Me Satan" was originally written by Irving Berlin and featured in the 1936 Fred Astaire/Ginger Rogers comedy *Follow the Fleet*, about a seaman who returns home from a long voyage in search of his former lover—a plot synopsis that figures into *The Master*'s dense matrix of inspirations. After a picaresque interlude that draws a bead on Freddie's competing temptations—not only his compulsive horniness, but also his alcoholism, which scuttles his date with the shopgirl and gets him kicked off a work gang in Salinas after his experiments in amateur mixology incapacitate an older man—he's shown returning, almost as if in thrall, to the ocean. Once again, Anderson places emphasis on *how* Freddie sees: Spotting Dodd's yacht in the harbor, he's drawn towards the coterie of well-dressed revelers on deck, whose appearance in luminous,

breathtakingly clear, deep focus throws light on his skulking shadow. Physical space is collapsed by covetous perception, with Freddie eventually moving away from the camera and into the alluring fantasy, his well-practiced agility as he hops aboard providing a bravura sequence with a comic punctuation mark.

"You're safe, you're at sea," Freddie is told by one of Dodd's followers (Katie Boland) upon waking disheveled belowdecks the next morning, a line with an unsubtle double meaning: To be "at sea" is to be confused and indecisive, which is to say that her assessment is accurate. The extended passage on the *Althea* not only introduces Freddie to Dodd but also—obliquely and gradually, in a set of judiciously miniaturized sequences—the aims and applications of the Cause. The dynamics of repression and temptation expressed in the shopgirl's vamp (and compounded by its musical curation) resurface as a running motif in Dodd's oratory, which preaches self-control: Officiating his daughter Elizabeth's (Ambyr Childers) wedding he likens mastering addiction to housebreaking a dragon, while Freddie—double-fisting drinks from his seat at the back of the room—looks on with an unreadable expression.

It is a central irony of *The Master* that Dodd, whose well-practiced spiel barely conceals his own fall-down-drunkenness is at once uniquely equipped and completely incapable of truly helping Freddie. The Cause's claims of returning converts to their "inherent state of perfect" is especially alluring to a man whose addictions and fixations have left him barely functional. (It's a running joke that Freddie is more interested in eyeballing the female disciples than absorbing the seminars and workshops about past life regression; "do you want to fuck?" he propositions one

↑ As the core text of the Church of Scientology, *Dianetics* has its place in the history of pseudo-religious tomes, filtering self-help bromides through the language of cheapjack science-fiction.

↑ The foundation of the so-called Sea Org in 1967 gave L. Ron Hubbard a floating home base that supposedly kept him safe from his landlocked enemies; in the film, Dodd's boat the *Alethia* stands in for Hubbard's fleet.

young woman in scribbled handwriting, like a kid passing a note in class.) And yet for all his fragility, Freddie just isn't the right kind of credulous. It's not the Cause that draws him in so much as Dodd and the multifaceted nature of their relationship: Surrogate father; drinking buddy; warped mirror image.

The pair's pathologies intersect in an intricate codependency that's as complex as Daniel Plainview's hatred-slash-obsession with Eli Sunday in *There Will Be Blood*. Daniel believes Eli to be an (un)holy fraud, watching contemptuously as he "exorcises" a demon by manipulating thin air (an antecedent of sorts to Dodd's *Dianetics*-esque talk of expunging the mind's detritus) and finally proving the supremacy of action over rhetoric. The power dynamic in *The Master* favors Dodd, who sees in Freddie a consciousness so broken that gluing it back together could vindicate his methodology once and for all, to his doubters but also to himself. This explains why he keeps a man who is so obviously a liability on such a long leash—Freddie is the dragon who will be taught to sit. The long middle section of *The Master*, which depicts Freddie's role as the Cause's mascot and enforcer, also takes care to show how much Dodd gets off on—and, to some extent, is totally consumed by—his attempt to assert his authority.

Richard Brody has written about how *The Master*'s centerpiece sequences of "processing," in which Dodd guides Freddie into a trance state to confront his bad memories, play up the theme of performance, with the push-pull between exhortation and revelation evoking, "Method acting classes, in which ordinary behavior . . . is linked to the deepest and most tightly buried personal experiences." Certainly, the focus on performance—of gradations of expression and cadence captured so intimately that even minor fluctuations register as an event—is an Anderson specialty, and the vague but calculated resemblances of each actor to a classical Hollywood analogue (Hoffman to Welles; Phoenix to a post-motorcycle accident Montgomery Clift) roots their exchanges in a cinephilic context.

More important than even the fanatical concentration of the actors, however, is the way Anderson plays with perspective. The first phase of Freddie's processing is shown in an unbroken close-up of Phoenix's face, with the real-time duration of the scene emphasized through the excruciating detail of Freddie not being allowed to blink. When he finally closes his eyes, we switch to an interior view, a remembrance of a sunny suburb cast in the same heightened glow as Freddie's department store photographs. Sitting on a park bench with his former teenage sweetheart Doris (Madisen

↑ *Above* The shot of the *Alethia* moving into open water (*top*) echoes a similar image in Orson Welles's 1947 noir *The Lady from Shanghai* (*bottom*), further connecting Dodd's showmanship to that of Welles.

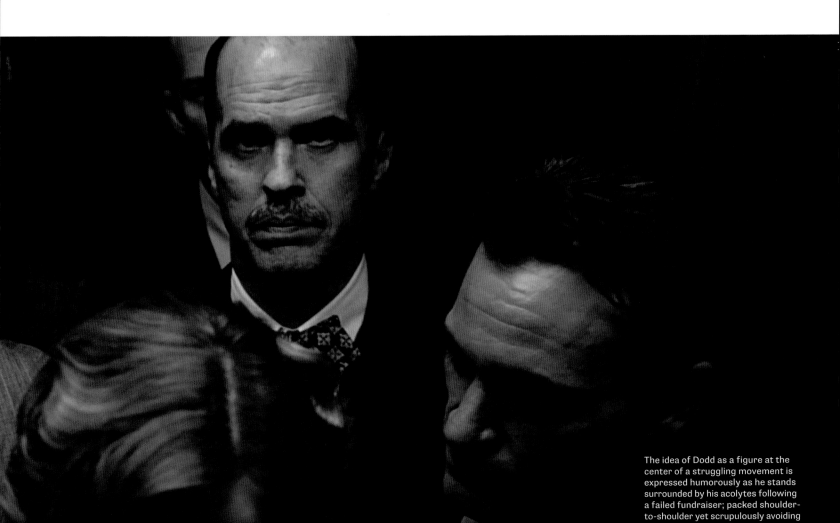

The idea of Dodd as a figure at the center of a struggling movement is expressed humorously as he stands surrounded by his acolytes following a failed fundraiser; packed shoulder-to-shoulder yet scrupulously avoiding

This brilliantly witty fixed camera setup emphasizes the theme of mutual entrapment between master and disciple: Hauled off to prison together, Freddie and Dodd react differently to imprisonment, with the latter pantomiming authority while his acolyte thrashes around chaotically—helplessly embodying his master's assessment of him as "an animal."

← **Left** The running motif of point of view shots in *The Master* reaches a delirious peak in the sequence where Freddie imagines a fully clothed Dodd surrounded by naked female followers; once again off to the side of the action, he's undressing the women with his eyes. Only Peggy Dodd meets his gaze—hinting that she's watching him carefully as he integrates into the Cause's surrogate family.

↓ **Below** As *The Master* progresses, it's implied that Peggy Dodd may be the real power behind the throne. Onstage (*center*), she assumes a deferential position to her husband, but in their bathroom (*opposite*), she masturbates him while insisting that he stays focused—a calculated show of physical and sexual control.

Beaty), who inexplicably towers over him like a giant while he's rendered even more childlike by his Navy blues, like a toddler in a sailor suit. It's a deeply subjective memory, with Doris's Amazonian proportions serving as a symbol of how large she looms over Freddie's psychic landscape.

The disparity in their sizes also twins Doris with the woman on the beach, at which point the film's pattern of statuesque, red-haired women, from the shopgirl to Elizabeth Dodd, becomes apparent. They're all reminiscent of Doris, the deserted lover in the narrative's epic, Freudian reworking of *Follow the Fleet*. Her manifestation through a procession of doppelgangers offers compelling evidence of how compromised Freddie's reality truly is, and how deeply we have been imbricated into that same perceptual space. In the film's most spectacularly executed set-piece, Freddie's various desires and fixations—his heterosexual lust; his feeling of being on the outside of fulfillment; his supplicance to Dodd as well as encroaching suspicions of the Great Man's hypocrisy—are interwoven in a surreal point of view shot showing Dodd reciting a song called "I'll Go No More A-Roving" at a Cause soiree. Like "Get Thee Behind Me Satan," it's an anthem of abstinence bristling with contradictions, pleading monogamous devotion while ceding the pleasures of screwing around—the latter embodied by the female followers he mock-seduces, each in turn, with every verse. Whirling through the room with boisterous aplomb, he's as transfixing in his dance as the shopgirl, except that Freddie's focus—and ours—is distracted by the fact that every woman he sees is stark naked, evidence not of an *Eyes Wide Shut* style cult bacchanal, but rather the culmination of an eyes-wide-shut-aesthetic.

The reduction of women to erotic props in this sequence is complicated by the presence of Peggy Dodd (Amy Adams), the de facto First Lady of the "Cause" and the only character in the "I'll Go No More a Roving" number to return his gaze. The coded implication of her direct-to-camera look is that she sees Freddie for what he is—a competitor for her husband's attention and a liability to his business—while also being exempt from Dodd's powers of persuasion. Peggy may even be the movement's actual prime mover. In the few glimpses of Dodd's family life we see beyond Freddie's purview, she is the one who wears the pants. She has also, to paraphrase Frank T.J. Mackey, tamed the cock: A scene where she rather violently jerks her

husband off over a bathroom sink while talking strategy is not a simple Lady Macbeth flourish but evidence of where all kinds of power in this film's universe resides. Even if it comes steeped in humiliation, Dodd is getting some; Freddie, as evidenced by his orgiastic fantasies, remains cock-blocked.

The bathroom handjob (and Dodd's hilarious, almost pre-verbal sigh of climax) chimes with the character's tendency to abruptly (and erruptively) lose his strenuously maintained composure. Hoffman's performance is a study in how calm can come unruffled. (Goaded into losing his cool by a critic at a fundraiser, Dodd bellowingly bestows upon his rival the title of "pigfuck," a show-stopping bit of imaginative profanity.) The unraveling of his authority—in relationship to Peggy, then his followers, and finally to Freddie—provides *The Master*'s second half with its broad, descending dramatic arc as well as some compelling showbiz subtext. Given the close proximity, historically speaking, of Scientology to the movie business, Anderson seemingly withholds direct commentary on the church's celebrity affiliations. But we are also shown, in surprisingly empathetic terms, the stress of functioning simultaneously as a religious movement's mysterious mastermind and its endlessly accessible spokesman.

When aboard the *Althea* or ensconced in the Cause's East Coast stronghold in Philadelphia, Dodd's control is absolute. Out in the world, attempting to promote his second book *The Split Saber*, his supremacy is contested and diminished. The title of *The Split Saber* is a nod to the Arthurian title (with its obvious phallic connotations) of Hubbard's unpublished 1938 book *Excalibur*, which was written after he suffered a "near-death experience" and contains the framework for *Dianetics*'s absolutist dialectic of "aberration" and "purity." What it also points to—right down to the castration-anxious illustration on its cover—is the reduced potency of the author's rhetoric. Longtime followers are shown pointing out the inconsistencies between his two texts. Speaking one afternoon with Freddie, Dodd's laconic adult son Val (Jesse Plemons) is succinct about his father's activities, exposing a con that's hiding in plain sight and in the process drawing another parallel to the artistic process: "He's making [it] all up."

It is this specific accusation that sets off Freddie's anger at regular intervals throughout the film, resulting in several physical assaults on apparent nonbelievers, and his incarceration alongside his "master" after Dodd is arrested in Philadelphia for financial malfeasance. Thrust into adjacent prison cells, the pair become props in Anderson's most strikingly static composition, occupying spots at either end of the widescreen frame roughly (and comically) corresponding to left-versus-right brain antagonism; the contrast between Freddie's animalistic thrashing and Dodd's static contemplation echoes and anticipates similarly schematic set-ups in *There Will Be Blood* and *Phantom Thread* respectively. In the cell, Freddie parrots Val's accusation almost word for word ("you're making this shit up")—his first expression of defiance.

The seeming irrationality of Dodd welcoming Freddie back into the fold after their mutual blow up in prison ("I'm done with you," says Dodd by way of farewell) is counteracted with the ruthless logic of what he does next, which is to thoroughly domesticate his overeager attack dog. Freddie's congenital sense of drift—his inveterate directionlessness—is literalized in a series of exercises based around his movement through increasingly capacious environments. Instructed to move back and forth between a window and a wall (a more kinetic variation on being sent to sit in the corner, infused with the usual transcendent mumbo-jumbo) he's like a rogue particle careening wildly in a confined space. Relocated to a set of salt flats and placed upon a motorcycle, Freddie is told to "pick a point" and drive towards it. That point, it turns out, is the vanishing point and, in a startling blast of existential slapstick—like a Looney Tunes cartoon lensed by Terrence Malick—he just keeps driving, out of frame, out of sight, and out of Dodd's life. That is, until the reunion in England, a meeting heralded by the final appearance of the wake, now indicating a trip across the Atlantic rather than the Pacific.

Like *There Will Be Blood*, *The Master* is a film with two distinct climaxes, each with its own dualistic dimension. Dodd's failed seduction via "Slow Boat to China" serves to conclude, if not necessarily reconcile, his relationship with Freddie, who, by rejecting not only "Master's" unmistakable emotional appeal but also his Cause-inflected talk about their both being locked in an ancient and recursive cycle

(continued on page 79)

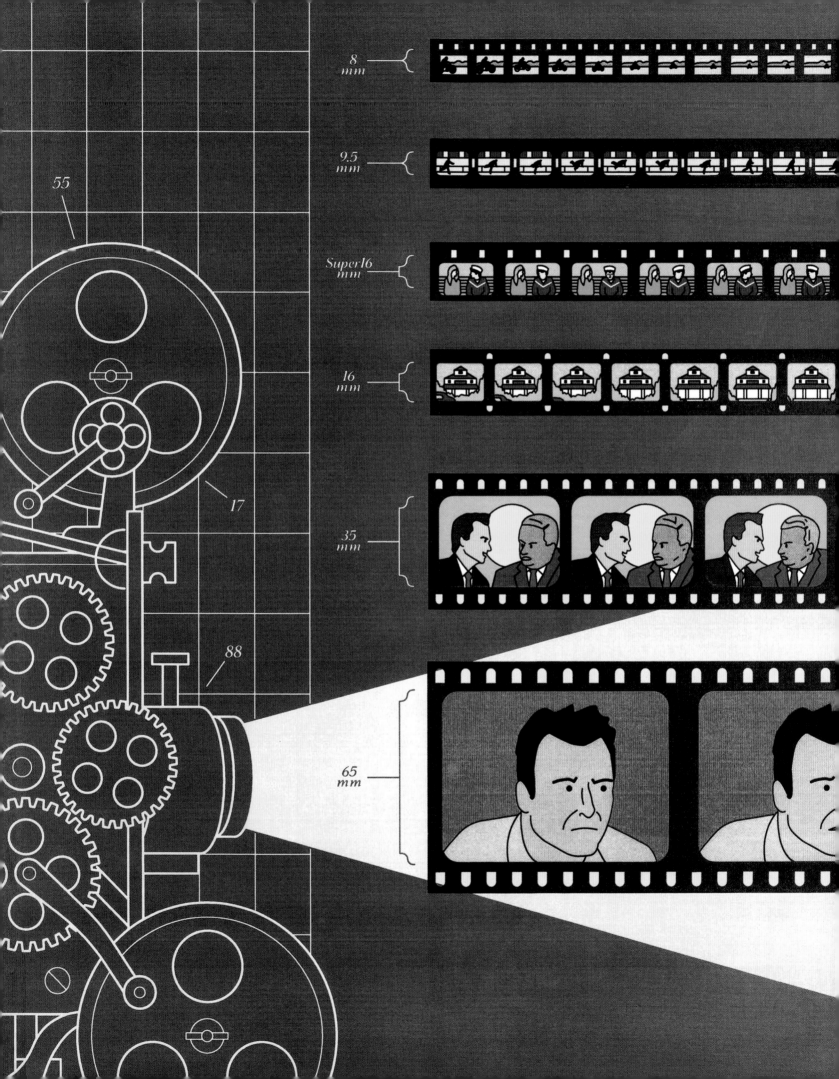

8
mm

9.5
mm

Super16
mm

16
mm

35
mm

65
mm

55

17

88

There may be no more dislocating sequence in early-sixties American cinema than the passage in *The Manchurian Candidate* where a meeting of the "women's garden club" is revealed, over the course of a languorous 360-degree pan, to be in fact a clandestine gathering of Russian and Chinese intelligence officials—a virtuoso act of unveiling that doubles as an encapsulation of the movie's themes. In John Frankenheimer's delirious thriller, US soldiers are systematically brainwashed to become assassins, programmed subconsciously in a slyly hyperbolic sci-fi satire of Cold War-era paranoia; the little old ladies talking about hydrangeas are really Soviet puppet-masters. The idea that susceptible Americans could succumb obliviously to foreign ideology gets audaciously visualized here, staged surreally via the memories of one of the hypnotized victims: Safe at home but still dreaming feverishly of Korea, Captain Bennett Marco (Frank Sinatra), can't believe what he's seeing with his own mind's-eye.

The stylistic similarities between this bravura set-piece and the hallucinatory "I'll No More Go A-Roving" scene in *The Master* are pronounced enough that the possibility of direct homage is in play, but there are subtler and more suggestive links between the two movies. Freely adapted from Richard Condon's 1959 novel and released in October of 1962 at the height of the Cuban Missile Crisis, *The Manchurian Candidate* offered a dazzlingly discombobulating take on the social and political tensions of the day. That the title character, a bloviating conservative senator (James Gregory as "Big" John Iselin) stage-managed by his wife (Angela Lansbury) and her Communist co-conspirators, was meant as a parody of Joe McCarthy was obvious enough, and yet the film also skewered the still-forming Camelot mythos splitting its JFK figure in two, between glamorous Rat Packer Sinatra and Laurence Harvey's Raymond Shaw, a telegenic war hero manipulated into a series of murderous outbursts.

Even leaving aside his being tricked into becoming a mind-controlled killer (JFK and Lee Harvey Oswald in one, long before the latter would emerge from obscurity for his real-life, walk-on role), Raymond's bitter mix of cynicism and vulnerability marks him as damaged goods. No less than *Let There Be Light*, *The Manchurian Candidate* hints that America's fighting men have come home in a state of disrepair, although his broken state is not solely a byproduct of his combat experiences. In Condon's novel, the incestuous backstory of the villainous

Mrs. Iselin and the way it bleeds over into her possessive, combative relationship with her son is explicit; George Axelrod's screenplay downplays these elements but they're still present enough that the film challenges *Psycho* as a perverse joke on the latent mania of a so-called Mama's Boy. Joquin Phoenix's eloquently halting body language as Freddie Quell is modeled on the documentary portraiture of *Let There Be Light*, but the more Gothic strokes of his performance—the flickers of a secret, shameful pain rooted in a lineage of incest (he tells Dodd he slept with his aunt) and mental illness ("loony bin," he rasps when queried about his mother's whereabouts)—are oddly synchronous with *The Manchurian Candidate*'s own shadow narrative.

The use of hypnosis in *The Manchurian Candidate* is not therapeutic, nor is it particularly realistic, although the well-known caveat that a hypnotized subject cannot do anything against his or her will—dutifully parroted in the dialogue by Khigh Dhiegh's Chinese Caligari Dr. Yen Lo—plays out interestingly in Raymond's decision in the end to kill his mother and father-in-law instead of his assigned target. It's an act of defiance rooted in a sense of personal rather than political emancipation, and his psychic liberation comes with a price—a gesture of suicidal contrition tied more to his earlier, horrifically detached and yet not fully repressed killing of his lover. ("They can make me do anything," he moans despondently to Marco, who can't tell him otherwise). In the end, Raymond fulfills his ersatz patriot-warrior persona by defending the republic from an invading (if internally located) force; he earns the medal he was given as part of a duplicitous cover story.

Freddie's arc in *The Master* is less dramatic or decisive, but it's similarly about a process in which synapses get cut like apron springs. It's hard to say whether he actively resists Dodd's tactics or else passively reveals their inherent phoniness, and yet by the end of the film, he is—for better or worse—his own man, unwilling to serve a master. He may still be haunted by what Yen Lo diagnoses at one point in *The Manchurian Candidate* as "those uniquely American symptoms [of] guilt and fear," but he's also learned that the cure may be worse than the disease: In both films, freedom is very much a state of mind.

If you come in five minutes after this picture begins, you won't know what it's all about!

when you've seen it all, you'll swear there's never been anything like it!

**Frank Sinatra
Laurence Harvey
Janet Leigh**

The Manchurian Candidate

Angela   Henry   James
Lansbury   Silva   Gregory

Produced by GEORGE AXELROD and JOHN FRANKENHEIMER
Directed by JOHN FRANKENHEIMER Screenplay by GEORGE AXELROD
Based upon a novel by RICHARD CONDON Executive Producer HOWARD W. KOCH
AN M-C PRODUCTION RELEASED THRU UNITED ARTISTS

The waning of Dodd's hold on Freddie finds eloquent and humorous visual expression when they journey to the desert to race motorcycles. After telling Freddie to "pick a point" and head towards it, Dodd can only watch as his protégé speeds away from him— a wayward dot against a distant horizon.

(i.e., that they actually met a century earlier as soldiers in the Prussian war) reveals himself as being capable of perspective and even detachment. His rejoinder, "maybe in the next life," is a dictionary-precise definition of irony, saying one thing while critically implying its opposite. That Freddie weeps at Dodd's song demonstrates, perhaps, a swell of feeling at the recognition that he's wanted; what empowers him is the realization that being wanted is not, in and of itself, reason enough to stay.

"You can't take this life straight, can you?" sighs Peggy when Freddie arrives. This might be the most charged line in the entire film, referencing Freddie's alcoholism, which shows no signs of abating, and teasing another interpretation of Dodd's devotion (an echo of *There Will Be Blood*'s barely sublimated queerness). It is also, on its face, a profound dismissal of the possibility that Freddie will get what he wants. And yet Anderson gifts his protagonist with a "happy ending" anyway. After stopping at a pub, Freddie ends up in bed with a young British woman named Winn Manchester (Jennifer Neala Page) whose physical appearance—tall, red-haired—connotes her as yet another one of his dreamgirls even as she is very much a flesh-and-blood reality.

No longer reduced to an onlooker through a camera lens or his own addled perceptions, Freddie is able to participate eagerly in an act which had previously remained in the realm of fantasy. What's even more liberating, though, is the way that a character previously shown following orders (in the Army, on the job, and in the service of the Cause) takes it upon himself to become "The Master," leading her through a version of Dodd's processing with the rules jumbled and the stakes reduced—just so much meaningless pillow talk, punctuated by his playful, self-deprecating instruction to Winn to "stick it back in, it fell out."

These are the last lines in the film, and maybe the last, giggly word on how much the Cause's pseudo-philosophy is supposed to matter—to Freddie, to Anderson, and to us. Long defined by his pent-up energy, Freddie finally seems at rest. And then Anderson cuts back to a shot of him beside the woman on the beach, a beautifully ambiguous gesture that feels out of nowhere, unmooring the film in time and space—an ellipsis that's also an ouroboros. *The Master*'s double vision comes into focus: It's a close-up and a two-shot; a dream and a reality; an ending and a return to the start. Is Winn, to use Freddie's words, "the greatest girl [he's] ever met" or just a placeholder for an ideal that can never be reached? In a film of interior landscapes, the beach is Paradise and Purgatory at the same time, a space of pure desire that leaves the possibility of consummation at arm's reach and yet forever in doubt. She may not be real, but Freddie has her all to himself, alone. And he always will.

T he first words of Thomas Pynchon's 2009 novel *Inherent Vice* are a slogan: "Under the paving stones, the beach." It's an epigram that derives from the May 1968 protest movement in France, in which students took to the streets of the French capital in defiance of American imperialism. The phrase, coined jointly by student activist Bernard Cousins and public relations expert Bernhard Fritsch, refers specifically to the use of forcibly torn-up sets to create makeshift barricades. Its metaphorical dimension transformed it into a widespread rallying cry.

The image of an unblemished natural expanse waiting to be rescued from beneath its suffocating enclosure signified on a social, cultural, ecological and even religious wavelength: A poetic rejoinder to history's inexorable forward momentum. Two years later, Joni Mitchell reworked the words into the hook of her hit single "Big Yellow Taxi," whose narrator juxtaposes the departure of her lover with the evils of urban sprawl: "They paved paradise and put up a parking lot."

"Big Yellow Taxi" was released in the summer of 1970, the same period dramatized in Pynchon's novel and Paul Thomas Anderson's 2014 adaptation, neither of which name-check it directly even as they embody aspects of its lyrical content. Under the guise of an environmentalist lament, Mitchell was writing about a more universal sensation: The feeling of something (or somebody) slipping away, articulated via the enduring, self-lacerating refrain "you don't know what you've got till it's gone." The elusive party in *Inherent Vice* is one Shasta Fay Hepworth (Katherine Waterston), the hippie ex-girlfriend of Larry "Doc" Sportello (Joaquin Phoenix), a self-styled private eye plying his trade in and around the outer edges of Los Angeles.

Doc's specialty is missing persons cases, and his gig takes on a darkly ironic tinge when Shasta, never one to be tied down, seemingly vanishes into thin air. This coming after an ominous visit to Doc's place during which she outlines a high-society kidnapping scheme and alludes to her own potential impending disappearance. Even though they're no longer a couple, Doc is in love with Shasta, and moreover he feels like it's his responsibility to find her.

Doc is played by Joaquin Phoenix, a piece of casting that can't help but connect the role (and the movie as a whole) to *The Master*. Like its predecessor, *Inherent Vice* begins with a shot of the ocean, except that instead of a bird's-eye, magisterial view, it opts for a shot wittily defined by horizontal lines: The Pacific is seen at a distance, bisecting the space between two ramshackle waterfront properties. In the foreground, the railing of a staircase invites us to climb down and head towards the horizon line, the same destination as Daniel Plainview and Freddie Quell. This inviting trajectory is an apt entry point for a movie whose narrative and themes are tied to the idea of questing—of Doc's search for Shasta, threaded as it is through a series of subplots about other characters who've become physically or figuratively lost amid the city's labyrinthine layout. It's a clever play on Pynchon's epigram, capturing a similar dynamic between civilization and the natural world. This sunblind stoner enclave of boardwalks and head shops exists at the edge of something huge and elemental. Under the paving stones, Gordita Beach!

The process of searching for something below the surface—of playing detective—is inherent to the storyline of both versions of *Inherent Vice*, which follow Doc as he attempts

to locate Shasta as well as billionaire land developer Mickey Wolfmann (Eric Roberts), who may or may not have been kidnapped and may or may not also be her new lover. But detective work is also embedded more abstractly in the relationship between the book and the movie. For viewers who've read the novel, the film's 148-minute running time is a staging ground for an investigation: Noting what's been included and excluded, what's been altered and what's been added, and mapping Pynchon's tricky, endlessly verbose prose onto Anderson's mise-en-scène.

The result is a movie that functions as a kind of reversible palimpsest, depending on which artist you're superimposing over the other. You can try to see Pynchon in the events on-screen (quite literally if the rumors of the famously reclusive author's unbilled, *Where's Waldo*–style cameo are to be believed) or else tally up the auteur touches: The roving

camera; the ghostly dissolves; the virtuoso juvenalia. With *There Will Be Blood*, Anderson showed no compunction about diverging from the work of Upton Sinclair, but his reverence for Pynchon's text, and also for a period closer to his own experience, yielded a sense of fidelity.

At least, up to a point. "You've got this great writer," Anderson told *Cineaste* in 2015. "[So] don't change a word. But you've got to change words. I think we've done a very faithful adaptation . . . but that's in tone and mood and everything else. There's tons that had to go. Pynchon aficionados will think 'who's this fucking character who fucked up our favorite writer?' You risk that."

In the same interview, Anderson admitted that he'd "kind of had enough of being left to his own devices," framing the decision to take on Pynchon—merely one of the

↑ **Above** "Under the paving stones, the beach": The rallying cry of May 1968 serves as the epigraph for Thomas Pynchon's novel of *Inherent Vice*, suggesting an Edenic Paradise buried beneath the concrete edifices of modern civilization—a metaphor for a natural order suppressed and waiting to break free.

↑ **Top** While Doc operates mostly on the right side of the law, he's consistently antagonized by super-cop Bigfoot Bjornsen—a Nixonian caricature of law-and-order who regards the private detective with contemptuous scorn. The LAPD are a constantly lurking presence throughout *Inherent Vice*, thwarting and hassling Doc's progress at every turn.

↑ **Bottom** The opening shot of *Inherent Vice* visualizes the opening lines off-handedly, showing neither the paving stones nor the beach, but rather land and sea, with the stairwell beckoning us invitingly down towards the oceanic expanse.

most distinctive, idiosyncratic American novelists of the twentieth century—as a "shot of adrenaline" after self-generating the screenplays for *There Will Be Blood* and *The Master*. Although the connection was not widely acknowledged, there was more than a little bit of Pynchon's 1963 debut novel *V.* in *The Master*: The book is about a discharged seaman who joins up with an eccentric, semi-bohemian collective known as the "Whole Sick Crew," rebels without a cause who nevertheless practice a form of psychological indoctrination.

"Shall I project a world?" asks Oedpia, the conspiracy theorist heroine of *The Crying of Lot 49* (1966). Her not-so-rhetorical question doubles as Pynchon's gleeful entreaty to his readership. Taken together, his novels constitute a relentlessly intertextual yet self-contained metafictional universe, one capacious enough to contain digressions on any and every possible subject but mostly focused on unfolding a counterfactual history of the United States from the 1700s onwards, from the Colonial satire of *Mason & Dixon* (1997) and terrifying turn-of-the-century modernity of *Against the Day* (2006), through the grotesque, poetic evocation of World War II and its aftermath in *V.* and *Gravity's Rainbow* (1973) and the 9/11 anxieties of *Bleeding Edge* (2013). Within this scheme, *Inherent Vice* constitutes both connective tissue—bridging the temporal and countercultural gap between between the Beatles-meet-*Lolita* sixties of *The Crying of Lot 49* and the Reaganite hangover of *Vineland* (1990)—while also functioning as an outlier: A relatively straightforward exercise in genre fiction by a writer determined to evade categorization. "*Inherent Vice* is a simple shaggy-dog detective story that pits likable dopers against the Los Angeles Police Department," wrote Michiko Kakutani in the *New York Times*. "It feels more like a Classic Comics version of a Pynchon novel than the thing itself."

Comic books definitely figured into Anderson's game plan for his version of *Inherent Vice*, specifically Gilbert Shelton's landmark underground cartoon *The Fabulous Furry Freak Brothers*, whose trio of stoner heroes—all bulbous noses, bulging bellies, and bushy, Jerry-Rubin grade facial hair—became the visual model for Phoenix's embodiment of Doc. Long and lanky beneath his beach-bum duds and handsome behind sunglasses and sideburns, he's as striking a presence as Freddie Quell, although conceived and acted in an adjacent behavioral register.

Where Freddie (and Daniel Plainview) were both shambling alcoholics, Doc is a pothead, a mellower affliction that leaves him addled but functional. He may be well and truly stoned in the majority of his scenes, but not in a way that limits his abilities as an investigator, and which also enhances his archetypal appeal. One year after the Summer of Love—and also the Manson Family murders, which are referred to several times in throwaway bits of dialogue—Doc's patchouli couture brands him as a stand-in for countercultural resistance in a country otherwise serving the will of its ruling silent majority via a foreign police action that has long since bled into a full-on military campaign.

It's not quite right to call *Inherent Vice* a Vietnam allegory, but the war—and the larger ideological divide it opened up on the homefront—is present as background texture. With his trusty notebook in hand, Doc is apt to search for connections, however tenuous, between the people he meets in the line of duty, and most of the chatter in East LA is all about a shadowy syndicate known as the Golden Fang, whose name and iconography hint at some sort of Oriental origin. From this xeonophobic angle, Doc is, in his own way, fighting the good fight in microcosm, but the Golden Fang ultimately isn't as exotic as it sounds, while his true rivals are local.

His clashes with the stone-faced LAPD detective Bigfoot Bjornsen (Josh Brolin), a physically imposing bully who burlesques Woodstock fashions on commercials for local businesses, are broadly representative of the period's schism between hippie hedonism and authoritarian machismo. When Doc's long and winding investigation of Mickey Wolfmann's whereabouts leads to his stumbling across the headquarters of aforementioned massive international corporatized criminal conspiracy—a towering, gilded building owned by the Golden Fang and located in the middle of Los Angeles—it becomes clear, in Pynchon's relentlessly dialectical conception that it's actually communism's evil twin that Doc's battling. The specter haunting the world is capitalism.

Same as it ever was: The noir genre has always reflected the social, historical, and economic conditions around its inception and development, rooted in the dislocation and fiscal inequality of the postwar forties and updated accordingly, whether via the Watergate fatalism of *The Long Goodbye* (1973) or the Desert Storm dementia of *The Big Lebowski* (1998). Both of these canonical LA stoner noirs became inevitable points of critical reference for *Inherent Vice*, but while Phoenix's performance arguably splits the difference between the fagged-out cool of Elliott Gould's Philip Marlowe and the hapless sweetness of Jeff Bridges as the Dude, Anderson's choices with regard to his hero take their cues directly from Pynchon.

The narcotic drift of Robert Elswit's camera and its recurring motif of slow-push-ins—ominous shots that probe unstoppably through space while paralyzing time—captures the novel's air of free-floating unease. The technique evokes the disequilibrium of being stoned as well the constant fear of losing sight of the bigger picture as it contracts towards a vanishing point. Trippiness is very much in Anderson's wheelhouse, and the portrayal of Doc and his medicinally enhanced paranoia follows the book almost exactly, providing the filmmaker with a steadily skewed frame on which to hang his myriad revisions.

The first and most apparent of these is the promotion of the minor character Sortilège (Joanna Newsom) into a position of prominence. She is the first person in the movie to speak, and when she does it is in the voice of the novel's omniscient narrator—as Pynchon himself. In the book, Sortilège is a sidekick who keeps Doc medicated and offers astrological advice; her hippie-chick tendencies make her

a mirror for Shasta, except that her relationship with Doc is purely platonic. If anything, she is Shasta's obverse within the narrative, a constant presence rather than a structuring absence. Anderson's decision to give her authority over the story is a canny one, dissolving the hard-boiled aura around the private eye genre into something hazier.

More practically, Newsom's expanded role allows for Anderson to retain snatches of the novel's dazzling language. For instance, it is via Sortilège's voiceover that *Inherent Vice* develops the crucial theme of Los Angeles as contested territory—a city long since carved up by various factions looking to control its resources and economy. The rapacious mindset dramatized in *There Will Be Blood* has not dissipated but thickened, hovering over pattern of land grabs authored by the spiritual descendants of Daniel Plainview: "Mexican families bounced out of Chavez Ravine to build Dodger Stadium, American Indians swept out of Bunker Hill for the Music Center, Tariq's neighborhood bulldozed aside for Channel View estates."

With his monstrous moniker and ruthless professional ethics—which involves using members of the Aryan Brotherhood as hired muscle—Mickey Wolfmann is the central Plainview manqué, but he's also a figure of pity and even pathos. What Shasta tells Doc during their first meeting is that Mickey's wife Sloane (Serena Scott Thomas) is fixing to have him committed to an insane asylum. Locked away in Chryskylodon, a luxurious compound catering to the extremely wealthy and spiritually bankrupt, Mickey finds peace in the relinquishment of his business interests. He's content instead to buy into the doctrine of selflessness preached by his new captor-mentors, making the alpha-wolf capitalist an unlikely but symbolically rich casualty of the era's vogue for cults.

Chryskylodon was modeled by Pynchon after the Big Sur–based Esalen Institute, founded by a pair of Stanford graduates determined to expand human consciousness: The list of celebrity practitioners over the years rivals that of Scientology. Anderson deviates from the novel again by having Doc actually find Wolfmann instead of having his imprisonment and carefully stage-managed philanthropy narrated to him by Bigfoot, and the scenes at Chryskylodon allow him to revisit the sinister placidity of the Cause's digs in *The Master*. The revelation that the self-help gurus are in league with (in actuality, fully subsidized by) operatives of the Golden Fang is not surprising, and neither is the suggestion that their methods are a sham.

The key to Pynchon's riff on noir is its lack of surprise at the idea that everything is connected, and that the hero's understanding of this synchronicity—i.e., learning that the disappearances of Shasta, Mickey, and the supposedly dead surf-trumpet player Coy Harlingen (Owen Wilson), whom he's simultaneously been hired to find by Coy's dubious, heartsick wife Hope (Jena Malone) are all part of the same case—yields not exhilaration but resignation. It's all just another byproduct of conglomeration: Of a vicious circle of supply and demand. "If the Golden Fang can get customers strung out," muses Sortilège, "why not run around and sell them a program to help kick. . . . As long as American life was something to be escaped from, the cartel could always be sure of a bottomless pool of new customers."

It's through this prism of addiction that *Inherent Vice* locates its hobbled, seriocomic soul. Doc's meeting with Hope (her name a movingly blatant synecdoche of her character) is punctuated by one of the movie's more outrageous gags—a Looney Tunes–style double take-and-scream by Doc after looking at a long-ago Polaroid of his client's heroin-addicted baby—now cleaned up, like her mother, into a perfectly normal-looking suburban moppet named Amethyst (a quartz that wards off intoxication). Doc's horror at the photographic evidence of the young man's past negligence is tempered by his desire

to help her out regardless, and of his general concern for fuck-ups trying to fly right, which reflects a degree of self-knowledge. "You can't take this life straight, can you?" was the key question of *The Master*, directed at Freddie, and Doc can't really take life straight either: His reliance on pot and the disintegrating effect it has on his consciousness is his *Inherent Vice*.

In interviews, Anderson has spoken about the zany comedies of Jim Abrams and David and Jerry Zucker as formative influences on *Inherent Vice*'s sight gag-heavy aesthetic, which overstates the case a bit. With the exception of Martin Short's manic, coked-out dentist Dr. Rudy Blatnoyd, the performances eschew blackout sketch wackiness. Where the idea of comic-book stylization rings true is the way Anderson depicts the LAPD as a swarming, authoritarian force, as its officers repeatedly impede Doc's progress and knock him to the ground. These vignettes have the clean, graphic power of an editorial cartoon. The image of the cops as faceless drones also serves Pynchon's larger conception of urban tribalism: In addition to the LAPD, the plot involves factions including the Black Panthers, the Aryan Brotherhood, the Chryskylodon cultists and, of course, the Golden Fang, whose chompers are engorged on all fronts.

But Doc stands alone, his independence emphasized throughout as a close cousin to his loneliness. Flying solo, he's able to access all of the hugely variegated habitats that make up the film's carnivalesque vision of Los Angeles. He slyly slides through the door at the Wolfmann mansion and breaks into Chryskylodon; he patronizes a suburban strip-mall massage parlor and breaches a drug-fueled house party in Topanga Canyon; he's on a first-name basis with the staff at police headquarters and the District Attorney's office. Doc's physical mobility, his determination to do the legwork demanded by his profession, is what gives the plot its picaresque momentum through a lovingly recreated Los Angeles. But it's his refusal to budge on his essential principles—to know the difference between simple temptation and the glossy decay represented by the Golden Fang—that makes him a hero.

To wit: Doc never receives any sort of compensation for his role in knotting the story's various dangling threads. Vice may be inherent, but virtue is its own reward—for whatever that's worth. During a late meeting with a malevolent businessman, he cracks wise, "How much money would I have to take from you so I don't lose your respect?" But he doesn't take any money—not even expenses. The actual dialogue is lifted straight from Pynchon, and it's as much a query to the reader/audience as it is to the antagonist: Doc is wondering aloud about the consequences of his steadfast refusal to (literally) buy into the system that keeps the Golden Fang in business.

A few scenes later, when we see him turning over several hundred pounds of shanghaied narcotics to some incongruously wholesome-looking operatives—a blonde-mother daughter duo in a station wagon—the visual joke is a killer: The hippie handing over the heroin to the suburban

*↑ **Above** Neil Young's haunting "Journey Through the Past" soundtracks a flashback showing Doc and Shasta in happier times, playing with a ouija board with Sortilège (opposite) and trying to score drugs in a rainstorm (center). Shasta's lyrically shot walk past an empty lot gives way to Doc moving through the same neighborhood years later only to see that the space has been colonized by the Golden Fang (left)—the freedom of the past buried by the contingencies of the present.*

This brazenly allusive tableaux evoking *The Last Supper* by way of a hippie pizza party—or a panel of the Fabulous Furry Freak Brothers—stands as *Inherent Vice*'s satirical centerpiece, an affectionate, empathetic jab at late-sixties iconography with comically (ir)religious undertones.

"Not hallucinating": Doc's notebook doubles as a chronicle of his investigation into Shasta's disappearance and his increasing paranoia about being at the center of a massive conspiracy involving the international crime syndicate called the Golden Fang.

squares, an early tactical surrender in the impending War on Drugs. "How long have you been working for the Golden Fang?" Doc asks, making conversation; when the little girl flips him off, he flashes a peace sign before returning the single finger salute.

This surreal tableau plays up the idea that Doc is, for all his hipster accessories, as inviolate as Raymond Chandler's original Philip Marlowe: A white knight in tarnished armor. His only request is that the Golden Fang release one of their undercover agents—that'd be Coy, who also happens to be a police informant—so that he can reunite with his wife and daughter. Anderson opts to shoot the subsequent reunion with Doc at a remove. Instead of going inside to observe the catharsis he's engineered, he stays in the car—another reminder of his solitary position.

Coy is one of two characters in *Inherent Vice* who can be taken as a doppelganger for Doc: In his case, he's what Doc could have been—or perhaps still could be—if he were to choose the safe harbour of hearth and home. The other, more significant twin is Bigfoot, who is probably the movie's most carefully modulated character, a foil who gradually takes on a tragic dimension. Initially, Anderson's strategy is to satirize Bigfoot's eight hundred-pound gorilla act, as in the profoundly adolescent shots of him sucking passionately and obliviously on a chocolate-covered frozen banana as he chauffeurs Doc through the city in his squad car: It's a juvenile way of suggesting sublimated homosexuality (or signalling homophobic panic, take your pick). But as *Inherent Vice* goes on, Bigfoot is shown to be no less a victim of external forces—including the Golden Fang, who conspired to have his partner assassinated—than Doc. And, despite his intimidating solidity, he may be less capable of holding things together in light of that knowledge.

Anderson's bold addition of a final tête-à-tête between the characters compresses Bigfoot's entire downward arc into a few broad, enigmatic strokes. In terms of the overall narrative, Bigfoot's final actions are deeply ambivalent: He helps Doc escape from the clutches of some neo-Nazi abductors working on behalf of a Golden Fang-affiliated loan shark, but the rescue is just a pretense to plant a shipment of heroin in Doc's trunk. After Doc successfully offloads the drugs in exchange for Coy's freedom, Bigfoot smashes his way into his house, leading with his size twelves, but his aggression is spent. "It's been a long and busy day of civil rights violations," he sighs. "I was in the neighborhood and I felt myself compelled to drop in."

The subtext seems to be that the supercop misses his punching bag, but it's more than that. Bigfoot is profoundly lonely (his wife, seen in fleeting glimpses, is named "Chastity," so we can perhaps assume some martial frustrations). Where Doc's paranoia is par for the course, Bigfoot's realization of his own insignificance in the larger scheme of things is deeply wounding, and his contempt for his opposite number is laced with envy. Inexplicably, their dialogue becomes synched and they speak as one, in unison, "Listen, I'm sorry about last night. You? Why

(continued on page 100)

Gilbert Shelton's underground comic strip *The Fabulous Furry Freak Brothers* was a key influence on Anderson's adaptation of *Inherent Vice*, both in terms of its slightly cartoony visual style and loose, anarchic tone; the strip's affectionate heroizing of anti-establishment outcasts made it a beloved under-the-radar publication of the early 1970s.

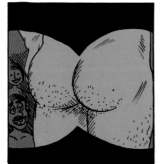

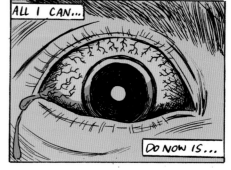

In 2014, following the world premiere of *Inherent Vice* at the New York Film Festival, Paul Thomas Anderson hosted a public salon discussing his various influences for the film, including the ABC procedural spoof *Police Squad!* and Alex Cox's deathless sci-fi punk oddity *Repo Man*. The strangest and most unexpected of these was the 1974 documentary *Journey Through the Past*, an experimental self-portrait directed by Neil Young under his long-standing pseudonym Bernard Shakey, which was represented in Anderson's presentation by a clip that reportedly left the audience somewhat bewildered; "they're not all going to be that fucking weird" the filmmaker offered by way of explanation if not apology.

In 1972, Young was at his commercial peak, having just released the acclaimed and best-selling *Harvest* album, a country-inflected collection whose intermittent provocations— baiting the unreconstructed American South through "Alabama's" regional put-downs and vexing feminists with the title and subtext of "A Man Needs a Maid"—couldn't staunch its melancholy melodicism: Despite their slow, stately pace, songs like "Old Man," "The Needle and the Damage Done" and "Heart of Gold" proved radio hits. *Harvest* made Young a household name as a solo act, and the combination of exposure and leverage may be what motivated him to release, as a follow-up, a two-disc audio collage whose contents were not new songs but older recordings culled from live radio and television broadcasts and rehearsal sessions with his former bandmates in Buffalo Springfield and Crosby, Stills, Nash, and Young. The record was described as a "soundtrack album" for a movie of the same name, but appeared in stores well ahead of its apparent inspiration; by the time the film version of *Journey Through the Past* was completed, it was 1974 and the LP had long since fallen off the charts.

The discontinuity between release dates is one oddity in the relationship between the two incarnations of *Journey Through the Past*; another is that the ostensible title track for both appears in neither. "I wrote it as the title tune for the picture, but then I found out that they had nothing to do with each other" Young told the *New York Times*, underlining the odd, contentious jumble of his multimedia venture. If anything, the lyric of "Journey Through the Past," with its ardent, questioning refrain of "will I still be in your eyes and on your mind?" syncs up perfectly with the content of the film, which in many ways resembles D.A. Pennebaker's 1967

Bob Dylan profile *Don't Look Back* while defying its titular edict: Here, every aspect of Young's music, career, and public persona are projected purposefully through the lens of the archive, eschewing forward momentum for the reverse trajectory of memory.

One way to look at the raggedly prismatic object that is *Journey Through the Past* is as Young's slightly premature reckoning with his own celebrity and mythmaking: In almost every jaggedly assembled sequence, the line between arrogance and self-deprecation gets warped and blurred. Another angle of approach would be to consider it as the singer's attempt to distinguish between his star persona and his private self (with "Bernard Shakey" as the guiding intelligence). The latter interpretation manifests most vividly in the footage of an outing pairing Young with his girlfriend at the time, the Oscar-nominated-actress Carrie Snodgress; they're shown driving together into the country and sharing a mostly wordless picnic lunch. "This scene in particular feels like my version of heaven," was Anderson's assessment. "Cruising round with your girl, parking your jalopy with a babbling brook nearby, taking a joint out, eating some strawberries . . . I don't know how it can get any better."

The use of "Journey Through the Past" to soundtrack Doc and Shasta's blissful afternoon in *Inherent Vice* cinches the allusion, but the effect goes beyond mere reference. Young's film balances its creator's desire to revisit his career against the desire to move forward—its nostalgia is tinged with anxiety and loss. "You want to keep going?" Young asks Snod-gress as they get up to leave their picnic, a simple query with answer whose inevitability encapsulates the meaning of "inherent vice" and also *Inherent Vice*: That the moment at which things can't get any better can only be a prelude to their deterioration.

JOURNEY THROUGH THE PAST
a film by NEIL YOUNG

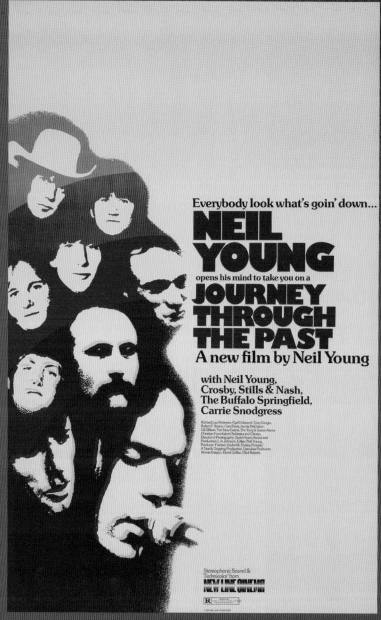

Everybody look what's goin' down...
NEIL YOUNG
opens his mind to take you on a
JOURNEY THROUGH THE PAST
A new film by Neil Young

with Neil Young,
Crosby, Stills & Nash,
The Buffalo Springfield,
Carrie Snodgress

Stereophonic Sound &
Technicolor from
NEW LINE CINEMA

should you be sorry?" Because they're also sharing a joint at the time, it's possible to read Bigfoot and Doc's mutual fugue of accusation and apology as something imagined—especially when Bigfoot makes good on his nickname and stuffs a handful or raw marijuana into his mouth. Brolin's cast-iron deadpan vulcanizes into something mournful. His face has become a devastated landscape to rival Lancaster Dodd's at the end of *The Master*, right down to the flickers of desperate surrender in his eyes, as if Jack Webb had become momentarily possessed by Frank Serpico.

The humanizing of Bigfoot is in line with Anderson's characteristic surfeit of empathy, which also informs a lovely flashback to Doc and Shasta, floundering together in "one of those prolonged times of no dope," running out into the rain to score—a plan cooked up after consulting Sortilège's ouija board. They end up empty-handed only to fall laughing into each other's arms under a strip-mall awning, seeking shelter from the storm. The use of Neil Young's "Journey Through the Past," underscores the scene's status as a fragile, sustaining memory, effectively italicizing Shasta's absence in the present tense while the camera's prowl along the length of a fence enclosing a vacant lot points similarly to something missing. The punchline—sudden, elegant, devastating—comes when Doc rounds the same corner on Sunset Boulevard to see that the space has filled in by a towering, brutalist office building erected in the name and curving, mercenary shape of the Golden Fang. It's not bad enough that they paved paradise and put up a parking lot—they went and built a monument to greed on top of it.

This moment is very much a point of no return: The beach is well and truly buried. On some level, the multi-directional futility of Doc's quest is known to us from the start, and yet it's still painful to watch how the sweetly idyllic sensations of the "Journey Through the Past" sequence get spoiled after Shasta returns. If Anderson's *Inherent Vice* is indeed a meta-detective exercise in trying to decide whether the filmmaker has hijacked the material or vice versa, the scene in Doc's house describing his reunion with his lover is at once inconclusive and definitive. It's modeled precisely on the novel while also manifesting something dark and disturbing on what would appear to be a more personal set of terms.

In the novel, Doc has been given information that she's back, but in the film she simply materializes—first in the foreground as a shadow out of a horror movie and then, just as unnervingly, as a placid, smiling vision. She brings her ex a beer, disappears to get change and emerges fully naked, asking in a lobotomized monotine: "What kind of girl do you need, Doc?" What follows is a one-take, tour de force sex scene with Shasta fully naked and draped across Phoenix's lap while recounting her adventures as a rich man's compliant plaything—a simultaneously erotic and disconcerting bit of exhibitionism that lines up snugly with Doc's most anguished fantasies (and Anderson's sometimes sentimentalized sexism). The basic choreography is Pynchon's, as is the suggestion that Doc is, at base, no different than the power-tripping masculine psychopaths he inwardly distinguishes himself from: No less aroused by "submissive, brainwashed, horny little teeners" than Charlie

Mason, and no less into power-tripping than Mickey Wolfmann or Bigfoot Bjornsen. In offering herself so completely to Doc, Shasta is enacting something between a come-on and a confessional, and the exchange that follows is more brutal and possessive than tender or erotic.

"When Doc finally caves and aggressively fucks Shasta, it's designed to be a illusion-shattering moment," writes Vikram Murthi. "The sixties are dead . . . instead of the two sharing kisses in the rain, they're sharing jaded sneers and aggressive power struggles." When Anderson cuts back to the pair in happier times on an (unpaved) beach, it's at once a saving grace and a twist of the knife, especially as Sortilège simultaneously explicates the meaning of the title: "Inherent Vice, in a marine insurance policy, is anything you can't avoid. Eggs break, chocolate melts, glass shatters. And Doc wondered what that meant when it applied to ex-old-ladies."

What it means is that things inevitably fall apart, and ultimately *Inherent Vice* is about the folly of nostalgia—for a culture, for a country, and for a lover—even as it luxuriates in its comforts. "Does it ever end?" Sortilège muses of her cohort's glory days, before correcting herself with the same abrupt velocity of that shot of the Golden Fang's tower. "Of course it does. It did." What Sortilège is describing isn't an ending but a point on a continuum whose contours are visible in retrospect, and which gains meaning from the fact that everything just keeps crumbling and rebuilding. Intimations of corruptibility and crime aside, what *Inherent Vice* really represents is the necessity of contingency, of not falling for the idea that people or ideology are truly immutable, and of toeing (without crossing) the thin line separating closely held principles for reactionary intractability (the distance, we might say, between Doc Sportello and Bigfoot).

The point is not that the heartless, profit-driven calculus of the Golden Fang adds up to anything new, just that it reincarnates something ancient and stubbornly enduring, which can't be toppled by a single knight-errant or otherwise—yet is subject to the same Inherent Vice as those who built it.

It preys on human frailty without transcending it, and the path of the practical radical is to wait it out, off the grid and for as long as possible—which is to say no path at all.

It may be a function of Anderson's abundant empathy that he refuses to let Doc go down that road alone, contriving a lovers-on-the-run ending where Shasta shacks up with Doc once and for all, even though he insists they're still "not back together." Pynchon's conclusion offers one last variation on the opening epigram's language of unveiling, as Doc waits, "for the fog to burn away, and for something else this time, somehow to be there instead." Anderson suggests that something is Shasta, but even so the morbid tenor of their sex scene, its lingering despair and fetishistic, necrophillic undertones hangs in the air. Her presence also means that Sortilège, Doc's voice of reason and the one person in the whole hazy caper that is *Inherent Vice* capable of seeing clearly, is nowhere to be found. Has he swapped out his dream girl for the real thing? Or has he abandoned his friend and navigator in an attempt to sustain an illusion?

It's also possible that Shasta isn't really there—that Doc is on a different kind of trip. In this case, Anderson's ending diverges from Pynchon and brushes up against *The Master*, with Phoenix once again stranded in a liminal space with a lover who completes him by being a projection—a phantom—of his own desire. "Remember the day the ouija board sent us off into that big storm?" asks Shasta, her head on Doc's shoulder. "This feels the same way tonight." To try to live inside a memory is to drift within a fog that never lifts; the headlight that catches Doc's eye before the final cut to black could mean that he sees through it, or else that he's happy to stay blind to the (un)reality of his situation. Either way, the scene is shot so that he's looking us, red-eyed but inquisitive, as if to scrutinize our responses: A detective down to the very last frame.

← *Left* Bigfoot Bjornsen's role as Doc's foil gets inverted in their final meeting, which Anderson scripted very differently than in the novel; here, the policeman seems to yearn for the hippie sleuth's lifestyle and freedom, animalistically devouring his pot stash as if it could transform him into a new person.

↖ *Opposite* When Shasta returns to Doc's apartment, she offers himself to him in an unsettling pantomime of physical submission that at once fulfills and undermines his self-image as her savior; the sex scene is shot so that the characters never make eye contact, complicating the idea of connection and implying instead a kind of base, impersonal exchange.

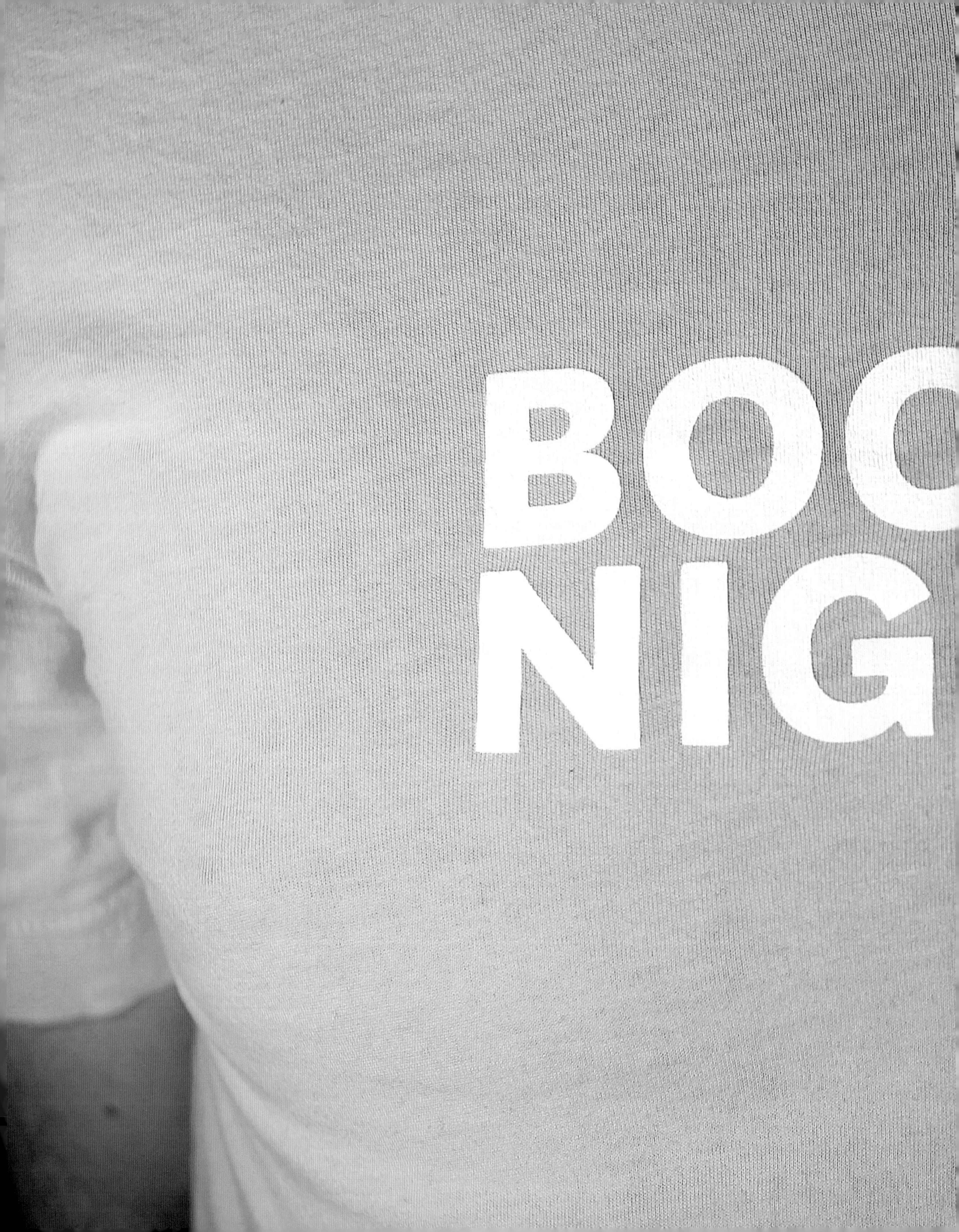
BOO
NIG

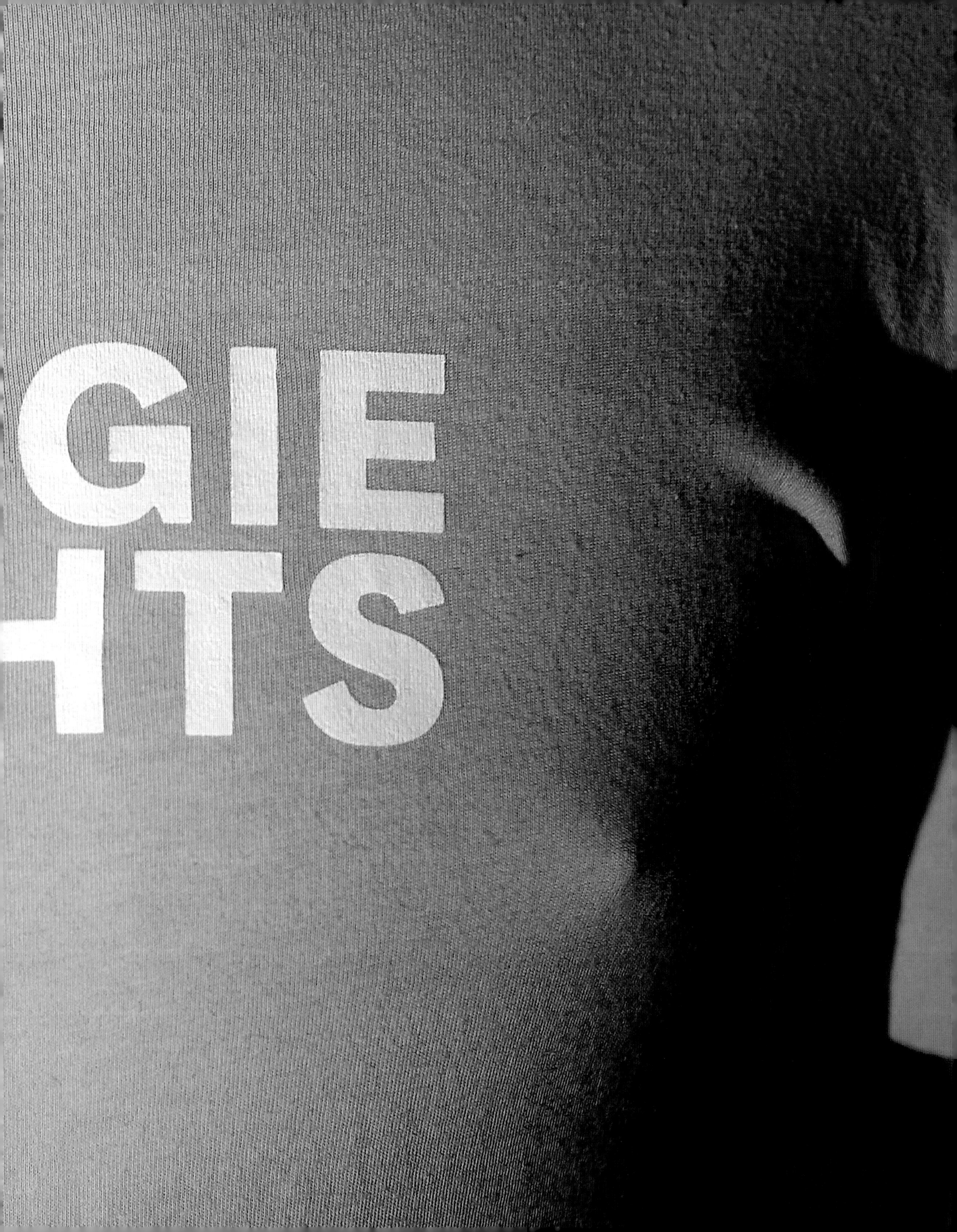
GIE
HTS

Fringed by mountains on all sides, the San Fernando Valley runs directly adjacent to Hollywood without officially being part of it. Its semi-tropical horizontal sprawl is fully visible from the long and winding Mulholland Drive—an appropriately downcast glance along a distinctly slippery slope of aspirations. Historically, the Valley is where movies too dirty for the light of day are made: the migration of the porn industry to Los Angeles in the wake of Hugh Hefner's innovations (and the erection of the Playboy Mansion in the Hollywood Hills) turned the suburb into a funnel for talent on both sides of the camera.

Jack Horner (Burt Reynolds) is a bit of a Hefner manqué, one whose eye for talent comes with a well-rehearsed gift for flattery. "A seventeen-year-old piece of gold," is his assessment of Eddie Adams (Mark Wahlberg), who buses to his dishwashing job at the Hot Traxx Disco in Reseda from not-so-nearby Torrance. It's an arduous commute for a crappy gig. "Can't you get a job like this in Torrance?" queries club patron Jack Horner (Burt Reynolds). He asks coyly, because he knows the answer. He can tell at a glance that Eddie wants to be where the action is. And in Reseda he's close enough.

Both of these men—the auteur and the ingenue—are playing their parts in a distinctly Californian narrative that predates porn: it's the same matter of prospecting and manifest destiny depicted in *There Will Be Blood*. If Jack, the surveyor of up-and-comers has struck gold, so has Eddie, who over the course of the film makes the most of his Lana Turner-ish "discovery," parlaying his diamond-in-the-rough origins into glittering marquee stardom.

That the name in lights is not actually his own is in keeping with the vicissitudes of showbiz. No sooner has Eddie been plucked out of obscurity than he's rebranded himself as "Dirk Diggler," an alliterative and allusive nom de plume riffing on the promise and prominence of his dick. The name is a joke and a boast, and also a carryover from Paul Thomas Anderson's 1988 mockumentary *The Dirk Diggler Story*, an assured short made when the director was seventeen. The rough-hewn mockumentary style is borrowed from *This Is Spinal Tap* (1984); its well-endowed protagonist is based on the adult film star John Holmes as depicted in the 1981 profile *Exhausted*. The relationship between these two films has been well-documented over the years in stories about Anderson's creative evolution, with the latter easily understood as a remake-cum-expansion of its amateurish inspiration; it's telling that in both versions of the story, the lead's given surname is "Adams." The suggestion is one of absolute, biblical innocence corrupted. "All I ever wanted was a cool '78 'Vette and a house in the country" sighs the original Diggler (played by Anderson's friend Matt Stein), a line that splits the difference between giggly irony and genuine pathos when it's revealed that it's been attributed posthumously.

It's hard to know what to make of the idea that a homemade thirty-two-minute pisstake written and directed while Anderson was a high school senior is ultimately more realistic (or at least fatalistic) about the fate of its protagonist than the two-and-a-half hour, Oscar-nominated epic that it begat. The frustration of *Boogie Nights* is that it tries to have it both ways: to be trenchant and sentimental about an era and an industry that were both hugely formative for its creator while lying just outside his lived experience, conflating history and fantasy under the sign of re-creation. The common auteur-biographical interpretation of *Boogie Nights* is that it uses Eddie/Dirk as a stand-in for, if not Anderson himself (the director would have been seven

when the story begins in 1977) then his artistic potency. This reading contextualizes the film's assertive technique as well as its relatively upbeat ending, which finds Dirk living in the country (chez Jack Horner), and still in possession of a '78 'Vette which, despite getting shot up during a botched drug deal, remains mostly intact. The hero is humbled in a strictly productive sense, and, crucially, eludes any sort of definitive literal or figurative emasculation. Eddie/Dirk is photographed full-frontal in the final shot to show that his penis (massive even only at half-mast) is still healthy enough to wield with impunity. Coming at the end of a movie whose aesthetic is defined simultaneously by size, rhythm, and duration—beyond-the-frame production design; excitably accelerated montage; elongated tracking shots calling attention to their own athletic stamina—the image seems coded as triumphant as well as promissory, as if Anderson were slyly advocating on his own behalf. It's an ending that suggests he's only just begun.

← **Left** The surrogate family: After leaving home, Eddie is absorbed into porn director Jack Horner's repetory company, which includes older porn star Amber Waves and fresh-faced starlet Rollergirl. Meeting at a diner to discuss an upcoming project, Jack and Amber look as much like a married couple out with their kids as purveyors of "adult entertainment," and the juxtaposition of the domestic and the risqué runs throughout the film.

↙ **Below** Of all of *Boogie Nights*'s metatextual casting choices, the selection of former under-wear model Wahlberg may be the savviest; as underaged Eddie cockily checks himself out in the mirror, it's impossible not to think of the actor's real-world Calvin Klein campaign and late-nineties sex symbol status.

Although not a debut feature, *Boogie Nights* was received with the language of discovery when it premiered in September 1997 at the Toronto International Film Festival. "I have seen the new Quentin Tarantino, and his name is Paul Thomas Anderson," wrote *Entertainment Weekly*'s Owen Gleiberman in a breathless dispatch modeled on Rolling Stone writer Jon Landau's review of a 1974 Bruce Springsteen concert: "Tonight, I saw rock 'n' roll's future and its name is Bruce Springsteen." In both cases, the artist in question was slightly more established than the rhetoric being used to herald them could admit: By 1974, Springsteen had already released the critically acclaimed (though initially low-selling) LP *Greetings From Asbury Park, NJ* while Anderson's résumé circa 1997 included the well-received crime drama *Hard Eight*. What Gleiberman was getting at was that *Boogie Nights*, like *Pulp Fiction* before it, had the potential to make its director a household name, and also to parlay a set of risque, explicit and even taboo elements into critical and box-office success.

The relatively generous $15 million budget bestowed by New Line Studios was a direct response to the success of *Pulp Fiction*. Executive Mike De Luca was still stinging from having passed on Tarantino's debut feature *Reservoir Dogs*, and looking to develop a movie with a similarly high-end return on investment. Jason Sperb writes that "[De Luca] was intrigued by the prospects of another hip, pop-song-driven retro film . . . like *Pulp Fiction*, *Boogie Nights* had the potential to make profits on soundtrack sales alone." In a post-Tarantino moment when the existence of a thriving, viable American independent cinema seemed more possible than at any time since the 1970s, and the cult of auteurism had been resurrected—with *Hard Eight* cited as a flashpoint—a filmmaker with ambition was a valuable commodity. Anderson's clashes with independent distributor Rysher over the editing and release of *Hard Eight* saw him labeled in the press as an *enfant terrible*; now they could be spun as a display of heroic principle rather than hubris.

The risks for an American movie using sex as its primary subject and texture were very real in 1997. Two years earlier, Paul Verhoeven's *Showgirls* (1995) had joined the ranks of *Heaven's Gate* (1980) and *Ishtar* (1987) as a canonical flop, effectively dissolving the cycle of profitable Hollywood eroticism sparked a decade earlier by *Fatal Attraction* (1987). *Showgirls*'s failure stemmed in part from Verhoeven's insistence on an NC-17 rating, and Anderson's original cut

of *Boogie Nights* would have probably secured a similarly scarlet letter from the censors (he wisely gave himself enough wiggle room to negotiate an R-rating while letting the MPAA feel it had done its due diligence). What eventually boosted *Boogie Nights*'s box office even more than the wave of admiring reviews or the hype over Anderson was how it seemed to be directly commenting on the climate of Puritan paranoia around the Bill Clinton-Monica Lewinsky sex scandal—not condoning or condemning, but instead offering a vicarious escape into an earlier era where judgment could be more easily suspended. The film's nostalgia was not only supremely marketable, but also a source of reassurance. No less than the biblical epics of the 1950s with their harems of loose women and prop-department golden calves collapsing the gulf between Hollywood and Babylon, *Boogie Nights*'s fixation on the 1970s as an idea as well as a setting, subsumed contemporary titillation into the anachronistic trappings of a period piece.

For Anderson, *Boogie Nights*'s setting and subject matter were a matter of personal history. He grew up in the San Fernando Valley surrounded by porn shoots, and wrote *The Dirk Diggler Story* as an homage to his father's extensive home-video collection (of which he displayed encyclopedic recall). When queried, Anderson expressed an unironic and unapologetic love for adult films, copping in particular to a fondness for the indefatigable, tragic Holmes, whose death from AIDS is alluded to in *The Dirk Diggler Story* but oddly omitted from *Boogie Nights*. The film pays no attention to the disease despite covering the period associated with its inception, an omission that undermines its attempts to fully evoke the era and its anxieties, consequences and casualties and indicates a timorousness at odds with the movie's overt boldness—a sanitizing impulse.

Beneath the nostalgia and fetishism of *Boogie Nights*'s origins lay thornier impulses. *Hard Eight* was harshly treated by its distributor—re-cut and re-titled, a symbolic circumcision— and Anderson's desire to make a follow-up on his own terms was unshakeable. "I wrote [*Boogie Nights*] fueled by a desire for revenge on all the people who told me I'd never amount to anything," he told *Creative Screenwriting*—an observation that connects to the petulance that manifests around the edges of the script. The first instance is Eddie's defiant tirade against his overbearing mother (Joanna Gleason) after she tells him he's a loser; in light of Anderson's comments, it's hard to not hear the filmmaker's voice in Eddie's response. "You don't know what I can do!" he bellows at her before

packing his bags to leave Torrance for good. "You don't know what I can do, what I'm gonna do, or what I'm gonna be! I'm good! I have good things that you don't know about! I'm gonna be something! I am! And don't fucking tell me I'm not!"

Much later in the film, after Eddie has adopted the decadent Dirk Diggler persona and enjoyed the spoils of his star-is-born narrative, he more or less repeats this outburst repeats this outburst, directing his energy instead at Jack, his surrogate father. Well past the need to argue for his own potential, he tries to assert dominance: "You're not the king of Dirk. I'm the boss of me. I'm the king of me. I'm Dirk Diggler. I'm the star. It's my big dick and I say when we roll."

That we are meant to sympathize and identify with Eddie in the first case but not Dirk in the second is in keeping with *Boogie Nights*'s underlying thesis about the thin line between desire and self-delusion, which figures into the psychology of almost all of its main characters. Eddie yearns for stardom, but once he achieves it the winning innocence that initially hypnotizes the camera becomes corroded and he's exposed as a limited talent—an archetypally cruel starlet narrative transposed, provocatively (if not necessarily more than that) onto a male ingenue. Jack sees himself as a principled artist deploying eroticism in the service of storytelling and whose dream is to "make a film that is true and right and dramatic," yet he more believably displays the traits of an exploiter and an enabler and, at his lowest point, capitulates to the sensationalism his oeuvre means to resist. Amber Waves (Julianne Moore) has styled herself as a sort of den mother for Jack's repertory—a rock of stability and support— while she struggles with the guilt of being separated from her biological son and the ravages of a cocaine habit (her yonic moniker signals maternal anxiety). Buck Swope (Don Cheadle) can't reconcile the flamboyance of his post–Cleavon Little "Black Cowboy" shtick with his wish to open a stereo equipment store. Hanger-on Scotty (Philip Seymour Hoffman) proffers macho camaraderie to Dirk in an attempt to disguise his deep-seated romantic attraction. "Little" Bill Thompson (William H. Macy), Jack's long-tenured assistant, leverages an easygoing swinger persona against the rage and paranoia building up every time he catches his wife (Nina Hartley) *in flagrante delicto* with a stranger (or two).

In a movie of symbolically ejaculatory outbursts, Bill's decision to commit an act of unfathomable savagery in the midst of a New Year's Eve party is the most startling, made more unsettling by the implications of its staging.

Jack Horner's insistence that he's making art as well as pornography functions as the philsophical fulcrum of *Boogie Nights*: Is it possible to achieve a version of personal expression through the lens of exploitation? The depiction of Jack's filmmaking process as an artisanal, communal, detail-oriented labor of love aligns the director and his aspirations with the auteurs of the New Hollywood—an allegory that leaves the movie open to accusations of sanitizing and romanticizing its chosen milieu.

"When I close my eyes, I see this thing, a sign, I see this name in bright blue neon lights with a purple outline": Eddie's dreams of being on a marquee come true when he changes his name to "Dirk Diggler"—a comic-book moniker that marks his pseudo-superheroic transformation into a very different, and ultimately less endearing, character.

When Jack apprises Eddie as a "seventeen-year-old ✂ piece of gold," it's in the aftermath of a virtuoso three-and-a-half minute take that prowls through Hot Traxx, introducing nearly all of the film's key players and emphasizing their tender, multi-directional affection: They're all happily caught up in the camera's swirl. As the Emotions's throbbing, upbeat disco hit "The Best of My Love" plays in the background, *Boogie Nights*'s opening conveys, in high style, a moment and a community where everything seems possible and permissible. It's a continuation—or reboot—of late-sixties Californian utopianism even after the nightmares of Altamont and Manson, events whose counter-cultural implications are absent in the shiny, accessible decadence on display. The idea lifestyle without limitations or boundaries is emblematized by Heather Graham's "Rollergirl," a porn starlet in Jack's stable whose gimmick is having sex in her roller-skates. In the opening

scene, she's like a cartoonishly obscure object of desire, careening through Hot Traxx with an intrepid, headlong momentum; her serene velocity suggests the thrill of the chase, or maybe the elusiveness of genuine fulfillment in a milieu calibrated in favor of all things fleeting.

The tracking shot during the New Year Eve party, meanwhile, reverses that heady sense of optimism, moving instead inexorably towards a set of consequences. Throughout the party sequence, characters are shown bumping up against the painful reality of their own desires, as in the moment where Scotty makes an ill-fated pass at Dirk and ends up crying alone in his new muscle car, helplessly consolidating his position as an outsider to a set of heterosexual revels. The sight gag of Buck, whose girlfriend has dumped him, sitting alone in Nile Rodgers drag similarly places him at the margins of his adoptive family; when he chats up his

William H. Macy's hapless cuckold "Little" Bill Thompson is figured early on as a victim of *Boogie Nights*'s free-loving setting; joining a crowd of onlookers watching his wife make love to a stranger at a pool party, he's reduced to the same spectatorial status as the consumers of the porn movies he helps to make, except that it's his personal life on display— a humiliation that catalyzes the movie's downward narrative turn.

sometime co-star Jessie (Melora Walters) it's only because the latter has, like Scotty, been rejected by Dirk, who has in turn just been seduced by Amber into trying cocaine for the first time. By the time the camera attaches itself to Bill as he walks in on his wife cheating on him yet again, stalks outside to his car (a path linking him subtly to Scotty) and returns with a pistol in hand, the film's trademark sense of momentum has become pressurized, and even weaponized: instead of being carried along on a wave of euphoria, we're trapped on a downward trajectory.

Bill's terrible act serves as a jolt at the exact midpoint of the movie, confirming *Boogie Nights* as a fully bifurcated work. The murder-suicide is staged as the grim herald of shifting decades: in the instant of Bill's death, Anderson throws up a title card reading, simply, "80s." The sudden introduction of this particular narrational device eighty minutes into a film that has not previously employed it is intentionally bewildering, recalling the irregular and eccentric use of title cards in The Shining, a horror movie that was set, produced and released in 1980. But the Kubrick joint that comes more readily to mind in the aftermath of Bill's act is *Full Metal Jacket*, both in the way Anderson copies the composition of the suicide itself—including the way blood and brain spatters against the back wall as in an action painting—and uses the imagery of "climax" to reset the narrative. In *Full Metal Jacket*, Pvt. Pyle (Vincent D'Onofrio) kills Sgt. Hartman (R. Lee Ermey) in ecstatic defiance of the Parris Island barracks's top-down, authoritarian sense of order before turning the gun on himself in a gesture of punishment and orgasmic release (paying off the Marine Corps's rhetoric of a rifle as an extension of the soldier who carries it). Bill's gesture signifies something else. Beyond its parameters as a completely localized act of vengeance and catharsis, it's like a general rejoinder to the gleeful hedonism of Jack Horner's little corner of the Valley: a money shot of a different kind.

The same complaints lobbed at *Full Metal Jacket* (1987)—that it's a distinctly lopsided piece of work—can be levied against *Boogie Nights*, which front-loads its showmanship at the risk of alienating its audience. With this in mind, the stylistic variance in the film's second half, which is more sparing with camera movement in favor of jagged cross-cutting, constitutes an alternate form of Anderson's aforementioned "revenge." It's a campaign by the film, via its writer-director, against its characters, its audience, and itself. Reviewing the film in the *Village Voice*, J. Hoberman observed that after a certain juncture, *Boogie Nights* "seeks to rub its viewer's nose in its characters' degradation," before wondering rhetorically "what makes it all go bad—is it drugs, video, old age, Reagan?" The answer (which Hoberman telegraphs by asking the question) is all of the above, and the way that a viewer responds to the second half's downward spiral—a veritable vortex of un-pleasure—depends on whether or not it seems duly prepared for and earned in retrospect.

The most malignant of these symptoms—even beyond the rampant cocaine use that brings out the worst in all who partake, Dirk in particular, directly demolishing his marketable virility—is "video," and *Boogie Nights* scans aptly as a parable about the inherent vice (and virtue) of different moviemaking formats. In a film filled with bruised, ambivalent characters who are shown to be more than their worst impulses (and also less than their best ones), the only obvious villain is Floyd Gondolli (Philip Baker Hall), a deep-pocketed impresario who shows up at the New Year's Eve party like a poker-faced angel of death: his appearance presages Little Bill's breakdown. He's there as an emissary of the future, trying to sell Jack and his financier The Colonel (Robert Ridgley) on the impending dominance of home video in the pornographic film marketplace; he presents his evidence flatly and without emotion, while Jack responds with a mixtures of prideful dismissal and anxious anger. In this equation, he's a stand-in for the brief moment in the early 1970s when X-rated films like *Behind the Green*

Door (1972), *Deep Throat* (1972) and *The Devil in Miss Jones* (1973) compelled unprecedented mainstream respectability and exposure (and box office), while Floyd advocates for a more anodyne, faceless and efficient approach that dovetails with consumers' wishes—supported by advances in home-viewing technology—to stay in with their dirty movies. "Video tape," he says, "tells the truth."

This seemingly minor disagreement between two differently inclined smut purveyors actually provides *Boogie Nights* with its central allegory. Nearly two decades before adapting Thomas Pynchon, Anderson was examining the same themes in the same California setting: a counterculture and its corporatization. In both *Boogie Nights* and *Inherent Vice* (and also *There Will Be Blood*) something pure becomes first diluted and then toxic. Floyd's bottom-line mentality is as slickly obstinate as Daniel Plainview; beyond his stated fondness for "people fucking onscreen") could just as easily be working for the Golden Fang. The main difference between *Boogie Nights* and *Inherent Vice* may be that at the time of the former Anderson's belief in that purity was itself a bit more pure. As clearly as the director sees his characters—and as impressive as his work with his skilled cast members is nearly across the board—his own naivete and narcissism competes with those qualities as they are figured in the story. There's no satirical perspective on Jack Horner, whose vision of pornography as a form of serious, principled, popular cinema is taken more or less at face value and, even more broadly, made to seem roughly analogous to the heroic mythology of the New Hollywood. Jack is a celluloid fetishist who wants to make work that'll be remembered long after he's gone; while the equation of Anderson-as-Eddie has some juice, his more idealized self-projection is via Jack.

Both Wahlberg and Reynolds were cast in *Boogie Nights* with an eye towards their established star personas. The scene of Eddie checking himself out in his bedroom mirror while wearing only a pair of briefs evokes Wahlberg's star-

making stint as a Calvin Klein underwear model. He is mesmerized by his own reflection in between Bruce Lee-style kung-fu moves—presented as an erotic icon. Meanwhile, we're being prodded to see the same glittering potential as Jack. While Wahlberg's performance drives *Boogie Nights*, Reynolds's presence adorns it, imbuing the halcyon, you-had-to-be-there approach with the lived-in credibility of the era's major box-office attraction. The model for this kind of self-reflexive lion-in-winter acting is probably Paul Newman reprising *The Hustler*'s (1961) "Fast Eddie" Felson a quarter-century later in *The Color of Money* (1986), except that Reynolds doesn't have to live up to an earlier part—he only has to evoke himself. Part of the calculus is that the actor works equally well as an avatar of decline: The slow fading of Reynolds's star in the 1980s (a decade that was considerably kinder to peers like Newman, Clint Eastwood, and Robert Redford) is in line with the film's desultory arc.

Boogie Nights increasingly comes to foreground Dirk's suffering, which deepens the further he gets from his director. What's really being mourned, though, is the death of the collective, collaborative creative ethos cultivated in Jack's productions, with their cozy all-in-the-family vibe. The theme of an ironic surrogate household is strong in *Boogie Nights*, which initially rewards Eddie's yearning for a group of people who will indulge and understand him—especially Amber, whose affection for the new initiate is even more complicated than Jack's. There are premonitory traces of *The Master* in *Boogie Nights*, with the wayward Eddie as its version of Freddy Quell and Jack as a saturnine father figure à la Lancaster Dodd. Sitting with Amber, Eddie, and Roller Girl at a diner as he outlines his latest project, Jack looks at a distance like a wholesome, distinguished figure—a prosperous pater planning a road trip to Disney World. That posture dissolves into something more incestuous back at his house, when he instructs Eddie and Rollergirl to get it on so that he can see how it'll look on screen. It's a moment that Anderson treats with studied restraint. Instead of focusing on the naked Wahlberg and Graham, we get a push-in on Jack studying their copulation with—what? Professional detachment? Personal interest? Directorial omniscience? Fatherly love? Reynolds's neutral expression betrays nothing; his close-up is one of the movie's only true, unreconciled mysteries.

The vignettes showing the making of Jack's pornos are played mostly for light comedy, with an idealized attitude about the treatment of the female performers that's a far cry from most documented histories of the industry. The fact that Jack is making porn allows for crude humour and copious nudity, but as much as the latter accounts for a portion of *Boogie Nights*'s success and notoriety, what Anderson is really interested in—and turned on by—is the filmmaking process itself. Whether or not Jack's film are actually "good," we're meant to see the way they're made, with a crew of talented professionals working harmoniously (and never autonomously) under Jack's direction, as a vindication of top-down artistic authority. By the time of *The Master* and especially *Phantom Thread*, Anderson's veneration of such set-ups is increasingly thorny and ambivalent; here, as he embarks on his own throwback ensemble drama,

↑ *Above* Little Bill's suicide is reminiscent of Pvt. Pyle's similar act of self-destruction in Stanley Kubrick's *Full Metal Jacket*, both in terms of staging and in the way it serves to stop and restart a fully bifurcated narrative.

← *Opposite* Jack's New Year's Eve 1980 party divides the narrative of *Boogie Nights* in half: as Rollergirl glides into view (*center*), she obscures the "o" in Hello, signalling the Stygian descent into a new, crueler decade. The suicide of Little Bill at the stroke of the midnight (*bottom*)—moments after murdering his wife in a rage at her infidelity—reinforces the theme of Paradise Lost.

he buys into Jack's mastery (and his own) without much self-interrogatory pushback.

The absurd "Brock Landers" pornos directed by Jack and starring Dirk as a 007-style operative become a staging ground for the creative break between auteur and star, neatly delineated in a fake-documentary-within-the-film attributed to Amber, whose attempt to honour both men ends up capturing their behind-the-scenes-power-struggles. (The doc is shot on 16mm, resulting in an authentically old-fashioned interlude in a movie deeply preoccupied with formats). From what we can see, the Brock Landers series becomes increasingly repetitive and redundant—as well as more steeped in misogynistic violence and rhetoric—as they go on. Here, the gleeful, lo-fi parody of *The Dirk Diggler Story* becomes interlaced with a more serious critique of the artistic and moral pitfalls of franchise filmmaking, which is to say the cinema of the eighties, which supplanted the stand-alone masterpieces of the New Hollywood. When Eddie shoots his first film for Jack, even before he's adopted the Dirk Diggler moniker, he wins plaudits via his willingness and ability to "go again" immediately after coming inside Amber. As the film goes on, however, the compulsion to "go again" becomes a locus of shame and degradation—a sign of helplessly recidivist behavior.

Anderson may see excess as a fault, but he's hardly immune to its lure; the second half of *Boogie Nights* plays out as two cautionary tales in one. There's what the film says about its characters and their various weaknesses, and the weaknesses it displays in the process. "I always thought the subtitle for *Boogie Nights* should be 'it's all fun and games until someone gets hurt,'" Anderson said in 1998, accounting for the movie's punitive aspects without necessarily making them seem persuasive after the fact. Where later in his career the director would prove adept at conjuring up conjoined sensations of ecstasy and despair—at discombobulating the viewer's responses—in his sophomore feature, he mostly settles for keeping his extremes segregated, and proves less adept at dramatizing the valleys than the peaks.

The sight of Dirk pathetically chasing pop stardom with a cover of the *Transformers: The Movie* (1986) theme song "You've Got the Touch" is a nod to *The Dirk Diggler Story* and a showcase for Wahlberg and Reilly's clownish chemistry; the scenes in the recording studio have the leavening effect of a blackout comedy sketch, as if the original cast of *Saturday Night Live* had been inserted in Robert Altman's *Nashville* (1975). Elsewhere, though, the movie's faith in its actors to make the thin material work through sheer force of will proves overly optimistic. The summit

where Amber and Rollergirl express their mutual desire to interact as mother-and-daughter puts dialogue around a dynamic that was already apparent and gains little from being verbalized ("I want you to be my mother"... "I'll ask you if you're my mother and you say 'yes,' OK?"). Buck's inability to secure a bank loan for his stereo business based on his sleazy previous career is more schematic than affecting. The doom-laden "December 11, 1983" segment interspersing three terrible encounters—Dirk's brutalization at the hands of a pick-up; Jack and Rollergirl nearly killing a stranger after a failed camcorder-porn experiment; Buck narrowly avoiding being murdered during a hold-up gone wrong—is so calculatedly abject and vicious that it's like the movie is succumbing to the same moralism potentially marshalled against it by conservative critics, getting its licks in against characters whose hubris has caught up with them.

Boogie Nights's lack of subtlety in the back half is a liability, and yet as it keeps pushing along an odd thing happens: Anderson goes so far over-the-top that the movie elevates along with him, owning its own excess in a way that swings the pendulum back in its favor. The extended set piece where Dirk, Reed Rothchild (John C. Reilly), and Todd Parker (Thomas Jane), descend on the Encino mansion of drug dealer Rahad Jackson (Alfred Molina) in an attempt to sell him $5,000 worth of phony cocaine is designed as the film's combination high-and-low-point, and it achieves the intended balancing act in a thrillingly self-contained way: It's an epic within an epic that feels out of control without actually being so.

The concentrated brilliance begins with the electric acting of Molina, who modelled Rahad's appearance and affect on the Palestinian-born nightclub owner and drug dealer Eddie Nash, rumored to be the mastermind of the 1981 Wonderland Gang murders in Laurel Canyon, another connection in the script to John Holmes and the seamy side of Los Angeles's adult film history, and an early example of how adroitly Anderson tethers his narrative inventions to established cultural myths. What Rahad ends up looking and acting like, however, is the embodiment of a decade's most decadent tendencies: He's the final act of Brian De Palma's *Scarface* (1983) as a one-man show, Tony Montana transplanted from Miami and given a Hollywood Hills makeover. Unshaven and bare-chested beneath a silver lame housecoat, Rahad stumbles and lurches through his lavishly appointed living room—the high ceiling is like a proscenium—in a fugue state, as if he's jacked up on the idea of being relaxed. The actor's splayed posture and movement are weirdly sympatico with Daniel Day-Lewis's

As an ensemble piece, *Boogie Nights* is concerned with tracing multiple character arcs over nearly a decade of screen time. In the first half (*above*), Rollergirl, Buck and Amber are shown balancing their onscreen personas as porn stars against real-world responsibilities (as a student, a salesman and a mother, respectively). After the switchover to the eighties (*right*), their struggles intensify as their professional reputations start limiting their options. Rollergirl's frustration at being objectified, Buck's thwarted attempts to start a business and a family and Amber's distance from her son leave them all in a state of mutual despair.

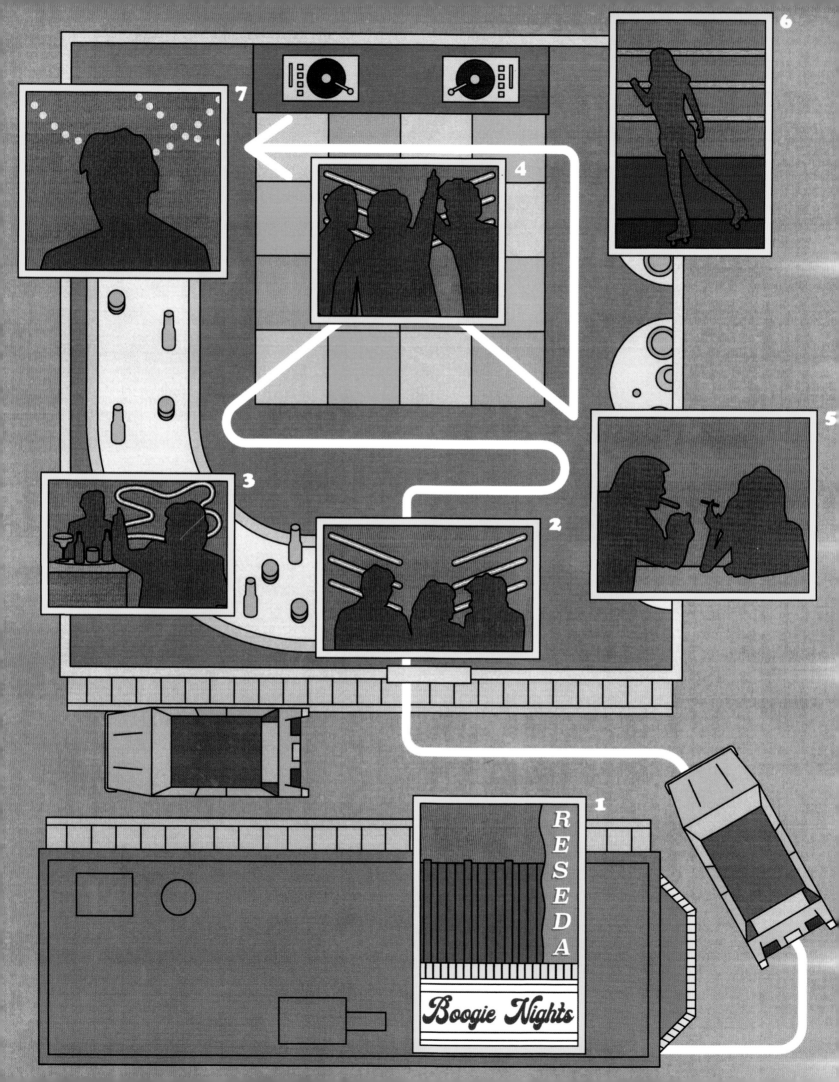

RESEDA

Boogie Nights

← **Left** The botched drug deal at Rahad Jackson's palatial home gives *Boogie Nights* an unlikely and hilariously parodic action movie climax. Alfred Molina's performance as a coked-out gangster (*top*) evokes Brian De Palma's *Scarface*, while Anderson's use of Top 40 music—all diegetically contained on Rahad's beloved "my awesome mixtape #6" (*bottom*)— similarly weaponizes mainstream eighties pop culture against Dirk and his friends, who barely make it out of the house alive.

comportment as Daniel Plainview near the end of *There Will Be Blood*—another isolated weirdo who acts out against a visitor he thinks is out to swindle him.

Rahad's disconnect from reality is signaled by his obliviousness to the firecrackers being set off at random intervals by his lover (?) Cosmo (Joe G.M. Chan), which remind Dirk, Reed and Todd of the very good possibility that they're about to be shot to death; the loud bursts are like extensions of their host's frayed, buzzing synapses. Just as the joy of the Hot Traxx scene mutated into the abrupt horror of Jack's New Year's Eve party, the stopover at Rahad's amplifies the terror of the Little Bill tracking shot so that there's no longer any dividing line between revelry and death. The exuberance of the movie's first half and the abjection of its second bleed together.

Above all, the scene at Rahad's is the culmination of the ugliness that *Boogie Nights* associates with the 1980s, exemplified by the three songs that play out almost in their entirety in the background: Night Ranger's "Sister Christian," Rick Springfield's "Jessie's Girl," and Nena's "99 Luftballons." Each song connects in some way to the dramatic and thematic content of the movie as a whole (coming-of-age; helpless yearning; sudden violence) but more generally, the effect that Anderson achieves is that of benign, ersatz Top 40 pop synced to appalling, hyperbolic carnage: an old, Kubrickian trick that works like gangbusters in context. By going out of his way to show that the songs are diegetic—choice cuts on Rahad's self-made mixes—Anderson continues the motif of tape (in this case, audio tape) as a harbinger of dark times.

On one level, it's hard to believe that even the vain, oblivious Todd—the main culprit in Dirk and Reed's cocaine addiction, and one of the only characters in the film defined almost solely in negative terms—would be so stupid as to go into the heavily fortified house of a rich drug dealer with fake coke, much less try to rob the place when escape with cash in hand is within his reach. At the same time, Anderson exploits the sheer improbability of the situation to give Dirk an epiphany that more indirect interventions by friends and loved ones couldn't achieve. Sitting on the couch next to Reed as Rahad's (armed) bodyguard counts out the money, Dirk's fear melts into pure, slack-jawed stupefaction, and as the camera slowly zooms in (a move indebted to the "I'm Easy" sequence in *Nashville*) we watch him gaze into space for a miniature real-time eternity. It's the thousand-yard stare of a drug addict, but also of somebody who has become a passive observer to his own situation—a guy watching a movie.

(continued on page 128)

The murder trial of porn star John C. Holmes, acquitted by a jury of participating in the retributive killing of four drug dealers during a violent home invasion in Laurel Canyon, received its share of sensationalistic media coverage in the summer of 1982: The combination of brutal violence and showbiz sleaze was irresistible for mainstream and tabloid outlets alike. As with the Manson killings thirteen years earlier, the victims in the so-called "Wonderland murders" registered as casualties in a larger culture war, and yet the trial's true significance, at least in legal terms, had to do with the submission of videotape as formal evidence: the first such instance of that format being entered into the official legal record.

Completed in 1981, Julia St. Vincent's homemade documentary *Exhausted: John C. Holmes, the Real Story* captures its subject at the last possible moment before his niche celebrity mutated into legitimate infamy. St. Vincent, who orbited the porn industry as an employee of the adult-entertainment distributor Freeway Films, had been romantically linked to Holmes at the height of his stardom—and his legendary promiscuity—and her motives were located somewhere between infatuation, exploitation, and prosperity. In the critical anthology *Grindhouse: Cultural Exchange on 42nd Street and Beyond*, she's quoted as saying "I started shooting these interviews with John mainly because I realized he was going to die someday . . . I would have the footage of him and I'd become rich."

Viewed alongside *Boogie Nights*, *Exhausted* reveals itself as a veritable style Bible for Anderson's film, especially the documentary-within-the-film directed by Amber Waves; Amber's outwardly worshipful, inadvertently damning profile of her co-star Eddie's ascendant under the stage name Dirk Diggler cannily reproduces the hapless, hilarious fascination of St. Vincent's amateur hagiography. For the most part, *Exhausted* takes Holmes's obnoxious braggadocio at face value, intercutting his (largely fabricated) account of his life story with scenes from his films, eagerly equating the actor with his onscreen persona as "Johnny Wadd." Co-stars praise his stamina and professionalism (and endowment) without evincing much personal affection (nor does he offer much praise for anybody but himself). More interesting—and revealing on a cultural level—are the "man on the street" segments in which various passersby are asked if they know who Holmes is, prompting a range of nonplussed responses that implicitly rebut Holmes's own suggestion that he's become bigger than porn: Whatever the filmmaker's intention, they generate the impression that if Holmes is a legend, it's largely in his own mind.

Anderson's recognition of the tragicomic potential in such delusions, combined with an eye for pastiche, led to the near-identical re-creation of several moments in *Exhausted* for *Boogie Nights*. These are helpfully annotated in a segment on the latter's DVD release in which Anderson provides commentary over selected scenes from *Exhausted*—an exercise that plays a bit like an X-rated version of *Mystery Science Theater*. Beyond copping to his fascination with Holmes in general and *Exhausted* in particular as an artifact from porn's pre-VHS glory days, Anderson points out all of the specific shots and lines of dialogue he hijacked for *Boogie Nights*; he's particularly proud of a random line stolen from one of Holmes's nastier, more action-inflected efforts (a subgenre within his output kidded via Dirk's "Brock Landers" series). "When I was writing *Boogie Nights*," he laughs over footage of Holmes, in character, shaking down an informant, "I realized that 'where the fuck is Ringo' was the key;" the line actually appears twice in *Boogie Nights*, once during Amber's documentary and again at the very end, as Eddie rehearses for his first scene back as a member of Jack's repertory.

It's telling that Anderson spares his Holmes manqué the shame, indignity, and physical decay of his real-life inspiration. While the scene at Rahad Jackson's house loosely evokes the Wonderland murders (with Albert Molina's Rahad styled as a version of club owner Eddie Nash, whom some suspected of enlisting Holmes to kill his enemies), Eddie doesn't get his hands dirty, fleeing the scene without consequences. His beauty remains intact, and he continues his career at the exact same mid-eighties moment when Holmes began his decline both reputationally and physically; in 1988, he died of AIDS at the age of forty-three. Viewed in light of his biography, Holmes's dead-eyed narcissism in *Exhausted* acquires a certain pathos. He's too busy burnishing his mythology to consider the grim realities of his lifestyle and their consequences, a great big shining star on the verge of implosion.

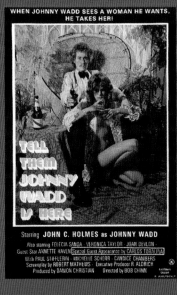

WHEN JOHNNY WADD SEES A WOMAN HE WANTS, HE TAKES HER!

TELL THEM JOHNNY WADD IS HERE

Starring JOHN C. HOLMES as JOHNNY WADD

Also starring FELICIA SANDA · VERONICA TAYLOR · JOAN DEVLON
Guest Star ANNETTE HAVEN · Special Guest Appearance by CARLOS TOBALINA
With PAUL STEFLEENN · MICHELLE SCHERR · CANDICE CHAMBERS
Screenplay by ROBERT MATHEWS · Executive Producer R. ALDRICH
Produced by DAMON CHRISTIAN · Directed by BOB CHINN

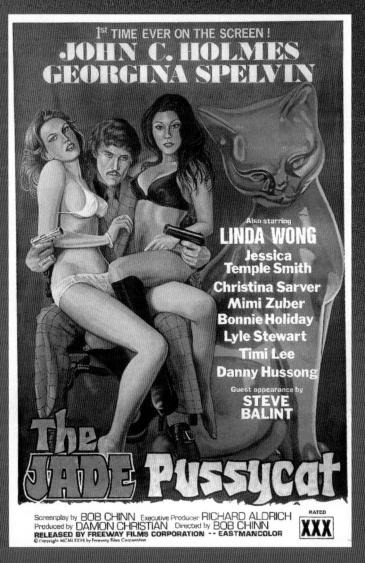

1st TIME EVER ON THE SCREEN!

**JOHN C. HOLMES
GEORGINA SPELVIN**

Also starring
LINDA WONG
Jessica Temple Smith
Christina Sarver
Mimi Zuber
Bonnie Holiday
Lyle Stewart
Timi Lee
Danny Hussong
Guest appearance by
STEVE BALINT

The JADE Pussycat

Screenplay by BOB CHINN   Executive Producer RICHARD ALDRICH
Produced by DAMON CHRISTIAN   Directed by BOB CHINN   RATED XXX
RELEASED BY FREEWAY FILMS CORPORATION -- EASTMANCOLOR
© Copyright MCMLXXVII by Freeway Films Corporation

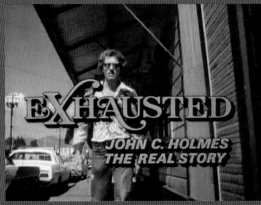

EXHAUSTED
JOHN C. HOLMES
THE REAL STORY

Every Woman's Dream's
Every Man's Fantasy

JOHN C. HOLMES IS THE
CALIFORNIA GIGOLO

STARRING JOHN C. HOLMES

↑ *Above* The final scene is clearly patterned after the epilogue of Martin Scorsese's *Raging Bull* (1980), suggesting that for Dirk—as for that film's emotionally arrested antihero Jake LaMotta—celebrity is a trap and true change is impossible.

→ *Right* Clad in a *Miami Vice* style white suit, Eddie finally looks at ease in the 1980s, rehearsing dialogue for his reunion production with Jack and reminding himself that he wants—and deserves—to be a star. The white suit could symbolize a clean slate, or else serves as a joke on the idea of purity and rebirth—a delusion shared narcissistically between an actor and his reflection.

In this case, it's a ridiculous action thriller with Todd pulling a gun and getting blown away by Rahad, who does everything but bellow "say hello to my little friend" to signal his transformation into a Tony Montana–style cartoon. The slapstick ridiculousness of Dirk and Reed dodging bullets as they flee the house brings *Boogie Nights* to a point of deliberate unhingement, which is ultimately what's needed to penetrate Dirk's self-perpetuated trance state. It's only by having seen his life transformed into a movie— a Brock Landers–style intrigue, starring Eddie Adams instead of Dirk Diggler and with real bullets instead of cap guns—that he's able to recognize and reconnect with reality—such as it is.

Boogie Nights's eleventh-hour embrace of artificiality is worth commenting on. The unlikeliness of Dirk showing up at Jack's door the morning after witnessing Todd's death (an event that Anderson never resolves, as if it happened in a nightmare rather than another part of the Valley) is part and parcel with a late-breaking metaphysics of deliverance that may actually be less believable than the shoot-out at Rahad's. In his desire to provide an all-purpose payoff, Anderson unravels a charming (if not cloying) montage scored to the Beach Boys's "God Only Knows" which catches up with the characters to show how in most cases they've moved on with

their lives and come out the other side of their respective freefalls. Rollergirl has gone back to school; Buck has opened a business and begun a family with Jessie; Reed is working as a musician; Amber seems to have cleaned up.

It's all rather pat and admittedly satisfying, and the same goes for the film's penultimate tracking shot, which describes the set-up for Jack's latest movie—his official reunion with Dirk—using the language of the Hot Traxx sequence. The mobility of the camera is comforting, inscribing the feeling that everything old is new again, and that everybody is (re)-connected—there's even a pan past a portrait of Bill, gone but not forgotten. The impression is of grace, bestowed not from within the people onscreen but from above, a gift from the filmmaker to his characters, as if in apology for putting them through the ringer, the coddling flip-side to his earlier callousness.

In this way, *Boogie Nights* muddles its own embedded critique by suggesting that the dire moral and artistic compromises of the eighties can simply be waited out, or else bought into (as in the case of Buck's new stereo store, which is paid for by stolen money and heralded with a chintzy hip-hop themed television ad). Even the gag of having Dirk dressed up like Don Johnson in *Miami Vice* as he rehearses for

his big scene is more affectionate than accusatory, and as obviously as his to-mirror-monologue is modelled on Robert De Niro's final scene in *Raging Bull* (1980) the impact is more glancing. Dirk is young and malleable, and even if his belief that he's a "a great big shining star" is just so much verbal self-fluffing, there's a logic to the idea that he can constantly reinvent himself around his "one special thing," since that's where power and agency lie in his world (and ours). But in Scorsese's film, Jake LaMotta's pitiful attempts to imitate Brando place his inadequacy as an actor in sharp relief. He's incapable of reinvention and doomed to literally and figuratively punch his way through a life that's closer to its end than its beginning, and a similar sense of regret will inflect the character at the center of *Hard Eight*.

HA
EIG

RD

HT

I t sounds like a porno," Paul Thomas Anderson joked about the title of *Hard Eight*, which was imposed on his debut feature by its studio, Rysher Entertainment. Anderson's preferred title was *Sydney*, in honour of the story's protagonist, an aged gambler who takes a young man under his wing in Reno for reasons more complicated than they initially seem. The battle over the title was symbolic in the context of a production governed by fractious behind-the scenes productions, with Anderson and Rysher split over the film's contents and the best way to market them to an audience. Beyond its sexual connotations, the title *Hard Eight* evoked something terse, the slang of hardcore gamblers and their gritty milieu. Conversely, a film called *Sydney* could be about anybody, an open-ended proposition that was either enticingly mysterious or off-puttingly anonymous. In commercial terms—a riskier bet.

Hard Eight is both of these movies in one: A genre piece that is also a character study, interwoven closely together. And despite Anderson's objections, it's not as if the alternate title was applied randomly. There are multiple scenes in the film featuring characters attempting to roll a "hard eight," which in craps terminology refers to a dice roll of two fours, a one-in-thirty-six possibility that adds up to the best possible outcome for any given turn. It indicates that the sum has been reached the "hard" way, before any other non-double combination of eight has been achieved. If the dice come up the "easy" way, in pairings of five and three or six and two, or if the shooter rolls a seven, the bet is nullified. Requiring no specific strategy, or physical or manual skill, the "hard" eight is above all a signifier of good luck, as well, perhaps, of the courage to submit oneself to the indignities of chance in the first place. It's also a twin: A doubled number imparting a sense of symmetry.

"Here we go, it's me and you," says the unnamed craps player (Philip Seymour Hoffman) who materializes to challenge Sydney (Philip Baker Hall). Sydney has bet $2,000 that the younger man is going to roll a hard eight, and the wager seems to enervate and energize the latter in equal measure, sending his already nervy vibe well over the top. Suddenly, it's as if a communal game has been reduced to a one-on-one duel. As a verbal skirmish, their clash is entirely one-sided: From his first moment on screen, Hoffman's character is compelled to taunt and antagonize Sydney, mocking his polished appearance and stoic demeanor while reminding him that a good roll will benefit them both. "Fucking forty-four, big time," he crows, holding the red-and-white dice up side-by-side so as to make them doppelgangers. Once released onto their separate trajectories, though, they diverge as surely and sharply as the appearances of the men waiting on the result. A five and a three: An "easy" eight, with no payoff. The shooter struggles to mask his disappointment and buck up his spirits, but Sydney's expression doesn't change. Without betraying his feelings, he simply walks away.

This scene takes place near the midpoint of *Hard Eight*, a film whose narrative intrigue lies mostly elsewhere. The craps game is little more than an interlude making time between the spacious, character-based action of the story's first section, which positions Sydney as a benevolent surrogate father figure to the young drifter John (John C. Reilly) as they work the casino circuit in tandem, and the more propulsive, noir-tinged action of its long mid-section wherein John and his new wife, Clementine (Gwyneth Paltrow), a cocktail waitress who moonlights as a prostitute, dangerously bungle a kidnapping scheme, resulting in a volatile situation ultimately defused by Sydney's surprisingly expert assistance. The question of how and why Sydney has experience with such matters, and how his past life intersects with the histories of both John and John's friend Jimmy (Samuel L. Jackson), a casino "security consultant" with a barely concealed agenda, is addressed in the film's final movement, by which time Sydney's loss at the craps table has been long forgotten. Still, despite its lack of import, the confrontation ranks among the film's most memorable moments, not least of all for the electric acting of Hoffman, who, according to Hall in a 2014 interview with *Rolling Stone*, improvised most of his dialogue. "At that point, I was older and he was very young... I was like, "Who is this kid... he was so aware of everything and had the instinct of an older trooper."

Hall's admiration for his late co-star, with whom he would again appear (although not in the same frame) in *Boogie Nights* and *Magnolia*, is rooted in a respect for the actor's craft. It also speaks to the scene's unmistakable subtext of intergenerational conflict, a clash of wills and styles and heightened by Hoffman's embodiment of overcompensatory cockiness.

For all the unpredictable energy that Hoffman brings to the scene, his exertions are still in the service of ideas that are present on the page, and it's this integration of something

Privately financed and shot over six weeks with a borrowed camera, *Cigarettes & Coffee* launched Anderson's career when it was programmed at the 1994 Sundance Film Festival, where its assured technique and deftly interwoven plotlines were seen by critics as heralds of a new, exciting directorial talent.

The first sequence of *Hard Eight* replicates *Cigarettes & Coffee*'s opening almost precisely, from the roadside diner setting to the casting of Hall, whose character in the short was also named Sydney. It also sets up the mentor/ protégé dynamic that drives the story forward, with Sydney emerging as a protector and instructor to the young man he's met (only seemingly) by chance.

genuinely spontaneous with premeditated finesse that results in combustion. The line "it's me and you" makes perfect sense for a guy trying to bait a stranger, but it's also a neat summation of the way that *Hard Eight* doubles down on the idea of pairings; the film is structured as a series of dialogue duets, first between Sydney and John, then Sydney and Clementine, then John and Clementine, and finally, Sydney and Jimmy. The common denominator in these conversations is Sydney, while other characters mostly make sense in counterpoint to him: John as his vulnerable but promising protege; Clementine as an object of ambivalent, protective fatherly affection; Jimmy as a rival and a reminder of his former line of work.

But what about Hoffman? It's obvious that this obnoxious upstart is anything but a twin for Sydney, who at this point is well established as a figure of rigorous and fastidious care, both in manner and appearance. At the same time, the force that draws both men towards the craps table— and specifically towards a game whose original name of "hazard" underlines its implicit quality of kamikaze risk— originates from the same double-edged compulsion: To exercise control by relinquishing it. They're not twins, but somewhere under the skin, they're the same. Which is why, when Sydney makes his exit, it's as if he's trying to do

something more than just quit while he's behind. He wants to leave everything about that encounter—and the part of himself that it represents—behind.

Not only is *Hard Eight* a crime thriller and a character study, it's also simultaneously an old man's movie and a young man's movie. Anderson's fascination with a character on the downward slope of his life belies his own precociousness as a first-time filmmaker, but Hall's smartly tailored performance tempers any sense of overreaching. "Philip Baker Hall has been in the movies since 1975," Roger Ebert wrote of the film, "he looks middle-aged and a little sad, and grown up . . . many Americans linger in adolescence, but Hall is the kind of man who puts on a tie before he leaves the house." Ebert's description of Hall as a figure out of *Father Knows Best* is apt while stopping short of the sense the actor gives of authority gone to seed—a diminishment that Robert Altman exploited when he cast Hall as Richard Nixon in *Secret Honor* (1984). There, Hall was able to convey not only Nixon's furtive mania but the disappointments of a decade where idealism was reshaped around the idea of skepticism; instead of placing their

En route to Vegas, John tells Sydney a story about a pack of cigarettes that ignited in his pants by accident (*center*)—an anecdote that encapsulates both his lucklessness and a more general anxiety about using matches tied by Anderson to the character's wounded masculinity ("it was this close to my dick!"). When Sydney asks John to briefly take the wheel, it's a gesture of trust in the younger man, while the ease with which he lights his own cigarette shows how much more composed and mature he is than his inadvertently incendiary protégé.

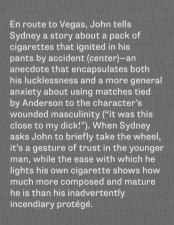

138

trust in all the President's men, Americans turned to the journalists charged with holding them to account.

Technically, *Secret Honor* is not a movie of the New Hollywood: It's an after-echo, thematically resonant but industrially muffled in the middle of the high-concept Reagan eighties. But as a living link to the cinema of Robert Altman, Hall's presence allowed Anderson to evoke his hero as surely as *Hard Eight*'s immersion in the world of gamblers recalls Altman's 1974 drama *California Split*. Before *Boogie Nights*'s full-scale glamorization of the 1970s as a kind of lost paradise, *Hard Eight* indulges a more modest—yet no less ardent—desire to resurrect the cinema of Anderson's youth. Although unmistakably set in the mid-nineties present tense of its production, the film still has the vague feeling of a period piece, of a story slightly unstuck in time. Where Anderson's backwards gaze is unmistakably fond, it's in the service of a story about the difficulty of reckoning with the past; Hall's Sydney is a compelling anachronism, but he's also a wreck. If *Hard Eight* is to some extent a young director's act of idol worship, it's a ritual performed in the shadow of ruin.

Hard Eight's fetishization of the style and sensibility of the quote-unquote "Seventies" was in line with any number of other heralded, up-and-coming American directors in the mid-nineties. What made Anderson a particularly irresistible figure for nostalgists—and a frustrating one for his financial backers—was how willing he was to take up the larger fight of the New Hollywood twenty years after the fact. The production of *Hard Eight* was an ordeal comparable, if not in scope and logistics, than in combative spirit, to the saga of *Heaven's Gate* (1980), the difference being that Michael Cimino was coming off a multi-Oscar-winning box office smash when he went to war with his studio. That impetuousness manifests in the movie in the form of Hoffman's pushy, patience-testing scene-stealer, an analogue for Anderson's defiant attitude towards his collaborators. In *The Sundance Kids*, James Mottram describes a fraught post-production process during which the filmmaker, who cut off communication after going on set, was reprimanded and even briefly fired by executives from Rysher Entertainment, after which he retaliated by "kidnapp[ing] an incomplete work print . . . and submit[ing] it to the Cannes Film Festival."

That Rysher's braintrust were reportedly nonplussed and even angered by the movie submitted by their flashy young hire could be seen, from an impartial vantage point, as an episode of schadenfreude. On whose behalf is the question: A case can be made that Anderson's consternation at the prospect of compromise isn't especially flattering.

"[They] hadn't read the script . . . all I could do was point to the script and say, 'This is what I shot, this is what you paid for, this is what you agreed to," Anderson was quoted as saying in the aftermath, insinuating that he'd done nothing more than deliver the film he devised. Jason Sperb argues that this much-publicized adversity, combined with Cannes's decision to play the director's cut over the one submitted by the studio, played into Anderson's favor reputationally beyond *Hard Eight*'s hard-luck box office: "It solidifie[d] Anderson's mythology as an emergent auteur struggling to create an independent vision in a system overrun by the meddling interference of moneymen."

The irony was that Rysher's investment in Anderson had been very much in thrall to the "mythology of the emergent auteur"—the everything-old-is-new-again mentality at work in the formation of a "New New Hollywood" in the mid-nineties. Their interest was specifically seeded by his 1993 short film *Cigarettes & Coffee*, an accomplished calling-card financed partially by credit card and showcased at the Sundance Film Festival, where it accrued critical buzz and industry attention. The film pulsates with an assurance that belies its maker's lack of actual experience, moving swiftly and with purpose through a contrived tripartite narrative set in and around a highway-side diner. At the Sundance Institute in Utah, Anderson would rework several aspects of *Cigarettes & Coffee* into a feature screenplay called *Sydney*, written specifically for Hall, who had appeared in the short after meeting Anderson on the set of a television show. After a workshopping process at Sundance that also involved Reilly, *Sydney* would be optioned by Rysher for production in 1995.

Viewed side by side, *Cigarettes & Coffee* and *Hard Eight* are not quite twins, even less so than *The Dirk Diggler Story* and *Boogie Nights*. If anything, *Cigarettes*'s intertwining plotlines and themes of coincidence (hinged, in a true coincidence, to the travels of a twenty-dollar bill in the same year as Keva Rosenfield's identically conceived feature *Twenty Bucks* (1993) more directly mirror the ensemble sprawl of *Magnolia*, with a sprinkling of crisply Tarantino-esque dialogue, much of it delivered by actor Kirk Baltz, whose ear is (in)famously sliced off in *Reservoir Dogs* (1992). Baltz's character relates a tale of woe involving his wife and his friend while Hall listens, evincing some of the same quiet authority as Sydney, although his first few lines of dialogue weirdly anticipate Hoffman's improv in *Hard Eight*. Hall's insistence that his seatmate, "wait until the coffee has been poured and the cigarette has been lit," gets rewritten at the beginning of the craps table stand-off, with the young shooter warning Sydney that he wants him to place a bet, "before I finish lighting my cigarette."

The language of instruction—of rules to be followed, with purpose and to the letter—runs throughout *Hard Eight*, originating with Sydney and the mentor-like role he adopts

with John during their meeting at the diner. He offers unsolicited advice on gambling protocol ("in my experience, if you don't know how to count cards, you should stay away from blackjack") and social graces ("never ignore a man's courtesy"), splitting the difference between benevolence and condescension as he goes. The film's opening is styled as an enigma, with John—and by extension, the audience—confused and intrigued by the question of why a total stranger would take an interest in somebody down on his luck, and offer, albeit in an indirect way, to help him with his plight. Upon learning that his new friend is broke and in need of $6,000 for his mother's funeral, Sydney insists that they drive back to Vegas, where he stakes John $50 and illustrates "what he did wrong" with an eye towards ensuring a more profitable return visit. Gradually, John's wariness about Sydney and his intentions dissolves, and by the time they leave the diner, he's already proven himself a potentially apt protégé by parroting back a rhetoric of rules: "A) you give me a ride; 2) you give me $50; and C) I sit in the back."

Because Reilly is a gifted comic actor—a natural clown able to stylize himself at the drop of a hat into either a Neanderthal caricature (*Step Brothers*, 2008) or a tragic sap (*Chicago*, 2002)—he's able to sell the over-deliberate goofiness of John's early dialogue: To make it seem like the dimness comes from inside the character rather than being imposed from above by the filmmaker. (There's no way that Reilly's line in *Step Brothers* about mastering martial arts isn't a callback to John claiming to know "three different kinds of karate" here.) A flashback to John accidentally striking the matchbook in his pants while waiting in line for a movie (1957's *Outlaw Queen,* a feminist western written by Ed Wood) conjures up a slapstick sight gag that seems to belong in a different movie while hinting, in metaphorical terms, that he doesn't yet have the dexterity to play with fire. "It was this close to my dick," he adds, clarifying the character's pervasive sense of emasculation.

John's anecdote about the self-igniting matchbook is about an accident, something uncontrollable and out of the ordinary. What Sydney is proposing to offer John is a way of navigating a path through life—represented in the film's universe by the casino circuit—that takes chance and contingency into account while attempting to mitigate them as much as possible. The passage in which John, following Sydney's instructions to the letter, enacts an elaborate comp hustle resulting in a free room and dinner is charged with a vicarious, illicit thrill ("I like movies that show me precisely how to get away with something," added Ebert supportively). But the comp hustle is also a victimless crime, especially in the context of an establishment designed to separate customers from their money. Sydney can't manipulate the fact that the house always wins, but he can explicate the benefits of looking and acting like a winner anyway. What he's really showing John how to do is to project a version of himself that gets the attention of the casino staff, who, by perceiving him as a high-roller, willingly and obliviously do their part in transforming that illusion into reality.

Insofar as *Hard Eight* is a showcase for its creator's talents—a venue for showing off—the bravura technique of the comp hustle scene clearly aligns Sydney's situational mastery with Anderson's formal control. The showmanship is more judicious than in subsequent works, owing to a lower budget and more compressed shooting schedule, and yet a ninety-second tracking shot of Sydney moving across the casino floor has as rich an economy of meaning as any of *Boogie Nights*'s more muscular curlicues. The shot communicates the character's aloofness and carefully cultivated anonymity while illustrating his fundamental comfort in his chosen environment; he's like a fish in water, cruising smoothly as the camera cruises dutifully, at a respectful middle distance.

To the extent that Sydney is "directing" John during their initial time together, their dynamic anticipates Jack Horner and Dirk Diggler in *Boogie Nights*, and also Lancaster Dodd and Freddie Quell in *The Master*, a film that is even more explicitly about the value (and cost) of buying into a life philosophy. Sydney resembles these characters insofar as he is a father figure, a role that extends beyond his arrangement with John to his relationship with Clementine—the least developed member of *Hard Eight*'s central quartet and a harbinger of the aggressively sexualized, undeniably well-acted yet underlyingly hollow female characters of Anderson's later films. In Clementine's first encounter with Sydney, there is a subtle inversion of the dynamic he'd established with John; she asks a series of probing questions that work to unravel some of Sydney's mystery. Her last question, however, clarifies her true place in the narrative: "Do you want to fuck me?" However ambivalently Paltrow delivers the line—somewhere between a come-on, a provocation, and a weary acknowledgement of her extra-curricular vocation—its purpose is to reveal Sydney's protective reticence. His gentle demural clarifies his position as the story's moral center (which will admittedly be complicated by the end) while Clementine is never permitted to transcend her status as an object of desire and a catalyst for male violence.

Hard Eight also prefigures the structural gambits of *Boogie Nights* and *There Will Be Blood* by deploying a surprising and substantial ellipsis immediately following the comp hustle. After John agrees to go watch Sydney gamble, the film cuts to "two years later," effectively wiping out one set of immediate narrative concerns—chiefly John's need to pay for his mother's funeral—and setting up a new set of variables: John's romance with Clementine; Jimmy's rivalry with Sydney; the explanation of Sydney's past transgressions. Following the almost real-time pacing of *Hard Eight*'s first twenty minutes, Anderson's bold use of

ellipsis confounds expectations: The large chunk of lost time ensures that Sydney's relationship with John, initially difficult to gauge, remains steeped in mystery.

It also stays mostly static: *Hard Eight* is not the sort of movie in which the student finally eclipses or even equals his teacher, and nor does John ever really threaten to come into focus as the true protagonist. His limitations remain consistent in spite of Sydney's tutelage, as evidenced by his clueless, impulsive actions when one of Clementine's clients—another, different kind of "John"—doesn't pay up: He beats the man into unconsciousness and tries to hold him for ransom from his wife. Arriving at the hotel room after a frantic call from John, what Sydney finds is literally and figuratively a mess—one that he is still motivated to clean up. That Sydney so willingly adopts this guardian angel role speaks to the guilt that's driving him throughout the movie, a burden which, once revealed, essentially "solves" the mystery of his character. After sending John and Clementine away to Niagara Falls until things blow over, Sydney is approached by Jimmy, who tells him they need to talk: The subject is Sydney's previous career as a mobster in Atlantic City, a history which Jimmy says includes his having killed John's father over an unpaid debt. Jimmy plans to use this information to extort $10,000 from Sydney, effectively leveraging the latter's guilt into a highly profitable position.

Jackson was easily the biggest star in *Hard Eight*'s cast at the time of its release, as well as a direct link to the critical and box-office success of Tarantino via his Oscar-nominated role in *Pulp Fiction* (1994), and his superb performance as Jimmy is curiously under-celebrated within his body of work. Jackson exults in the role's exaggerated potency. In his first appearance, Jimmy is shown dominating John, who submissively lights his cigarette where Jimmy had once lit his; he's similarly overpowering in the way he talks to Clementine, and also to Sydney, whom he taunts using loaded language about diminished virility. He recalls watching Sydney play craps years earlier, and a certain "big ball bet" on a Hard Eight that didn't come through. "So you gave up on big ball bets on the hard way to play Keno, huh?" he smirks.

In a film filled with twins, Jimmy can be taken as a parallel for multiple characters, starting with Hoffman's gambler. Jackson's ecstatic alpha-male display at the craps table late in the film rhymes closely with Hoffman's posturing, and Anderson shoots both characters the same way, placing them dead-center of the widescreen frame against blurry neon backgrounds. He's also a modified double for John: Both characters attempt blackmail schemes, and Jimmy's confrontation of Sydney is obviously more carefully calculated than John's desperate attempt to get money out of a deadbeat trick. Because of his criminal connections, Jimmy is also close to Sydney, whom he treats with hyperbolic nastiness not because he disrespects him but because he knows what he's truly capable of. Where John and Clementine are shown the tender, supportive side of Sydney, Jimmy knows better. What links the two men is their lack of naiveté.

(continued on page 148)

↑ *Above* Philip Seymour Hoffman
made his first appearance for
Anderson as an unnamed and
spectacularly obnoxious gambler
determined to hit a "hard eight"
at the craps table (*top*). While the
scene is developed to make him
seem like Sydney's temporary
nemesis, the symmetrical shot-
reverse-shot between the two
men emphasizes their underlying
similarities: Sydney's deadpan
non-reaction shots (*bottom*)
only barely conceal his own
internalized self-disgust.

"Luck plays a part in nine-ball, but for some players, luck itself is an art" explains Martin Scorsese in the opening voice-over to *The Color of Money* (1986), a drama set in the world of pool hustling. The major difference between the movie's two major characters is that where one is seasoned enough to know that things won't always break his way, the other thinks he's so skilled that even chance itself has no chance against him; the contrast is that of innocence versus experience. Over the course of the film, Paul Newman's silver fox "Fast" Eddie Felson will take the opportunity to instruct hotshot Vincent Lauria (Tom Cruise) on the art of luck, becoming his mentor and, later, his rival—a dynamic that reawakens Eddie's own self-absorbed cockiness about his mastery with a cue.

The Color of Money has its place in film history mostly for earning Newman his first acting Oscar—appropriately enough for a role many believed he should have been rewarded for twenty-five years earlier in Robert Rossen's *The Hustler* (1961), the first installment of Eddie Felson's story. In the sequel-happy 1980s, the after-the-fact serialization of a standalone sixties masterpiece was seen by some as a sign of Hollywood's creeping commodification, while the roping in of Scorsese after a series of commercial flops (*The King of Comedy* [1983], *After Hours* [1985]) appeared like nothing so much as a gifted veteran seizing the opportunity to make a little money. This mercenary subtext goes a long way towards elevating *The Color of Money*, as does Scorsese's expert, virtuoso direction and the performances of Newman and Cruise, whose partnership is made in context to seem symbolic of the passing of the torch between two generations of heartthrob leading men.

There are no such stakes in *Hard Eight*, whose stars are of a lower wattage: while in the context of Anderson's career, the hookup between Philip Baker Hall and John C. Reilly is of considerable importance, they don't possess even a fraction of the other pair's brand-name fame. *Hard Eight* is also less explicitly about competition, wrong-footing the viewer in the opening twenty minutes to think it's going to be a *Color of Money*-style caper in which an experienced gambler grooms his protege to help him take down a big score, or else ends up facing him in a craps table showdown. But Anderson's debut defies our expectations by rerouting away from Scorsese towards something disconnected from literal ideas of winning and losing and not even all that much about luck: The gamble it describes is a matter of intimacy rather than instruction.

Where the two movies converge—and where Anderson, who would tribute Scorsese more fulsomely in *Boogie Nights*, owes the master a debt—is in their mutual absorption with codes of masculinity. *The Color of Money* draws its tension (and its humor) from the collision of two alphas: at sixty years old when the film was shot, Newman's preternatural beauty refuses to cede supremacy to Cruise's younger, smoother features, and the movie presents them physically as equals. In *Hard Eight*, Sydney's elegance is slightly rumpled in line with Hall's creased countenance, and the character doesn't have to hold his own with his apprentice because the younger man is so meek: where Vincent shows off martial arts moves at the pool table, John can only unconvincingly claim that he knows "three different kinds of karate." Vincent is a force of nature, while John is an unformed lump; where *The Color of Money* vibrates with exuberance and aggression, *Hard Eight* is resolutely downbeat, denying John any moment of true mastery or heroism and contaminating Sydney's version of the same by revealing him as a stone-cold killer—a distressing variation on Eddie's climactic reclamation of mojo in Scorsese's film: "I'm back."

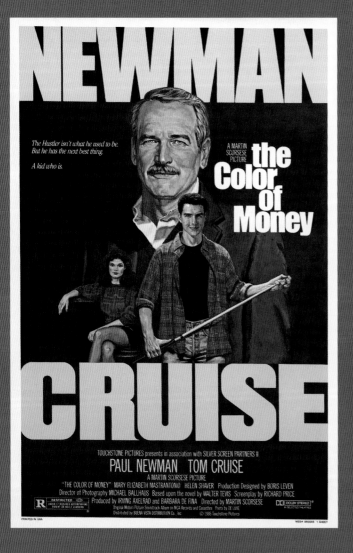

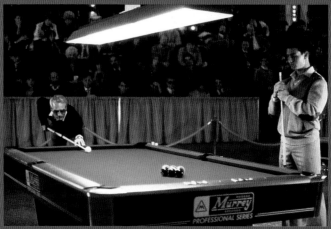

It's telling, within the macho world of *Hard Eight*, that it's only through being threatened—not just with death but a loss of authority—that Sydney reluctantly engages with the softer part of himself. Hall's best acting moments are ones where Sydney's trademark calm either comes unruffled or when we can, for once, sense the strain of its maintenance. When Sydney is confronted with the truth about John's father, he's shaken and overmatched; the seen-it-all look he'd maintained at the craps table or even after going into John and Clementine's hotel room to find a man handcuffed to the bed is gone, replaced by an uncharacteristically rattled expression. Having his back forced to the wall will ultimately bring out Sydney's ruthlessness, but it also unlocks his compassion. In one of the script's most effective bits of doubling, he tells Jimmy that he "loves John like he was my own child" before telling John the same thing on a phone call: "I love you like you were my own son."

The repetition is not redundant: While the two scenes both pivot on the same line, they're not quite a matched set. With Jimmy, Sydney is actually being fully honest, explaining that he loves John but is not willing to die for him: He'll pay up to keep the secret, but also mainly to keep himself alive. With John, the affection is sincere, but it's only a partial confession—he's unable to open up fully. If it's possible to put your cards on the table while also keeping them close to your chest, that's what Sydney is doing, permitting John some kindness and himself a catharsis without being fully truthful. Because we know from an earlier conversation with Clementine that Sydney's actual children are no longer in the picture, his words to John have extra resonance—he means what he says—and yet he's still lying by omission. As moving as John's reaction is, the emotion is undermined by our knowledge that on the deepest level, he's still being lied to, and that he'll never know better; he's arguably no wiser as he exits the story than he was in the opening shot.

Sydney, meanwhile, proves even more ruthless and capable than we suspected. While predicated on self-preservation, his final act of violence is, in its way, as much about asserting his masculinity as anything else—the grim flip side to his tender exchange with John. Everything about the staging of Jimmy's murder is intriguingly coded, beginning with the slow push-in from Sydney's point of view on the hotel room door as he waits armed in the dark in which the camera catches sight of a logo for the rock band Big Black—a suggestive and discomfitting sight gag in light of Jimmy's race that also ties back to the idea of potency. "Hard eight, just like mine," crows Jimmy during a run of luck at the craps table; when he gets home, he's with a female companion (Melora Walters) and in the process of unzipping his fly when Sydney rises to shoot him—catching him, in effect, with his pants down. The shock of seeing the quiet, reserved Sydney transform before our eyes into a hardened killer is balanced against the satisfaction of watching big-mouthed Jimmy get punished, as well the way Sydney calmly instructs the woman to leave, a gesture of mercy that takes a little edge off of his lethal show of force.

The intricacy of *Hard Eight*'s structure is such that this finale, besides resolving the complications of the plot—i.e., defusing the threat posed by Jimmy to Sydney's life and to his relationship with John—is how it functions abstractly as a flashback to an unseen event: Sydney's murder of John's father. If it's supposed to be a surprise when we learn that this quiet, watchful and seemingly passive character—a man who has traded in "big ball bets" for Keno, submerges potential sexual urges beneath paternal concern, and takes verbal abuse at the craps table—has a violent past, the shock is redoubled when he shifts definitively back into that mode. Sydney's assertion of power at the end of *Hard Eight* is thrilling and discomfiting at once, because there's nothing actually heroic about it; while we're sympathetic to his position as a man being blackmailed, all he's truly doing by killing Jimmy is recovering money earned by chance and keeping the facts of his past safely tucked away.

The film's final shot, showing Sydney pulling his suit jacket sleeve over his bloodstained shirt sleeve—residue from Jimmy's murder—serves as an elegant synechdoche of this repression.

By placing Sydney back in the same diner where he first met John, Anderson resolves *Hard Eight*'s doubling motif while also significantly contradicting it: This time, Sydney is alone. "You look like you could use a friend," he tells John shortly after offering him coffee and cigarettes, an act of generosity predicated on ulterior motives that pointed towards contrition or redemption without ever really getting there. John may be a static figure—an arrested man-child incapable of growth—but so, in his way, is Sydney, whose entrapment towards the end of his life is considerably more pronounced. The same detachment that makes him a fearless, successful gambler has guaranteed his isolation, and while he thus has the ability (and agility) to walk out of any situation on his own terms, what he can't actually get away from is himself. Killing Jimmy hasn't extinguished that part of Sydney so much as proven its durability.

"I know all those guys you know," Jimmy tell Sydney during their confrontation. "Floyd Gondoli, Jimmy Gator . . ." These are throwaway lines, but they retrospectively get at something about Anderson's use of Hall as an avatar of moral compromise—a man whose outward elegance conceals inner rot. In *Boogie Nights*, the actor plays "Floyd Gondoli," the porn magnate trying to tempt Jack Horner into making videos rather than films—an emissary of collapse.

As for "Jimmy Gator," he'll show up at the center of *Magnolia* as yet another one of Sydney's distorted twins, a paternal figure wracked with guilt over a different and more disturbing transgression towards his real child—one that can't be hidden up his sleeve, but once fully exposed instead seems to rend the fabric of the universe, and sends things falling from the sky.

← *Opposite* Samuel L. Jackson brought his associations with Quentin Tarantino and *Pulp Fiction* to *Hard Eight*, contextualizing his character Jimmy's streak of violent calculation. In a movie of doubles, Jimmy is in some ways Sydney's evil twin—a criminal with the means and ruthlessness to rattle the older man's calm via an extortion plot, which in turn rouses Sydney's vengeance and turns him back, necessarily, into a stone-cold killer.

↑ *Above* "I love you like you were my own son": the submerged paternal subtext of *Hard Eight* surfaces definitively in Sydney and John's final phone conversation (*top*), a farewell that is also a confession, but only to a point. While Sydney can tell John how he feels about him, he can't reveal the true nature of their connection— it's an act of kindness shadowed by a larger denial.

→ *Right* Sydney's outward elegance is blemished by the murder of Jimmy; the stain on his cuff is evidence of a violent nature that can be concealed, but not necessarily ever washed away.

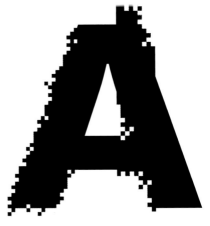nd if he's worth being hurt, he's worth bringin' pain in. When the sunshine don't work, the good Lord bring the rain in. Now that shit will help you solve the case."

The "case" referred to in the freestyle rap delivered early in *Magnolia* by ten-year-old Dixon (Emmanuel Johnson) is the murder of an unknown man discovered in the closet of Dixon's mother, Marcie (Cleo King). The words are directed at the investigating LAPD officer, Jim Kurring (John C. Reilly), who shrugs off the kid's display; "cut it, Coolio" he says sarcastically before moving on. In a film that seems determined to deracinate its San Fernando Valley setting, the subsequent near-total sidelining of Dixon and Marcie—both of whom are black—is worth noting. In the first draft of the screenplay, these characters played a larger role, only to see their subplot discarded. As a result, Dixon's rap plays like a digression even though it's been woven indispensably into the film's thematic fabric. It has the ring of prophecy, both with regards to the literally torrential nature of *Magnolia*'s climax and its subtext of karmic retribution and closure.

"Partly cloudy, 82% chance of rain," reads the first of several weather reports relaying what might be referred to as *Magnolia*'s meteorological narrative (rain being so rare in LA that even its suggestion is cataclysmic—a local in-joke raised to apocalyptic stakes). As hinted by Dixon's rhymes, the best perspective on events and their significance in this toweringly high-concept film can be found by watching the skies. The flat, low-rise architectural topography of the Los Angeles locations (including the eponymous Magnolia Avenue, which intersects with Venice Boulevard) keeps the horizon line visible in establishing shots, and the all-in-a-day narrative transforms the Valley's ever-shifting quality of light into a supporting character. The sunshine has a touch of grey; overcast clouds grow swollen and black. The film is framed by a prologue relating three stranger-than-fiction tales whose commonality is the image of bodies dropping from a great heights: Three criminals hanged in a gallows; a scuba diver scooped up out of a lake by a firefighting plane and posthumously deposited in a treetop; a man accidentally gutshot out the window of an apartment building in mid-descent from a rooftop suicide attempt. The other linking device at play in this deceptively self-contained curtain-raiser is a proliferation of coyly displayed eights and twos—adorning everything from the placard around one of the convict's necks to the side of the airplane to a coil of rope—alluding to *The Book of Exodus*, chapter eight, verse two, about God's threat to the Pharaoh to unleash a plague of frogs on Egypt: The good Lord bringin' the rain in.

Apocalyptic visions were in vogue in the late 1990s: Think of the invading aliens of *Independence Day* (1996) and *Mars Attacks!* (1996); the hurtling meteors of *Armageddon* (1998) and *Deep Impact* (1998); or, on the artier end of the spectrum, the melancholy resignation of Don McKellar's end-of-the-world-as-we-know-it drama *Last Night* (1998), which drew on Ray Bradbury's short story *The Last Night of the World* to imagine a whimper in place of a bang. The thematizing of Y2K anxieties also extended to several titles in the auteur-forward bumper crop of 1999, including David Fincher's *Fight Club*—a comedy-thriller about domestic terrorists attempting to hotwire a devastating economic collapse—and the Wachowskis' paradigm shifting sci-fi parable *The Matrix*, which posits that civilization has been transmuted into a virtual-reality illusion, while in the physical realm the planet lies in ruins. The incongruous Old Testament callback of *Magnolia*'s climax, meanwhile, rhymes with the quasi-mysticism (and ominous numerology) of Darren Aronofsky's *Pi* (1998), released to critical acclaim one year earlier. In that film, a lowly mathematician comes to believe he's stumbled upon a number that unlocks the secrets of the universe, from the stock market to God's will; in *Magnolia*, the onus of interpreter is transferred onto the audience. More than *Hard Eight* or *Boogie Nights*—and more for that matter than any other American film in its immediate vicinity—Anderson's third feature is styled as an enigma, an epistemological mystery to be puzzled over and decoded. Speaking to the *Village Voice* on the eve of *Magnolia*'s release, the director fondly recalled a childhood viewing of *Close Encounters of the Third Kind* (1978), and even if it would be a stretch to call his new movie sci-fi, its portentous-slash-pretentious aspirations channelled the mantra of Steven Spielberg's classic: "This means something."

This insistence on significance separates *Magnolia* from its predecessors in Anderson's filmography while hinting at the more metaphysical dimension of the movies that followed. *Hard Eight* touched lightly on the theme of chance, stranding its characters in Reno—a city erected under the glowing neon sign of contingency—and sending dice tumbling through the narrative at regular intervals. One could read *Magnolia* as an attempt to double down on the idea of hard-luck in

Hard Eight while exponentially multiplying its parental/paternal pathos play across a larger gallery of characters—an approach closer to the everything-is-connected shtick of *Cigarettes & Coffee*.

In light of this ambition, *Magnolia*'s present-tense setting also signified differently from *Hard Eight*'s. Nothing in the narrative of Anderson's debut was specific to 1996; if anything, its nods to the American cinema of the 1970s made it feel like a bit of a reactionary gesture—a love letter to the New Hollywood and its desperate, downwardly mobile characters. *Magnolia* casts its share of glances in the rearview mirror, and one crucial line of dialogue, repeated at different times by different characters, insists that "we may be through with the past, but the past isn't through with us"—a sentiment that Sydney in *Hard Eight* would surely sympathize with. And yet without denying the past its power (and in a few cases, giving it its due in the form of characters swallowed up by their transgressions), *Magnolia* is defined by its fleet, hurtling sense of purpose. The film is constructed out of what Kent Jones calls an "ecstasy of cross-cutting," but no matter how many lateral moves Anderson and editor Dylan Tichenor keep making across its duration—relentlessly subdividing narrative space until it seems we're watching nine different movies side by side—there is always the sense of moving towards something: Some big, foreshadowed impending reckoning.

That constant, relentless feeling of imminence is *Magnolia*'s greatest feat, marking it as an attempt to reckon with social and cultural transition—an echo of *Boogie Nights*'s fateful crossover between the 1970s and eighties. There, Anderson was working with the benefit of rose-colored corrective lenses. *Magnolia* shivers with intimations of the not-yet-known. Viewed in a millennial context, those jumping, plunging bodies—human and amphibian alike—allude to either a great leap forward or else the bottom falling out entirely, a vertiginous condition experienced in different ways by characters whose lives keep spinning out of control.

"Consider this [film] written completely from the gut," writes Anderson at the outset of *Magnolia*'s published screenplay—a statement of intent that could be interpreted as a mea culpa. It's common to read *Magnolia*'s overweening scope symptomatically, as Anderson's response to his struggles over creative control with Rysher Entertainment on *Hard Eight* and the subsequent respect (and clout) afforded him by the critical and commercial success of *Boogie Nights*. It's one thing to not want to cut anything out of a film and another to not have to, and New Line's decision to let Anderson have the final say—meaning that their big Christmas release clocked in at 190 minutes—was a leap of faith even in the context of 1999's consensus banner year, which manifested a disproportionate number of well-financed, stylistically experimental films: Not only *Fight Club* and *The Matrix* but also *Being John Malkovich*, *Three Kings*, *Election*, and *Eyes Wide Shut*.

← The preponderance of apocalypse-themed narratives like Michael Bay's *Armageddon* (1998) in the mid-to-late nineties contextualizes *Magnolia*'s millennial end-of-days subtext; released at the end of 1999, the movie reckons with its characters' histories while gesturing at an uncertain future—"we may be through with the past, but the past isn't through with us."

↑ John C. Reilly's LAPD officer Jim Kurring is charged with solving a literal mystery when he discovers a murder victim in an apartment building, but his encounter with Dixon (Emmanuel Johnson) presents him with a more interpretive enigma; Dixon's freestyle rap alludes to impending events in the movie's narrative, justifying the boy's claim that listening will help the cop "solve the case."

More than his own track record or perceived talent, Anderson's true ace in the hole was Cruise, whom he'd met on the London set of Kubrick's swansong. Kubrick had screened *Boogie Nights* during the making of *Eyes Wide Shut*, and would end up doing a similar dance with the MPAA over avoiding an NC-17 rating; both he and Cruise had enjoyed the film, and the story goes that the actor—at that point arguably the biggest movie star in the world, and certainly among the most bankable—told Anderson he wanted them to work together. "Getting *Magnolia* off the ground was very much the direct result of star power," writes Jason Sperb; while the script that would eventually become *Magnolia* was already underway, Cruise's offer resulted in Anderson writing a character directly for him—- a strutting peacock whose ostentatious displays could almost be taken as a parody of the actor's past performances. *Magnolia* doesn't have a lead character as such, but

Cruise's Frank T.J. Mackey is its most spectacular creation, a swaggering, self-styled self-help specialist promising strategies to "tame the pussy." His more predatory insight though, is towards heterosexual male fear of inadequacy: Onstage at his seminars, he presents himself to his clientele as both a shoulder to cry on and a hardbody to aspire to. In 1999, the reference point for Frank's commodified pop psychology would have been the innocuous, inoffensive Anthony Robbins; twenty years later, he's caught up with his more sinister context in the age of Men's Rights Activists' grievances, Proud Boys, red-pill rhetoric and Jordan Peterson.

Especially in its early stages, Cruise's performance seems to ignite or exorcise something within the actor, tapping the same vein of performativity as his roles in *Top Gun* (1986), *The Color of Money* (1986) and *Cocktail* (1988) and exposing its hollowness in the process. For an actor at the peak of his popularity to commit so fully to a role coated in a thin layer of sleaze was a bit of risky business. At the same time, Cruise was, in effect, Anderson's safety net—collateral he could leverage against the eccentric and deeply personal details of the film. This specificity was something new: Not the coyly mediated, symbolically bifurcated self-portraiture of *Boogie Nights*, with Dirk Diggler and Jack Horner representing two sides of Anderson's projected artistic persona (or, more modestly, manifestations of his teenage fixation on porn), nor an affectionate nod towards the New Hollywood à la *Hard Eight*. Leaving aside the obvious touchstone of Robert Altman's similarly roving Los Angeles–set ensemble piece *Short Cuts* (1993), a virtuoso adaptation of several short stories by Raymond Carver that served as a clear structural model for Anderson's script (and on which Tichenor had worked as an assistant editor), *Magnolia* was lighter on cinematic allusions than either *Hard Eight* or *Boogie Nights*. (There are, admittedly, a few small visual and musical parodies of *2001: A Space Odyssey* that play like friendly winks at Kubrick— Frank comes out on stage to "Thus Spoke Zarathustra," for instance, in effect turning the movie star into a monolith— but little more than that.)

In lieu of older movies, *Magnolia* draws heavily on its creator's own autobiography, starting with his experience in the television industry as a production assistant on a Los Angeles–based kids' quiz show—a gig that came about partially because of his father Ernie's connections. The elder Anderson's blink-or-miss-it cameo in *Hard Eight* during the flashback to John's matchbook mishap was keyed to that film's fixation on father figures, and the ambiguous daddy-knows-best vibe projected by Jack Horner in *Boogie Nights* mined a similar vein. *Magnolia*, though, was written following Ernie's death from cancer, and so the front-and-center presence of the disease within the narrative—as well as the fact that the two characters afflicted by it are both older men with

→ **Opposite** As in *Hard Eight*, Philip Baker Hall appears in *Magnolia* as a flawed paternal figure. The incestuous transgressions of his Jimmy Gator can be neither repressed nor forgiven; in a film without heroes or villains Jimmy comes closest of all to being a fully abject character.

↓ **Below** One of *Magnolia*'s several surrogate father-son relationships involves Big Earl Partridge (Jason Robards), who has transferred his love for his absent, estranged son Frank onto his caregiver Phil Parma (Philip Seymour Hoffman); Phil's desperate attempts to locate Frank as the movie goes on can be read as an earnest, selfless attempt to cede his adopted position.

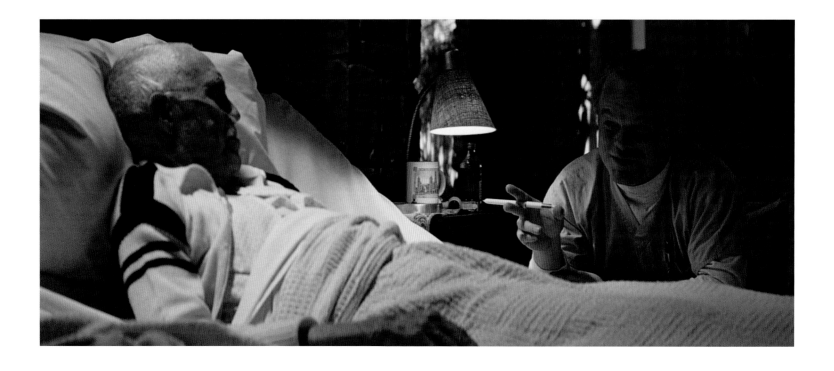

entertainment industry legacies—redoubles this idea of "personal" filmmaking. It would be presumptuous to suggest that either or both of Earl Partridge (Jason Robards) and Jimmy Gator (Philip Baker Hall), the producer and host of a fictional game show entitled *What Do Kids Know?*, are stand-ins for Anderson's father, but the correspondences are hard to ignore, especially in light of *Magnolia*'s local showbiz milieu.

The absurd contrivance of *What Do Kids Know?*, which pits underage prodigies against grown-up trivia buffs in a *Family Feud*-style format, gives *Magnolia* a sturdy allegorical framework: Innocence versus experience. It also permits Anderson an outlet for all kinds of artistic arcana and ephemera. The questions posed and answered during the taping that serves as the center of *Magnolia*'s concentric storytelling structure include references to classical music, poetry, theater and opera—incongruous annotations that, like Dixon's rap or all of those pseudo-surreptitious eights and twos, serve as motivators towards a more fully attuned viewership. (Case in point: Anderson makes a cameo as a PA removing an "Exodus 8:2" sign from the hands of an overzealous fan.) It's telling, however, in light of Anderson's claim of writing "from the gut" that most of this ostentatious cleverness was added mostly after the fact. The Bible passage in question was not actually among his initial influences; instead, he came across Exodus 8:2 after hitting upon the idea of ending the film with an inexplicable, semi-religious event. Anderson's inspiration for the rain of frogs were the writings of Charles Fort, whose 1919 text *The Book of the Damned* provides an inventory of strange phenomena. Intrigued by Fort's accounts of the paranormal, he utilized one of his more bizarre case studies in the service of making a larger social commentary: "I began to decipher things about frogs and history, like this notion that as far back as the Romans, people have been able to judge the health of a society by the health of its frogs," Anderson has said.

↑ The scenes of Earl in his sickbed manifest a gentle visual parody of the climax of *2001: A Space Odyssey*, in which an old man confronts his mortality— the same prospect stares Earl in the face for the duration of *Magnolia*.

"The frogs are a barometer for who we are as a people. We're polluting ourselves, we're killing ourselves and the frogs are telling us so, because they're getting all sick and deformed."

If *Magnolia* has a true scriptural inspiration, it's the work of the singer-songwriter Aimee Mann—to the point where Anderson has said the film could "for all intents and purposes be called an adaptation of [her songs]." The deepest of these cuts was made by a slow, rolling piano ballad called "Wise Up," which was actually originally written for a different film: Cameron Crowe's 1996 comedy *Jerry Maguire*, starring Cruise as a high-powered, ethically flexible sports agent who precipitates a professional crisis and comes out the other end stronger for it. The song makes sense in the context of *Jerry Maguire*'s narrative of self-improvement; the plot hinges on the eponymous protagonist's realization and redressement of his flaws, after which he is permitted to live happily ever after in the glow of his newfound wisdom.

Crowe didn't use the song, and by some of the same serendipitous coincidence harped on during *Magnolia*'s opening voiceover, Anderson heard it while deep in the screenwriting process—at which point he was moved to let "Wise Up" more or less hijack the film. It soundtracks an extended parallel montage in which each of the story's nine protagonists is compelled to spontaneously sing along regardless of his or her immediate surroundings or circumstances; inexplicably, characters in a realistic drama are transformed into their own Greek Chorus. "I wrote as I listened," Anderson has explained, "and the most natural course of action was that everyone should sing . . . I was either too stupid or not scared enough to hit *delete* once done."

Magnolia is a film made without a *delete* button. It shows no restraint, and kills no darlings, closely reflecting Anderson's stated dichotomy between foolishness and fearlessness—between his gut and his brain—without landing decisively on either side of the equation. In the context of the film's daunting size, "Wise Up" takes on an unintentionally self-deprecating dimension: Mann's repeated, sweet-voiced assertion that "it's not going to stop" becomes a commentary on the idea of some oppressive encroaching force, with "it" potentially legible as the film's own sense of inflation—the feeling that its action might actually extend into infinity. For those on Anderson's wavelength though, the scene's communal affirmation of the helplessness to act—the inability, despite our best efforts, to "wise up" the way people do in crowd-pleasing movies like *Jerry Maguire*—produces an affecting, irresistible melancholy—the same kind evoked in Jake Scott's 1993 music video for R.E.M.'s hit single "Everybody Hurts." The clip, which shows a series of sad-eyed Angelenos lost in private reveries during a freeway traffic jam, has never been acknowledged as a reference for *Magnolia*, but seems like a plausible candidate. The same goes for Michael Stipe's mid-song exhortation to the listener to join in: "Now it's time to sing along."

In truth, "everybody hurts" is as succinct a description of *Magnolia*'s contents as one could hope for. Some of the characters wear their pain on their sleeves, like Donnie Smith (William H. Macy), an electronics store employee

William H. Macy's "Quiz Kid" Donnie Smith (*opposite*) is *Magnolia*'s emblem of squandered potential—a melancholy man-child trapped by his almost-famous childhood persona. His inability to grow and mature also informs his unrequited affection for Brad the Bartender (Craig Kvinsland), an alpha-male object of desire whose braces give him his own touching, adolescent vulnerability (*below*). (The dynamic recalls Scotty's impossible crush on Eddie/Dirk in *Boogie Nights*.)

The fictional game show "What Do Kids Know?' exists at the centre of *Magnolia*'s swirling, concentric narrative structure, providing a diegetic link between Earl (the show's producer) and Jimmy (the host) and thus connections to all of the major characters. Its title is also suggestive of the movie's deeper themes about childhood trauma and how it lingers and manifests in adulthood—in Anderson's script, kids know more than their parents think (or want to believe) and that knowledge isn't always empowering.

whose childhood celebrity as a local game show champion places his adult failures in sharp relief ("I used to be smart, but now I'm just stupid"), or lonely cokehead Claudia (Melora Walters), who sublimates the trauma of her childhood molestation through bouts of anonymous, unsatisfying sex with strangers. Others have adopted hard outer shells to cover up their weak spots: Mackey's whole public persona is predicated on an impenetrable, Nautilized charisma, while Jim uses his police uniform (and its embedded sense of authority) to disguise beta-male deference. Frank and Claudia provide direct links to Earl Partridge and Jimmy Gator; they're both estranged adult children unwilling to forgive their differently distant, abusive fathers. When Jimmy comes to Claudia's apartment to reveal his cancer diagnosis, she refuses to speak to him and throws him out. Frank, who hasn't seen Earl in decades, has gone so far as to change his name and alter the details of his biography, adopting performance as a coping mechanism and cover story by which he can absent his authentic self.

Earl's orbit also includes his guilt-stricken, prematurely grieving wife Linda (Julianne Moore), a self-described gold digger wrestling with late-breaking feelings of genuine love (and medicating herself accordingly with over-the-counter pills), and his in-home caregiver Phil Parma (Philip Seymour Hoffman), a gentle, willing receptacle for the dying man's anguish (as well as Linda's mania). Most vulnerable of all in *Magnolia*'s menagerie of damaged creatures, though, is Stanley Spector (Jeremy Blackman), a ten-year-old in the midst of a record-setting run on *What Do Kids Know?*—a show dominated once upon a time by Donnie, whose apartment wall is adorned with the oversized novelty cheque for $100,000 he earned as a child prodigy. Stanley's father Rick (Michael Bowen) treats him like a meal ticket, gleefully monetizing Stanley's preternatural intelligence. He's just a link in a chain of exploitation that also includes Jimmy, the show's host, and Earl, its producer. As soulfully played by Blackman, owl-eyed beneath a furrowed brow, Stanley is one of Anderson's more vivid creations, a prodigy entrapped rather than liberated by his genius.

"Quiz kids" Stanley and Donnie are obvious doppelgangers, as are Jimmy and Earl—two hobbled, philandering, second-tier Lears trying to make amends. Comparisons just keep manifesting across the ensemble; one could just as easily pair Donnie with Claudia, adult infants paralyzed by their treatment by their parents, or Stanley and Dixon, twin possessors of some secret knowledge to the point of seeming like holy figures. ("It is not dangerous to confuse children with angels!" insists Donnie during a barroom argument.) Frank's hyperbolic misogyny includes consistent reference to his penis as a weapon; his catchphrase is "respect the cock." The phrase calls to mind Jim losing his gun while trying to chase down a suspect—a symbolic emasculation straight out of an LA noir like *Chinatown* (1974) where Jake Gittes's slashed nose signals his castration (and which also deals significantly with incest and water, featuring a malevolent patriarch named for the survivor of a flood).

As a coruscating weave of incidents and motifs, *Magnolia* is something to behold. The parallel montage in the back half of *Boogie Nights*, while impressive in its own right, is a mere precursor to the electrifyingly achieved simultaneity in his follow-up, which heightens the implicit tension of its linear narrative via a set of pressurized subplots. A high-stakes taping of *What Do Kids Know?* plunges Stanley and Jimmy into simultaneous emotional crises; Donnie's visit to a bar to gaze at the hunky bartender on whom he has a hopelessly unrequited crush is a preamble to a planned robbery of his workplace; Frank's fractious sit-down interview with a television journalist (April Grace) probing his past keeps him from receiving Phil's frantic calls to visit Earl on his deathbed; and so on. "And so on" is the organizing principle of *Magnolia*, a Matryoshka soap opera that just keeps going in the name of forward propulsion, all, in the words of Aimee Mann, for the sake of momentum—a veritable marathon of melodrama run

← *Left* Julianne Moore's Linda Partridge exists at the melodramatic edge of *Magnolia*'s behavioural spectrum: Her guilt over gold-digging in her marriage to Earl has led to a severe drug addiction, which in turn heightens her feelings of self-loathing. The casting of Moore as an unfaithful wife alluded to her role in Robert Altman's *Short Cuts* (1993), a major influence on *Magnolia* as a whole.

→ *Opposite* Anderson's powerful use of close-ups is emphasized in the interview between Frank (*bottom*) and Gwenovier (April Grace) (*top*), a television journalist who challenges and undermines his machismo. The casting of a mostly unknown actress to go head to head with Tom Cruise charges their scenes with suspense and tension; when Gwenovier ultimately wins the battle of wills, the deflation of Cruise's movie-star charisma has its own potent effect.

THE WEATHER CHANNEL

STORM ON THE MOVE

Extended Forecast

SAT

PARTLY
CLOUDY

RAIN	HI
82	92

SUN

LIGHT
SHOWERS

HUM	WIN
99	SE 12

MON

RAIN
CLEARING

LO	HI
79	90

SAN FERNANDO VALLEY

LAUREL CANYON

MOBIL

Current conditions on the ground ● LIVE

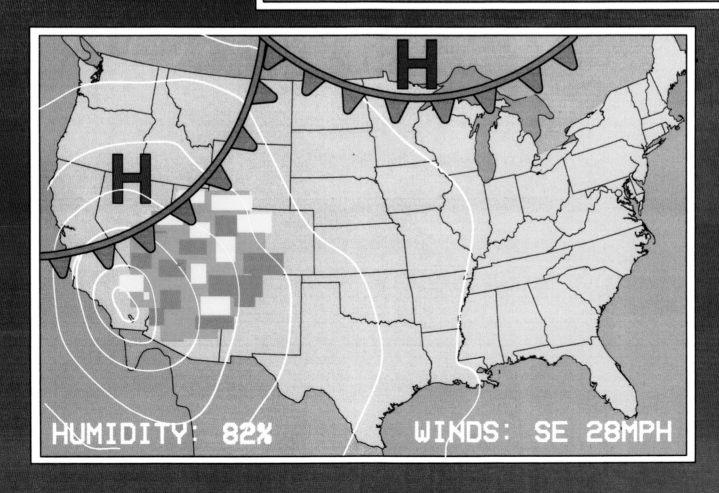

H

H

HUMIDITY: 82%   WINDS: SE 28MPH

under the rules of relay, with the characters passing the baton of identification back and forth between them in a mad dash to the finish line.

That threshold is the aforementioned rain of frogs, which functions similarly to the "Wise Up" scene: It punctures any traditional sense of realism, even as the event itself is depicted realistically, with metallic, clattering sound design that overwhelms and replaces Jon Brion's omnipresent score. In rhythmic terms, it's *Magnolia*'s equivalent to the Rashad Jackson sequence in *Boogie Nights*—a fugue of panic, confusion and disorientation.

In an essay on Anderson's films for *The Point* magazine, Nick Pinkerton characterizes *Magnolia*'s ending as a "last-minute gambit [that is the] trademark of Anderson's films," adding that "where some see derring-do, I find a hint of desperation . . . I get the feeling that Anderson, having painted himself into a corner, is turning to the grand gesture to make his escape."

Pinkerton's observation is difficult to gainsay in the sense that *Magnolia* does indeed have so much going on—so many characters in play, with so much at stake between them—that anything short of a literal showstopper would be insufficient to bring the proceedings to a close. Can't the same be said, though, of the earthquake in *Short Cuts*, a geographically specific deus ex machina that winkingly evokes the all-star disaster movies of the 1970s? Or what about the mid-concert assassination that knots together Altman's earlier *Nashville*'s? In its way, the killing of Ronnee Blakely's country star Barbara Jean is as carefully prepared as *Magnolia*'s deluge, and beyond its deliberate evocation of JFK (and weird prescience with regard to John Lennon), it's just as open-ended in its meaning. The communal sing-along of "It Don't Worry Me" that immediately follows Jean's death works as a spontaneous expression of Southern pride or just so much whistling in the dark at the edge of the bicentennial.

Magnolia isn't as all-American a vision as *Nashville*, which played smartly on the showy, in-your-face patriotism of the country music industry; the small section of Los Angeles in Anderson's film isn't meant as a microcosm of the country as a whole. The director's comments about the frogs as a symbol of a deformed society overreach in that Los Angeles is not synonymous with America. It is, however, plausible that their appearance represents a more localized comeuppance against the city's insidious celebrity culture. Read this way, *Magnolia* is much closer than it initially seems to *Boogie Nights*, offering a variation on its *Paradise Lost* riff with the television business swapped for the porn industry. The two most famous characters are Frank, a wannabe inconoclast who's high on his own supply (although the character predates Lancaster Dodd in Anderson's filmography, he's legible as his historical descendant, peddling self-actualization through sexual

mastery) and Jimmy, a trusted game show host whose endless knowledge base is really just a matter of reading answers off cue cards. Stumbling through the taping of *What Do Kids Know?* in the wake of his encounter with Claudia, Jimmy's status as both star and putative authority figure is diminished (a quality directly in Hall's wheelhouse as an actor); viewed in the light of his off-camera conduct, he looks and sounds like nothing so much as a practiced phony and barely functional drunk.

Confined to a sickbed, Earl is an even more vivid emblem of ruin, shrunken from his former status as "Big" Earl Partridge (note the surname's connotations of prideful plumage) and reduced from a purveyor of daytime entertainment to a passive viewer of the soap opera that is his life—and Moore's performance as Linda is plenty soapy. As much as *Magnolia* aspires to be a critique of individual and structural misogyny—centered, obviously and effectively, on Frank's repellent philosophy (inhabited fully by the uninhibited and extraordinary Cruise)—it has the same shortcomings in its female parts as *Hard Eight* and *Boogie Nights*, and, as in those films, even the excellence of the actors (an excellence derived in part from how well Anderson directs them) can't transcend those parameters. The extremity of Claudia's victimhood and Linda's self-loathing, both rooted in the characters' sexual experience, renders their characters almost unbearably shrill regardless of the context of empathy around both of them; Moore's breakdown is less attenuated than her role in Todd Haynes's *Safe* (1995), which also used Los Angeles as the locus for a grim end-of-the-century environmental metaphor. The one exception, the television journalist Gwenovier, is drawn as an expert circumspect professional, but it's a role in service of Cruise's character—she's there to prompt his revelation that he needs to visit his father before he dies. As with Dixon, Anderson uses an African-American character as an avatar of truth-telling without letting her be anything else. His real investment lies with flawed, tragic white males, a cohort he scrutinizes without idealizing or imparting validation.

It's also hard to know what to do with Donnie's closeted agony, which recalls the angst of the lovelorn Scottie in *Boogie Nights* and is only slightly less of an afterthought in the big picture. Donnie is a casualty of childhood celebrity, flailing aimlessly for decades after the conclusion of his fifteen minutes of fame; as such, he's a cautionary tale for Stanley. He's also, unfortunately, something of a figure of fun, mockingly heralded everywhere he goes by the lyrics of his favourite song (Gabrielle's upbeat, follow-your-heart nineties pop hit "Dreams") and incapable of following through on any of his plans. *Magnolia*'s other designated soft-bodied punching bag is Phil, and Hoffman's performance is exemplary, deepening the theme of physical suffering by showing the impact on those in its orbit; although he is not a son to Earl, his proximity to the older man means that he's absorbed aspects of his

condition. Phil's desperate attempts to reach Frank provides the film with some of its most inspired comedic moments, forcing the seemingly sexless nurse to consult pornographic magazines and 1-800 numbers to locate the contact info for a man who coined "respect the cock," as well as its most self-reflexive dialogue: "This is the part in the movie where you help me out," he pleads over the telephone, gently rapping against the fourth wall. And it's Hoffman's wordless background acting during the encounter between Frank and Earl that makes for *Magnolia*'s most indelible moment, perfectly encapsulating what it feels like to bear witness to something that doesn't involve you directly yet takes full possession of your emotional identification—precisely the kind of mesmerized, affective viewership *Magnolia* is chasing for its duration.

"How are there frogs falling from the sky?" That's Phil again, looking out the poolside window of Earl's palatial digs and once again taking on the role of dazed audience surrogate, putting his mouth around the proverbial $64,000 question. In one of the *Magnolia*'s most beautifully conceived bits of patterning, Phil's frightened agape at the outset of the downpour is answered at the end of the cross-cutting by Stanley, seen watching the incident serenely from inside a quiet library (the frogs shown as shadows descending in a steady stream against the back wall) who says to himself—but really to Phil—"this is something that happens." Earlier in the movie, Stanley has been shown as somebody who either always has the right answers or else declines to speak, so his pronouncement has its own disproportionate weight, with added ballast in the form of the ethereal lighting scheme and a glimpse of his reading material on "prodigal children." Reading between the lines of Anderson's filmmaking choices, it's the last word on the subject and the answer to the menacing, aching rhetorical question "What do kids know?" Turns out it's a lot.

Stanley also gets the last word on the topic of familial dysfunction, awakening his dead-drunk father early in the morning after the storm to tell him flatly, "You need to be nicer to me, Dad." Here, Stanley speaks for himself and on behalf of any number of the film's other characters: For Frank, for Claudia, for Donnie. In other words, Stanley is telling his father to "wise up," and his request works in the same way as the sing-along sequence to level out the film's characters and plotlines despite their wildly different

Anderson wrote several scenes in *Magnolia* specifically to cue up with songs by Aimee Mann; the three-minute sequence in which all of the movie's characters sing along to Mann's ballad "Wise Up" transforms the film from a melodrama into a kind of surreal musical, piercing the veneer of reality to access a larger, universal emotionalism—shades of the end of Altman's *Nashville*, where "It Don't Worry Me" is used ironically to express a community's collective anxiety.

details and outcomes; it reveals *Magnolia* as nothing more (or less) than a call for kindness. In the end, Anderson leaves no wound uncauterized; even the sexual predator Jimmy is spared—however randomly—when a frog smashes through his skylight and interrupts his suicide attempt (although this outcome is admittedly ambiguously staged, as he is not glimpsed during the redemptive "morning after" montage that shows every other surviving character picking through the wreckage and getting on with their lives). The startling anti-grace note at the end of *Hard Eight*—that bloodstained shirt sleeve—suggested that some sins can't be washed away. In its final moments, *Magnolia* wipes the slate clean, permitting its most damaged character, Claudia, a beatific, smiling close-up—a ray of sunshine after a night of rain.

The question of whether Stanley's soft-voiced ultimatum can serve as a load-bearing rationale for such a big, unwieldy film—that it can "close the case," as prophesied by Dixon— is as open to debate as anything else in *Magnolia*. The disparity between the film's expansive size and relentlessly foregrounded complexity and its simple, ostensible moral can make it seem, for all its dazzling moving parts, like a work whose proportions are ultimately out of whack. For instance, as invigorating as the prologue is, its percussively edited O. Henry tales are never really persuasively integrated with the more mundane convergences that make up most of the movie's action, and while Ricky Jay is wonderfully cast to play the narrator-as-confidence-man, his detachment is at odds with the overwrought tone of the film as a whole. The showmanship is undeniable, and also maybe extraneous. Its true function is to introduce *Magnolia* as a film preoccupied with metaphysics instead of letting that interest manifest more organically, and while it makes the movie seem "smarter" it doesn't necessarily raise the level of its intelligence.

Magnolia's critical reception was mixed, with the *New York Times*'s Janet Maslin opining that it "torpedo[ed] itself in its final hour," while Andrew Sarris—a long-standing advocate for the kind of from-the-gut auteur filmmaking practiced by Anderson—invoked the cliche "you can't break an omelet without making some eggs" to express the dialectic between *Magnolia*'s strengths and weaknesses (he also anticipated the ending of *Phantom Thread*—these strange things happen). Anderson's own position on the film has shifted over the years. In 1999 he bristled at the suggestion made by collaborators ranging from Tichenor to New Line head Robert Shaye that

(continued on page 176)

Few American authors were so well-monikered as the late Raymond Carver, a short story writer and poet whose prose at its best imparted the clean, precise sensation of a scalpel slicing through skin: The title of Robert Altman's 1993 omnibus *Short Cuts*—freely adapted by the director and Frank Barhydt from ten previously published Carver pieces can be taken as a pun on its inspiration's surname. Altman's movie was at once a tribute to Carver's writing and a statement of purpose following the surprising and career-resurrecting success of 1992's *The Player*, a barbed Hollywood satire bemoaning the state of the movie-industrial complex. Where in that film Altman kidded the steady erosion of serious, adult movie-making in favor of high-concept properties, *Short Cuts* reached back directly to his seventies heyday, weaving a massive, intricate interpersonal tapestry in the style of *Nashville* but set (like *The Player*) in Los Angeles.

In an essay for the *Criterion Collection*, Michael Wilmington smartly places *The Player* and *Short Cuts* in conversation with one another, noting that where the former "deals with upper-level LA, the world of studios stars and executive deals . . . *Short Cuts* focuses on the middle-class world that surrounds them. "Both movies," he adds, "are fed by the same perception, that beneath the thick veneer of glamour and artifice beats a heart of darkness, emptiness, and even despair." As despair was Carver's forte, his stories of loners, failures and fuck-ups—mostly situated on the page in the Pacific Northwest—were well-suited to a milieu rendered by the director with a genuine sense of pestilence. "There is no purity here," said Altman of his adaptation, referring to the license taken with the material, but the statement also works literally; the film opens with a brilliantly designed sequence depicting a fleet of helicopters spraying for medflies, suggesting a city in the throes of infestation.

This is not to say that *Short Cuts* views its characters, who run the gamut from police officers and television broadcasters to phone-sex operators and petty criminals, as anything less than human; even (and sometimes especially) when at their worst, they're fully recognizable. Altman's exalted status in contemporary American cinema has always been tied to his messy, bottomless indulgence for frailty and foibles (among his actors as well as his characters); among his champions, Pauline Kael was drawn most strongly to the choral, polylot nature of Altman's films, with overlapping dialogue tracks serving as a metonym for a multifaceted perspective on the world. *Short Cuts* is at once less raucous and more precise than those seventies movies, replicating Carver's penchant for paring big, unwieldy feelings and ideas down to the bone through a visual language attuned to disorder and decay. A shot of a woman's lifeless body floating in a rocky outcropping of a river—shades of *Twin Peaks*—

initiates a mystery that winds its way through the film's narrative maze while also serving as a stark, polyvalent symbol of loss and vulnerability—of something submerged under the sunshine.

It's hard not to think of that body during *Magnolia*'s bravura opening sequence, where an unlucky scuba driver is scooped up and deposited posthumously in the trees: an emblem of horror reworked into a whimsical enigma. *Magnolia* is a movie with *Short Cuts* on the brain, and it's almost easier to list the things the movies don't share than the ones they do, including themes of familial dysfunction (and incest); critiques of showbiz hypocrisy; Julianne Moore playing an unfaithful wife; and, most notably, mutually cataclysmic endings, with *Magnolia*'s rain of frogs answering *Short Cuts*'s all-obliterating earthquake. Both films feature song scores dominated by a lone female voice (with Altman's use of jazz singer Annie Ross anticipating Anderson's deployment of Aimee Mann) and both are constructed via a complex network of cross-cutting, with the difference being that characters drift in and out of *Short Cuts* while *Magnolia* keeps bringing people back into the story after they've seemingly wandered off; where Altman emphasizes the fleeting, arbitrary nature of his characters' comings and goings—of lives glimpsed in *media res*, most denied even the sense of an ending—Anderson keeps pushing the idea of fate via dialogue and voice-over until the connections between the film's characters, their occupations, their backstories, their fears, their interpersonal vertices, can't help but add up.

The feeling among some critics that *Magnolia* wasn't just an homage to *Short Cuts* but an act of theft was summed up in a withering *New York Press* essay by Armond White, who believed that the newer film fell short of its predecessor's "Olympian view of American crisis." White's thesis was that where Altman had diagnosed disconnected-ness as a dire and divisive national condition—the malady of the nineties—Anderson was trying earnestly to apply a band-aid. It's a comparison that's apt enough in terms of the two movies' philosophies, if reductive: *Magnolia*'s relationship to *Short Cuts*, like that of Altman's movie to Carver's fiction, has its impurities but it exists more in conversation than as a bad-faith act of appropriation. For his part, Altman was taken by the younger director's work, to the point that they became good friends; when they met, Anderson supposedly told his idol "all I'm doing is ripping you off." He was on set for the production of Altman's valedictory *A Prairie Home Companion* (2006), selected for insurance purposes as a "backup" in case the director fell ill. In 2007, *There Will Be Blood* was dedicated to Altman's memory.

the film needed to be cut down (he's quoted as smugly telling Shaye, "Bob, I have two words for you: Final cut," in Sharon Waxman's *Rebels on the Backlot*) and said he'd never make a better movie. In a *Reddit* AMA conducted in 2017, however, he answered the question of what he would tell himself if he could go back to reshoot the movie with "Chill the Fuck Out and Cut Twenty Minutes."

This self-deprecation could be taken as a sign of a filmmaker who's distancing himself from the undisciplined overreaching of his early work and also the unsettled time of life that produced it—as evidence of a mature, wised-up perspective. But even after Anderson put *Magnolia* behind him, its unruly emotionalism resurfaced in a more streamlined (yet also more experimentally infected) form in a film set in the same neighborhoods on the other side of millennium—one where strange things happen not in counterpoint to the everyday but in a sort of warm, ephemeral harmony.

← **Left** The rain of frogs that concludes *Magnolia* derives from the writings of Charles Fort, a scholar of strange phenomena; Anderson had been reading Fort's work while writing the script and incorporated the frogs into the movie's action, using the storm and its bloody aftermath to unite the movie's characters.

↓ **Below** The sunlight streaming through the blanket over Claudia's (Melora Walters) window means that dawn has broken on "tomorrow" after *Magnolia*'s overcast-then-black all day narrative; the lighting is that of a happy ending, with Claudia's sweet, weary smile providing its own form of illumination.

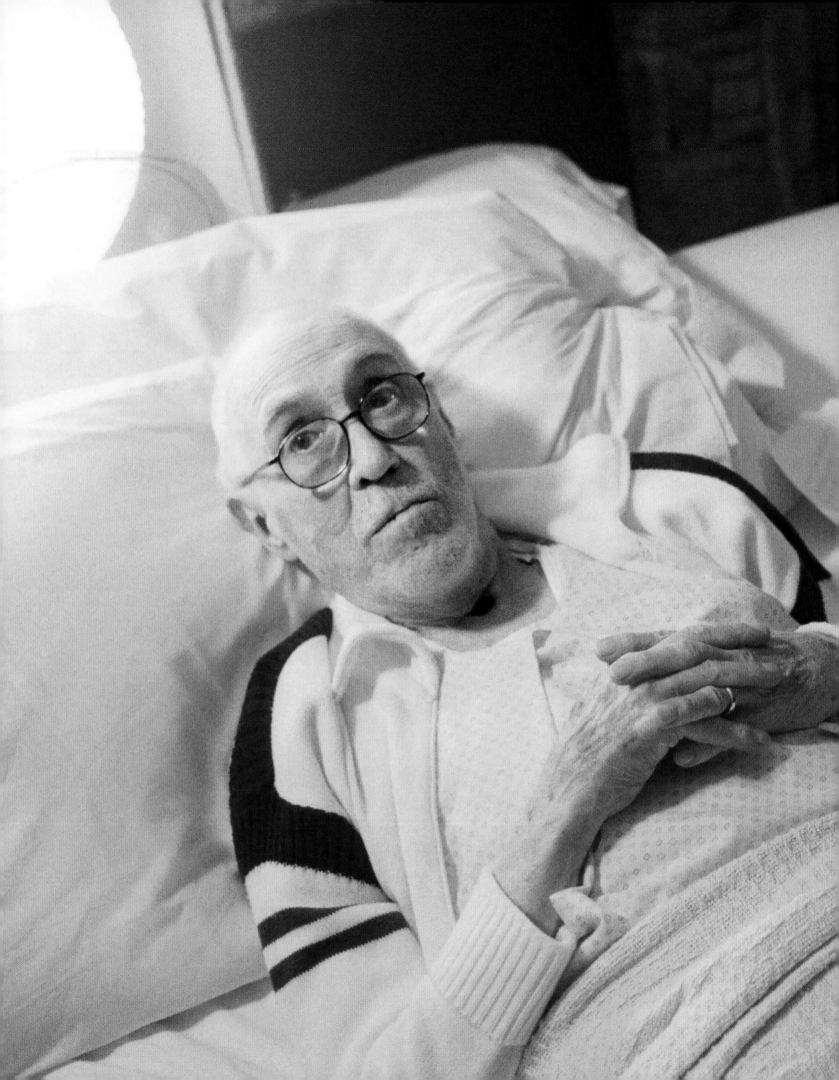

ver the course of *Punch-Drunk Love*, Barry Egan (Adam Sandler) destroys several objects with his bare hands, including a sliding glass door, a restaurant bathroom, and a rotary telephone. He also lays waste to several thugs with the aid of a tire-iron in a scene out of a balletic action slapstick movie, Buster Keaton possessed by Charles Bronson. After receiving some bad news at work, he impulsively wheels around and throws a hard right cross at the back wall of his office, caving in the plaster.

The impression is of a man acting out without intention, and yet the collateral damage caused by his blow is suggestive. Barry strikes a paper map of the Continental US with the western states—including his native California—circled in red ink; a prominent visual detail to this point in the movie, it drops to the ground with the force of a gauntlet. As the (unconscious?) gesture of a man stifled by his surroundings, Barry's haymaker could indicate a desire to get out of town, and in the next sequence, he flies to Hawaii, his first time on an airplane, conveyed beyond the map to an island Paradise that becomes the first stop in his self-actualization. He'll complete the process later on during a far less pleasurable, all-business trip to Provo, Nevada; for Barry, the San Fernando Valley is trap.

Movement is key in *Punch-Drunk Love* (the first of Anderson's movies to feature any scenes outside of the American Southwest) and anticipates the transatlantic peregrinations of *Phantom Thread* and *The Master*, though the version of Hawaii Barry visits is very different than that experienced by Freddie Quell half a century earlier. The film stands as a transitional work between Anderson's intimate LA-based productions—and their inherent showbiz

metaphysics—and the broader leaps in time and space supported by the later historical period pieces. In the years since 2002, Anderson has yet to make another movie set in the present, rendering Barry's story his most contemporary narrative by default. There are things that fix *Punch-Drunk Love* in the early 2000s—the logistics of a telephone scam based around landline usage; the novelty of frequent-flyer miles; a featured appearance by the Clapper—but the only thing that really dates it is Sandler himself, who, caught at the peak of his stardom, is not really used as a culturally or historically representative presence. Like the purposefully abstracted Valley locations, he's just sort of there.

There is perhaps a twinge of *Magnolia*'s millennial anxiety in *Punch-Drunk Love*, although not on the same apocalyptic scale. In that film and its predecessors, a case could be made that Anderson, for all his singularity, was surfing the pop-cultural zeitgeist, with *Hard Eight* and *Boogie Nights* both easily recouped under the sign of post-Tarantino postmodernism. It's harder to place *Punch-Drunk Love*, tonally or stylistically, on a continuum with anything else in early-2000s American cinema. The Best Director prize copped by Anderson at the 2002 Cannes Film Festival was rendered less surprising by the identity of the jury president: David Lynch, who was well-equipped to process and appreciate the film's surrealist streak. But while *Punch-Drunk Love* found a coterie of critical defenders, like *Salon*'s Charles Taylor, who called it a "new-fashioned love song," the general impression was one of bewilderment. By rerouting away from the seventies references of his first three movies, Anderson was risking the critical and audience admiration that came from evoking a heroic era in American moviemaking; referring to his new movie as "referenceless"—a designation that isn't quite true but testifies nevertheless to his intentions—the director seemed

← **Top** The opening shot of *Punch-Drunk Love* buries Barry at the back of the frame; between the blue color of his suit and that of the warehouse wall behind him, it's as if he's been painted into a corner. As a visual correlative to the character's sense of claustrophobia, Anderson's first composition sets a high bar that the rest of the movie strives to match.

← **Center** Lena's arrival in Barry's life comes complete with a lens flare—a motif expressing moments of pleasure, energy and revelation throughout *Punch-Drunk Love*. The rainbow between Barry and Lena doubles as a color spectrum, with his blue suit and her red dress at opposite ends, waiting to be blended together.

↙ **Bottom** The flat emptiness of the San Fernando Valley makes *Punch-Drunk Love* into a film of stark, horizontal camera set-ups; here, as in several early scenes, the camera is distanced from Barry to emphasize his solitude, while the harmonium's placement on the empty street works as a non-sequitur sight gag—it's as out of place as Barry, with whose posture and position it seems to align.

↑ *Above* Robert Mitchum's evil preacher in *The Night of the Hunter* has "Love" and "Hate" tattooed on his knuckles, prefiguring the appearance of bloody wounds reading "love" on Barry's hands after he punches his office wall.

to be implying that after the skilled ventriloquist act he'd cultivated previously, he was going to try to do something entirely in his own voice.

To wit: *Punch-Drunk Love* is where Anderson decisively detours away from the ensemble cast model and towards a solo protagonist, to the point of contouring the movie entirely to Barry's inner life. The later film it most resembles in this regard is *The Master*, and Barry's inchoate emotionalism—his propensity to lash out and/or implode—is of a piece with Freddie Quell's, as is his essentially questing nature. But there's also a connection to be made with *There Will Be Blood*, which comes immediately afterwards in Anderson's filmography but works retrospectively to contextualize *Punch-Drunk Love*'s themes of commodity and consumerism. Like Daniel Plainview, Barry is a salesman, although in a more modest register; his novelty items are not the makings of a West Coast empire, but an example of the free-for-all-entrepreneurship flourishing a century after the consolidation of top-down industrial capitalism. Barry isn't driven like Daniel (and to paraphrase *The Master*'s Peggy Dodd) to "dominate his environment" but to make minor incursions by addressing banal, everyday needs. The fragile, fiberglass toilet plungers ("fungers") he's mass producing are trinkets rather than monolithic monuments, reminders of physical indignity, prone to breaking apart at inopportune moments; they are as much mirrors of their maker's goofy frailty as *There Will Be Blood*'s towering oil derricks double Daniel's ambitions.

Barry, we might say, is breakable, a condition that *Punch-Drunk Love* gradually exalts into a state of grace: An alternate title derived from the filmography of Anderson's hero Jonathan Demme could be *Handle with Care*. After he assaults the wall, we see Barry and the poster crumpled side by side in a crowded medium-close up, with California—and its collapsed possibilities—prominently visible on the left. Any appreciation for the significance of the map, however, is undermined by a bizarre detail in the foreground. As Barry's right hand comes into view, we see the word "love" spelled out in jagged letters on his knuckles, an uncanny special effect recasting his outburst in viscerally empathetic terms. The blood on his hands is his own; he wears his battle scars like a heart on his sleeve.

"These strange things happen all the time" as the narrator of *Magnolia* reminds us, and one way to look at *Punch-Drunk Love* is as a thorny strand pruned from that movie's overgrown narrative thicket. It's possible to imagine Barry's story, with its roiling themes of familial dysfunction, and inventory of symbolic objects (to the map and Barry's iconic dark-blue suit we can add single-serving pudding cups,

toilet plungers and a discarded harmonium) integrated into *Magnolia*'s orgy of contrapuntal cross-cutting. (It even features a sleazy phone-sex subplot, with Philip Seymour Hoffman shifted from the role of shame-faced caller to that of minor porn magnate—a contemporary of Frank T.J. Mackey). Conversely, *Punch-Drunk Love* can be said to play on some level as a more streamlined version of its supersized predecessor, zeroing in—in its zany, abtruse way—on the emotional truths that Anderson had attempted to express by drawing them out with an improved efficiency. When, at the film's climax, Barry declares to a rival "I have a love in my life, it makes me stronger than anything you can imagine," he echoes and revises Donnie Smith's assertion "I really do have love to give . . . I just don't know where to put it," while the two men share a similar problem, the solution is ultimately a matter of focus.

Barry's discovery of where to put his love—of where it, and he, fits—comes as the resolution to *Punch-Drunk Love*'s confounding series of narrative enigmas, and yet also as no surprise at all. From the moment that Lena (Emily Watson) enters the film bathed in one of the bright, multihued blue lens flares that Anderson and cinematographer Robert Elswit use to establish and heighten the film's magic-realist texture, it's apparent that she's there to deliver Barry from

his loneliness and isolation; she's the dream girl he hasn't met yet. Lena is, in her way, as unnatural a phenomena as the rain of frogs in *Magnolia*, minus the implied sense of collective punishment: She is a strange thing that happens, and a good one too. While Barry will ultimately be tested during their courtship, his obstacles are either profoundly internal (his problems with anger and phobia of intimacy) or so mechanically plot-driven (his battle with Hoffman's venal 1-900 number puppetmaster) as to be absurd; for her part, Lena makes everything, from a first date to a first kiss to a first night together, seem impossibly easy. For all the tension in *Punch-Drunk Love*—its skittery pacing and clattering sound design; its snatches of startling, gory violence; the battered dry wall and smashed glass; those weeping, bloody knuckles—the film mostly takes the form of a wish-fulfillment fantasy in which the aspirations of the protagonist and the filmmaker are poetically and beguilingly aligned. It's a buoyant movie, carried aloft on twinned sensations of flight and arrival; it's designed like an escape hatch opening up out of a series of propulsive tunnels towards an unforeseen but inevitable safe haven.

"Coming out of making *Magnolia* and living with that for a while, I went 'God, I would really like to take a left turn and make myself happy, get rid of all this cancer and

Barry's dangerous fragility is represented by the shattered glass door at a family party, becoming collateral damage in one of his tantrums. The bisected framing indicates division from his family while also making a visual joke of the portrait in the far right quadrant: Note that even in the photo, Barry is wearing the same blue suit.

crying,'" Anderson told Roger Ebert in 2002, an admission that accounts for the massive shift in tone and scale—as well as style, if not sensibility—that manifested in his next project. At a fleet, trim ninety-five minutes, *Punch-Drunk Love* is exactly half as long as *Magnolia*, suggesting that for all his anxiety (and bravado) about earning final cut on the former, the filmmaker was aware that he had perhaps tried to do too much. "I wish I could take ten or fifteen minutes out," he admitted to James Mottram, adding that "in ninety minutes, you have to get to it, say what you've got to say and get the hell out of there." *Magnolia*'s gigantism had provided a more than ample arena for what Anderson had to say—articulated most succinctly in Stanley Spector's meek-shall-inherit rallying cry "I need you to be nicer to me"—as well the myriad and intermittently ingenious ways he devised to say it. It was a showcase for his gifts that also exposed his weaknesses. By setting himself a baseline goal of brevity, Anderson ensured that *Punch-Drunk Love* would propose a different set of creative and logistical challenges, and also exercise a different, subtler set of muscles, conjuring up a lean, middleweight contender instead of a steroidal giant.

The boxing analogy suits the film and its two-fisted protagonist; the working title was *Punch-Drunk Knuckle Love* and Anderson told *Variety* that the character was "a bit confused and a bit angry . . . it's about that feeling when you can't say something and you just start to throw punches." Emotionally impacted characters were not new for Anderson, nor were the kind of furious outbursts that

comprised Sandler's star persona; on *Saturday Night Live* and in the series of thrifty, high return-on-investment frat-demographic hits he'd made after exiting the show, the actor's go-to move was to play simple, unprepossessing types who exploded at irregular intervals into incandescent rage (e.g. *The Waterboy*'s (1998) Bobby Boucher, a gentle, Gumpian savant who transforms into a gridiron hero whenever anybody makes him angry). No less than Cruise, Sandler is an actor whose success had to do with wringing variations on a formula, but where Cruise decided early in his career to take risks—answering the high-flying, straight-saluting pilot of *Top Gun* (1986) with the embittered Vietnam vet in *Born on the Fourth of July* (1989), or risking his leading-man virility to play *Eyes Wide Shut*'s bewildered existential cuckold—Sandler seemed content to say in his lane, replicating the man-child-versus-the-world formula of *Billy Madison* (1995) ad infinitum.

George Toles observes correctly that the Sandler brand is associated with "mock outbursts of essentially harmless anger"; the tantrums thrown by the title characters of *Billy Madison* and *Happy Gilmore* (1996) are pretences for indulgent mugging and cartoonish slapstick (as when the latter attacks Bob Barker at a charity golf tournament), with no real sense of consequence. As an actor, Sandler's appeal is uniquely juvenile—he's a figure of pure id, albeit one lacking the surface sophistication of more acclaimed mainstream subversives like Groucho Marx (whose contempt for bourgeois mores marks him as an agent of real

EAT PUDDING—TRAVEL THE WORLD

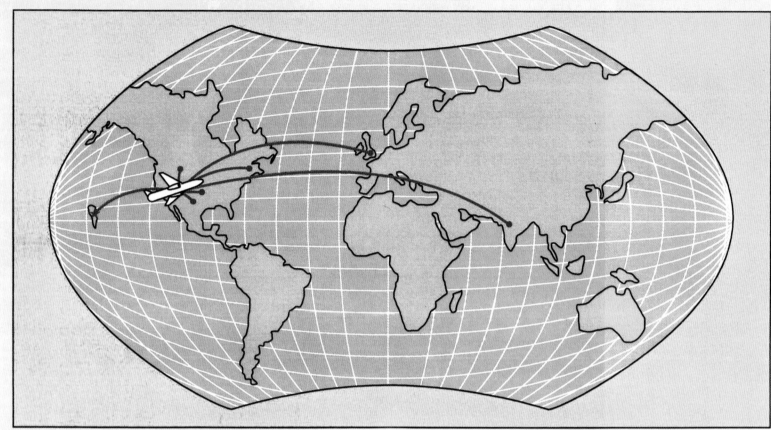

Puddings Per Destination

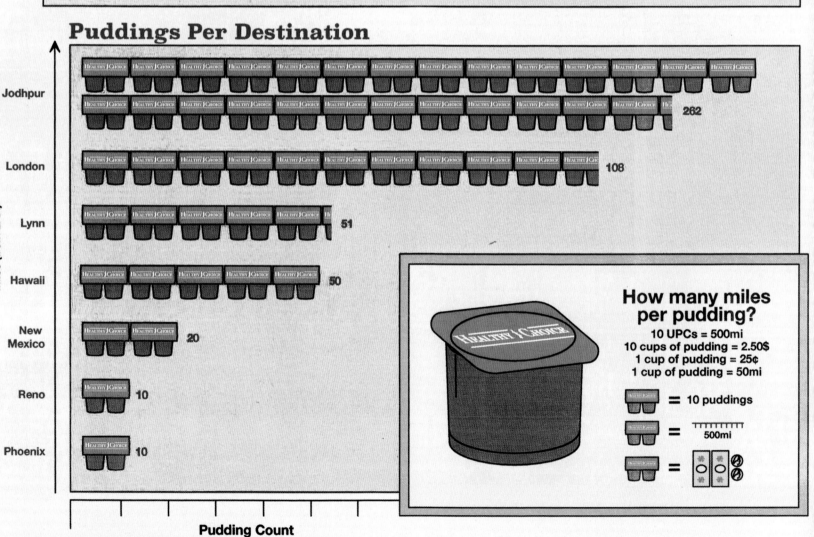

Miles (from LAX)

Destination	Count
Jodhpur	262
London	108
Lynn	51
Hawaii	50
New Mexico	20
Reno	10
Phoenix	10

Pudding Count

How many miles per pudding?

10 UPCs = 500mi
10 cups of pudding = 2.50$
1 cup of pudding = 25¢
1 cup of pudding = 50mi

= 10 puddings

= 500mi

=

anarchy) or Jerry Lewis (a class-conscious comic driven by a perfectionism far removed by Sandler's slobby populism). The lazy contradiction of Sandler's early comedies is how their plots variably demand that his character "grow up"— most directly in *Billy Madison*, which forces Billy to relive the entirety of his education in a compressed period to access a family fortune—while asserting and reveling in the grotesque spectacle of immaturity; the teenage boys who made up their target audience knew what they were really rooting for (or against) when it came to the prospect of their hero embracing adulthood's complexities. Only 1998's *The Wedding Singer*, which cast Sandler as a self-loathing, cut-rate entertainer yearning to transcend his own cover-band mediocrity, made effective use of the actor's sweetness, including a final serenade of co-star Drew Barrymore featuring the incongruously thoughtful refrain, "I want to be the one who grows old with you."

Sandler's musicality—a major factor in his rise on *Saturday Night Live* via the jokey baritone of his recurring "Opera Man" character and goofy, self-penned ukelele ditties like "The Hannukah Song"—is not on display in *Punch-Drunk Love*, even as the film makes allusions to and plays with the form of classic musicals. "Paul was looking at a lot of old MGM stuff," recalled Jon Brion in an interview with *Vulture*, who explained that the film's swirling, percussive score was recorded with fifties-era RCA microphones. In one sequence, Barry tap-dances in a 99-cent store, Fred Astaire in spirit if not in grace; elsewhere, Lena is

The contrast between the "Healthy Choice" coupons and the 1-900 advertisements generates a satirical dialectic between "wholesome" and "sleazy" purchases. At the same time, Barry's coupon-clipping frequent-flyer miles scheme has some of the same subterfuge as the phone-sex operation—it's an attempt to game the system.

seen in a white dress identical to one worn by Cyd Charisse in *The Band Wagon* (1953). As in *Magnolia*, Anderson uses orchestral music to propel the action forward and pop to comment on the action: The deployment of Shelley Duvall singing "He Needs Me"—a song composed by Harry Nilsson for Robert Altman's ill-fated movie version of *Popeye* (1981)—is as overt as any of Aimee Mann's tunes in *Magnolia*, its reedy-voiced refrain spelling out the emerging codependency between Barry and Lena with something like the opposite of subtlety. Indeed, it is this lack of understatement—and a correspondent embrace of the brazenly, exuberantly stylized and artificial—that confirms *Punch-Drunk Love*'s tonal debt to classic musicals, with their privileging of feeling over plausibility, and which also accommodates Sandler's acting choices, which don't so much deviate from his usual shtick as force identification and empathy with its private, primal sources. Rather than making an arty version of an Adam Sandler movie—or even just depositing Sandler in an art film to fight his way towards thespian respectability—Anderson recognizes and reconciles disparate forms of cinematic excess—the sublime, hyper-real tactility of Technicolor musicals and the unrepentant ridiculousness of twenty-first-century multiplex comedy crowd-pleasers—into something that feels unhinged from moment to moment and yet also more of a piece than the bifurcated *Boogie Nights* or the florid, flowery *Magnolia*; a surpassingly gorgeous, oddball fantasy that locates its continuity in the idea that anything can happen at any time.

The crazy rhythms of *Punch-Drunk Love* are established at the very outset, with Anderson hearkening back to *Magnolia*'s curtain-raiser via the juxtaposition of two bizarre events: A one vehicle car crash in a desolate back alley abutting on Barry's warehouse space and the arrival, simultaneously, of a taxi cab whose unseen driver deposits a small organ—a harmonium—on the curb before driving off. The crash, undoubtedly the more startling of the two occurences, is never referred to again, while the harmonium, which Barry rescues in lieu of investigating the (fatal?) car accident, remains present throughout the remainder of the present, looming un-threateningly in Barry's office. Still and impassive in the face of confusion and carnage—the warehouse is a Tati-esque breeding ground for accidents

↑ *Above* The dancers on the street (*left*) in Hawaii are dressed in red and white—Lena's colors—indicating Barry's increased proximity to his beloved. Framed against the ocean in the film's most iconic shot (*opposite*), Barry and Lena's silouhetted heads seem to form a heart—a surpassingly romantic image styled and color-coded in contrast to the drabness of the Los Angeles locations.

← *Left* The brothers (*below*) who menace Barry at the Mattress Man's behest are like comic-book henchmen, as well as distorted mirror images of Barry's overbearing sisters: Sibling relationships as sources of fear and anxiety.

→ *Opposite* Lena can be seen wearing a white dress modeled on Cyd Charisse's costume in the vintage Vincente Minnelli musical *The Band Wagon* (1953), one of several allusions to an affectionate artificiality in *Punch-Drunk Love*'s style and conception.

and catastrophes—the harmonium stands for equilibrium and order, as well as mystery: Its catalyzing function weirdly recalls the severed ear discovered by Kyle McLachlan in *Blue Velvet* (1986). Barry can't play it properly, but he *wants* to. Hence the instrument's association with Lena, whose own arrival a few scenes later into Barry's life is just as random and fortuitous, offering Barry a challenge and reward in the same form. If the harmonium heralds Lena and her almost magical transformative properties, then the car crash is a prescient synecdoche for Barry's potentially self-destructive anger.

Punch-Drunk Love is pressurized by the proximity of these two possibilities. Although we're never shown Barry's left hand after he wallops the wall, the implicit visual reference to Charles Laughton's *Night of the Hunter* (1955), with its indelibly, tattooed villain, means that we can guess it has "hate" written somewhere under the skin. "These fingers, dear hearts, is always a-warrin' and a-tuggin', one agin' the other," crows Robert Mitchum's sociopathic "Preacher" Harry Powell, expressing a Manichean view of the universe that belies the more elastic (and even Lynchian) possibility that each extreme exists inside the other—a duality that

certainly holds true for Anderson's protagonist. The first time that Barry loses his temper is during a birthday party attended by his seven sisters, whose collective attitude towards Barry—the baby of the family, like Anderson himself—is simultaneously protective, overbearing and enervating, a nightmare of possessive and infantilizing affection—the kind of love that could easily generate hate. Their pet name for their little brother, "gay boy," uttered by each in turn upon his arrival, is so overtly antagonistic that it's hard for us to perceive any good-natured kidding in it, while the language they use to describe him after he smashes the sliding glass door—"you retard, Barry"—is similarly incideniary and politically incorrect.

Why are Barry's sisters so grotesque? Julian Murphet contends that the group's threat resides in their "copiously breeding, indelibly *familial*" qualities—that in a movie that takes leave early and often of conventional realism, the Egan girls are, no less than the harmonium or that aforementioned map, a wholly symbolic element within Anderson's narrative universe: They represent Barry's fear of, in some intertwining order, family, femininity, and intimacy and sureveillance. As in the obsessive, desirous lover's quest

The forbidding expanse of the Mattress Man's headquarters in Provo, Utah, creates a visual double for the strip malls and warehouses of Barry's natural habitat in the Valley; it's also a comic book–style image, a tacky, suburban fortress of solitude, inviting Barry to enter and settle accounts.

↓ **Below** Dean "Mattress Man" Trumbell (*top*) (Philip Seymour Hoffman) is an unlikely but perfectly designed nemesis for Barry: A small-time salesman who seeks to punish clients for being "perverts" as an extension of his own fetishistic cruelty. Barry's arrival (*bottom*) to confront him gives *Punch-Drunk Love* a showdown ending worthy of an old Western (or a superhero movie), with the violence of combat negated and subsumed into a war of words that Barry wins through a raw confession about the "love he has inside [him]."

of *The Master*—and arguably also via the feminine lack of *There Will Be Blood*, with its phallic derricks and frustrated male strivers—women possess a disproportionate amount of power in *Punch-Drunk Love*, albeit distributed across a cross-section of regressive archetypes: The nagging Egans; the duplicitous phone sex worker, "Georgia" (Ashley Clark), who inveigles Barry in a blackmail scheme after their first $1.99-per-minute conversation; even Lena, whose essential perfection—embodied in her willigness, against all common sense, to indulge Barry's nervous lies about his life and behavior and reciprocate his terrifying pillow talk after they make love ("I want to smash your face in with a sledgehammer") makes her a memorable character but only in counterpoint to the movie's anguished, psychologically complex male lead. Without Barry, Lena makes no sense—in fact, she may as well not exist.

Plunge deeply enough into the dark corners of the Internet and you'll find a welter of fan theories—posted on message boards, some of which are dozens of entries long—theorizing that Lena is, in fact, an alien, one whose function is to help Barry realize his own potential; in some versions of this theory, her alliterative initials (Lena Leonard) are juxtaposed against Barry's blue suit and a few stray, strained details (his prodigious strength; the constant lens flares) to construct a reading in which she is "Lois Lane" and Sandler is playing an unofficial version of Superman. While such analyses are in line with both the boldly appropriate nature of online fandom and the burgeoning twenty-first-century obsession with superhero narratives, such thinking reduces *Punch-Drunk Love*'s ambiguities rather than honoring (or persuasively solving) them. At the same, the application of comic-book logic to some of *Punch-Drunk Love*'s visual and dramatic choices is not entirely out of bounds. Barry's blue suit may evoke Superman, but the more on-point corollary for his shifts between mild-mannered shyness and inarticulate freakouts would be the Incredible Hulk. "I don't like myself sometimes," Barry confides to one of his brothers-in-law after destroying the glass door, a line that echoes (however unconsciously) Bruce Banner's trademark threat "you wouldn't like me when I'm angry;" in both cases, the characters are acknowledging their basic helplessness in the throes of uncontrollable feelings.

One of the ways that Anderson signals Barry's growth over the course of *Punch-Drunk Love* is to show how he's able to more successfully channel his rage, moving from the senseless—if satisfying—demolition of environments and objects to focused acts of aggression against deserving parties. The film's morality is not particularly sophisticated on this point; the four blonde siblings that Dean Trumbell unleashes on Barry to collect on his (illegitimate) "debt" to Georgia are moronic mercenaries, as well as bullies who have no compunction about roughing him up four-on-one. (In this way, they're also gender-flipped mirror images of Barry's sisters—another monstrous embodiment of familial

closeness and continuity.) But in their second encounter, after the brothers have injured Lena by driving their car into Barry's (shades of the opening smash-up)—and, within the movie's overall logic of male fantasy, following his first sexual encounter with Lena in Hawaii, which may or may not have been his first sexual encounter ever—he transforms into a virtuoso of violence, dispatching them precisely and wordlessly with a tire-iron. The ease with which Anderson aligns us with this act of vengeance is undeniable and disturbing: It suggests that all that's needed for Barry to go from misfit to hero is the right context.

"Healthy Choice" is the name of the pudding company that Barry is trying to systematically defraud in order to accumulate a near-infinite amount of frequent flyer miles (a plot point Anderson adapted from a real news story, truth being as always stranger than fiction). Barry's embrace of physical violence in the home stretch its own "healthy choice?" Tellingly, Anderson stops short of turning *Punch-Drunk Love* into a vigilante narrative, staging the ultimate showdown between Barry and Dean at the latter's headquarters in Provo as a war of words—one in which Barry's assertion about the strength gifted to him by love is enough to make the apoplectic "Mattress Man" (a pretty good name for a comic-book villain) stand down. Throughout the film, Barry's demeanor while talking on telephones has been anxious and deferential; now, clenching a broken rotary phone in hand (how he got from California to Utah without relinquishing the receiver is perhaps the most quietly hilarious of the film's logistical ellipses), he assumes a dominant position, whereas Dean's over-the-phone bluster shrivels up in person. "You tell me 'that's that' before I beat the hell from you," Barry growls, a threat that one can hear hissing through the clenched teeth of *Happy Gilmore*: As much as the film has conditioned us to anticipate—and cheer—Dean's own beating, the violence never materializes. (The short, repetitive phrase also echoes Barry's strangled "bye bye" after departing Lena's apartment for the first time, a failure to verbalize recast as getting the last word).

Where Hoffman's supremely empathetic acting was central to *Magnolia*'s affective power, in *Punch-Drunk Love* he's more of an adornment—a bizarre character who, like Lena, really only makes sense in counterpoint to Barry. Both men are salesmen, but Dean, who is further along in his entrepreneurship, represents the corrosion of the profit motive. "Think you can be a pervert and not pay for it?" he queries Barry, a statement that not only implies a punitive attitude, but the idea that "unhealthy choices" are just another commodity. Dean's dual empires—the mattress store and the phone sex line—emblematize sleaze and passivity versus the hypothetically unclogging properties of Barry's "fungers." It's prurient fantasy set against earthy reality, harmful, targeted grifting and blackmail versus the essentially victimless crime of finding a loophole in a corporate promotion.

(continued on page 202)

"I refused to be a prisoner of my own first success," said François Truffaut of his motivations for making *Shoot the Piano Player* in 1960 after the widespread embrace of *The 400 Blows* (1959) made him one of the most celebrated young film directors in Europe—along with his colleague and collaborator Jean-Luc Godard, the face of the cresting French New Wave. The question of where a young, gifted, ambitious filmmaker might go after crafting such an undeniable debut was encoded in the final, freeze-framed shot of *The 400 Blows*, in which Jean-Pierre Léaud's Antoine Doinel gazes out at the audience. The image is meant to convey unknowability of the character's future—what does he see ahead of him? It's equally legible, though, as a (self)-portrait of the artist, wondering plaintively where to go next.

Truffaut's instincts led him away from childhood as a subject, at least for a short while (he would return to the character of Doinel in a series of sequels, as well as other stand-alone portraits of youth in revolt and transition, including 1970's beguiling *The Wild Child*). Instead, he gravitated towards noir, reflecting the same fascination for American genre cinema that informed his script (co-written with Claude Chabrol) for Godard's epochal *Breathless* (1960) and haunted the Nouvelle Vague as a whole: While the Cahiers critics ultimately subsumed a whole host of influences into their moviemaking work, the fleet rhythms and terse, unnerving fatalism of postwar B-movies proved irresistible, both to replicate and to complicate.

Shoot the Piano Player's roots are literary: Truffaut was a fan of David Goodis's *Down There*, a Philadelphia-set thriller about two brothers—Turley, a deadbeat, and Eddie, his scarcely more solvent, piano-playing sibling—involved in a game of cat-and-mouse with violent assailants; set in the down-and-out neighborhood of Port Richmond, the book was praised for its lean, hungry style and embedded class consciousness (Henry Miller was reportedly a fan). For his adaptation, Truffaut kept aspects of the plot but reimagined the musician protagonist as a less two-fisted type, renaming him Charlie, casting the elegant singer Charles Aznavour, and directing him to act hapless in the midst of an otherwise propulsive, perilous narrative—the deadpan eye of the storm.

A wry burlesque of gangster movie conventions that gradually achieves screwball velocity in between a series of self-aware interruptions—doubling back and flashing forward in time with the same aplomb as *Citizen Kane* (1941)—

Shoot the Piano Player is a film made under the sign of postmodernism, a gateway to the gamesmanship of Godard, De Palma, Tarantino, and others. With *Punch-Drunk Love*, Anderson claimed to reduce the ratio of his own intertextual referentiality, but he uses what few allusions he has to evoke *Shoot the Piano Player*. The homage begins with the harmonium deposited on Barry Egan's doorstep; his reverence for—and gradual mastery of—this heaven-sent keyboard helps to define his heroism. If Aznavour's weary resignation as Charlie is more controlled than Sandler's raw anxiety, the performances have plenty in common: Both riff on the performer's established showbiz persona while tapping a rich vein of passive, lovelorn masculinity. Both Charlie and Barry become infatuated with mysterious women named Lena, played in Truffaut's film by Marie Dubois, who makes her barmaid character into a sweet, steady, resourceful romantic presence, not an angel like the Lena played by Emily Watson but a potentially redemptive figure all the same.

Anderson's most evocative quotation of Truffaut comes when Barry escapes the first ambush by the Mattress Man's henchmen; the chaotic framing recalls Charlie's brother Chico (Albert Remy) being similarly pursued by goons at the outset of *Shoot the Piano Player*, a burst of headlong momentum that establishes the movie's mandate to rush from scene to scene and trope to trope—to throw caution (and conventionality) to the winds and play fast and loose with the rules of filmmaking. It's a cause taken up in *Punch-Drunk Love*, which laces its psychodrama with a playful spirit; it even ends with its protagonist as a kind of maestro, serenely making music with his new harmonium as Lena looks on. Barry! The piano player!

Dean's tendency to throw temper tantrums—"shut up shut up shut up shut up" he sputters into the phone after Barry calls to complain about Georgia's extortion, with Hoffman turning each syllable into a masterclass in exposed-nerve fury—marks him even more clearly as Barry's double, and as another avatar of weak, inadequate masculinity in a movie that's ultimately too insistent on this point to dismiss as a macho fantasy. Anderson's use of the song "He Needs Me" is instructive here: The enmeshed irony of Olive Oyl's anthem references Popeye's inability to look after himself despite his super-strength and seaworthiness. The way Duvall's vocal performance is mixed into the action in *Punch-Drunk Love* is one of Anderson's great stylistic coups; she provides aural accompaniment for Barry's trip—in comic-book terms, his flight—to Hawaii, her voice at once a stand-in for the absent Lena and a vocalization of his inner monologue. (Like Aimee Mann's songs in *Magnolia*, the lyrics are woven into the dramatic texture of the work; they say what he cannot, and with a childlike simplicity that suits this material as surely as Mann's complex, lurching verbiage fits *Magnolia*). Stumbling blindly through long, winding airport corridors before emerging into the South Pacific sunshine, Barry is an addled, determined Romeo, and Anderson and Elswit reward him with a shot whose pure Pop Art perfection suggests Roy Lichtenstein stripped of irony—which is to say, a comic-book panel. It's a frieze of the two lovers in silhouette, framed against a technicolor backdrop of sea and sky; a rare example in Anderson's work of beauty fully unencumbered by menace "it really looks like Hawaii here," says Barry, as if amazed to encounter a place that delivers on his promises.

Beauty does not want for explanations in *Punch-Drunk Love*: It simply asserts itself, as in the abstract canvases by artist Jeremy Blake that appear at irregular intervals throughout the film, transforming the screen into a field of pure color forms, or the lens flares devised by Elswit, which serve to almost electrify the imagery (they're like intermittent injections of voltage into the mise-en-scène); or the motif of alternately shadowy or overbright corridors that keep depositing Barry into new realms and realities like a side-scrolling video game character; or the harmonium, whose tones are eventually integrated into the gorgeous cacophony of Brion's score. The movie ends with Barry, seated and at rest, plucking the harmonium in sync with the soundtrack as Lena embraces him from behind; it's as if the different elements of the movie, with its fleeting hints of symmetry across its widescreen frames, have all finally aligned.

Where the violent protagonists of *Hard Eight* and *There Will Be Blood* are left to literally wallow in the gory aftermath of their actions—the spot of blood on Sydney's collar multiplied into the ocean of plasma flooding Daniel Plainview's basement bowling alley—Barry is content to holster his temper. His dominance duly asserted via a Western-style showdown, Barry holsters his temper; he swaps out the broken telephone and its intimations of troubled communication for the harmonium, which he brings to Lena's apartment as if returning to its rightful owner. Still, he's figured as a distinctly beta superhero, clipping coupons so that he might fly alongside his lover wherever *her* job takes her. "So here we go," she whispers, a call to adventure that propels the couple beyond the frame of the narrative.

In both *The Master* and *Inherent Vice*, Anderson will complicate the blissful implications of this kind of male-female two shot, stranding Freddie back on the beach with his imaginary dream girl and cozying Doc Sportello up to somebody who may yet be a figment of his imagination. (The flicker of sunlight that plays on the latter's face as he drives off into the fog could almost be a refraction of one of *Punch-Drunk Love*'s lens flares). This configuration will occur once more at the end of *Phantom Thread*, the film which truly answers *Punch-Drunk Love*, offering a differently stylized variation on romantic comedy tropes, arrayed in period finery and tilted—for the first time in Anderson's filmography—towards a distaff point of view. If the director's first seven features are all in some ways about male desire, with women as either its explicit objects or structuring absence, *Phantom Thread* reverses polarities to gradually and significantly privilege female subjectivity,

← *Opposite* Arriving at Lena's apartment after the confrontation with Dean, Barry apologizes for abandoning her at the hospital, taking responsbility for his actions and her trust; once he's said he's sorry, she lets him in, an invitation to share not only her space but her life.

↓ *Below* "So here we go": Barry and Lena are together and in sync, a conditioned confirmed by Barry picking out the melody of Jon Brion's score on the harmonium: After so much dissonance and chaos, the elements of his life find themselves—finally—in harmony.

a move that undermines our expectations about its individual narrative as well as the filmmaker's work as a whole. The sweetness of the sentiments expressed by Duvall-as-Olive Oyl on *Punch-Drunk Love*'s soundtrack are in harmony with the film's euphoric whimsy. By the time of *Phantom Thread*, our memory of those lyrics takes on a darker, more satirical—though no less plangent—cast. "He needs me," is the barely restrained subtext of everything that *Phantom Thread*'s intrepid heroine does for—and to—her partner: Even if it's bad, it's for his own good.

ITOM
EAD

n a 1996 interview with the *Paris Review*, Billy Wilder recalls coming to Los Angeles as a German émigré in the 1930s and meeting with his countryman Ernst Lubitsch, who needed an opening scene for his adaptation of a French play about a serial monogamist who keeps trying and failing to marry for love. "A 'meet-cute,' was a staple of romantic comedies back then," explains Wilder, who improvised for Lubitsch a set-up in which the male lead, an eccentric millionaire, goes to a high-end store seeking a pajama top only to meet a woman determined to purchase the bottoms—a pointed, anatomically charged detail hinting at his emasculation and her imminent desire to "wear the pants" in their subsequent relationship.

The film in question, *Bluebeard's Eighth Wife* (1938), is not considered one of Lubitsch's great masterpieces; Wilder and his writing partner Charles Brackett would go on to greater glory with the scripts for *Ball of Fire* (1941) and *Sunset Boulevard* (1950). It does, however, offer an interesting variation on the so-called "comedy of remarriage" theorized by Stanley Cavell. While Cavell did not include *Bluebeard's Eighth Wife* in his landmark text *Pursuits of Happiness*, a study of the form and ideology of 1930s screwball comedies, its storyline both fits and complicates his model, offering up two lovers whose passionate, bickering ambivalence gives way to mutual affection and devotion, while adding the wrinkle that Gary Cooper's wealthy businessman Michael Brandon is not so much commitment-phobic so much as commitment-obsessed. When he meets Claudette Colbert's Nicole, he's already been married seven times, offering each of his wives a valuable prenuptial agreement and watching them in turn heartlessly cash in; when Nicole proves to be a difficult partner, he suspects she's trying to do the same. Really, her desire is to keep him flustered and thus interested in her long enough to break his habit and allow true love to bloom.

A dark-hued comedy of remarriage set in mid-twentieth century England, *Phantom Thread* features a heroine with similar aims, as well as a Bluebeard figure in the form of Reynolds Woodcock, and a decisive meet-cute in a country hotel restaurant. Catching Reynolds's gaze while bussing tables, Alma Elson collides knee-first with a table, stumbling badly before regaining her feet and her composure. Almost. The giveaway is that—in a superb bit of full-bodied physical comedy by Vicky Krieps—she's blushing the same shade of burgundy as her waitress uniform, her cheeks glowing hot red against the muted blue wallpaper of the restaurant's dining room. As she heads back into the kitchen, we see Reynolds enact his own version of cooling down; Anderson frames him in profile as his smile shrinks and hardens and something troubled plays across his face. It's an odd, unnerving shot, suggesting the ingrained reticence of a "confirmed bachelor" trying to repress the the effects of love at first sight. When Alma returns, so does his mask of charming civility, except that we're aware of the efforts being made to fasten it safely in place.

As Anderson's most critically and commercially successful film since *There Will Be Blood*, *Phantom Thread* was hailed as, if not a "return to form" after the more oblique accomplishments of *The Master* and *Inherent Vice*, then at least to mainstream celebration—the director's "most outwardly accessible film in ages" as per *IndieWire*. *Phantom Thread* amassed six Oscar nominations including Best Picture, Director, Actor and Original Screenplay, and won one for Mark Bridges's costume design—an appropriate citation for a movie about a master dressmaker. Working for the first time as his own cinematographer, Anderson crafted his first-ever chamber piece, eschewing exterior locations in what the *Hollywood Reporter* called a "a singular work played out mostly in small rooms." In the process,

Phantom Thread drew numerous comparisons to a group of movies quite apart from the All-American touchstones attributed to the director's LA-set work. Picking up on cues stitched directly into the material, critics alluded to Alfred Hitchcock's *Rebecca* (1940) as well as the films of British masters Michael Powell and Emeric Pressburger, Max Ophüls, and Lubitsch, a more continental set of references for Anderson's first foray outside the United States.

Like the unofficial trilogy of *There Will Be Blood*, *The Master*, and *Inherent Vice*, *Phantom Thread* is a period piece requiring a certain amount of imaginative projection on behalf of the filmmaker and his collaborators; "it was not the Valley," joked Anderson to the *East Bay Times* of shooting in the UK for the first time. There is an element of fidelity to *Phantom Thread* with respect to Bridges's costume designs (scrupulously modeled on the fashions of the period and wedded to expert production design by Mark Tildesley) and the class divisions separating its two main characters. But the spectacle of a society in either formation or transition—a condition so central to the American films—is more understated here: Not absent, perhaps, but blended almost invisibly into the background. Curiously given Anderson's interests, there is no sense of an emergent British counterculture in *Phantom Thread*, which is set at the last possible moment before the seismic impact of British popular culture—mostly the rock 'n' roll mainstreamed by the Beatles, but also the "kitchen sink" realism of novelists, playwrights and filmmakers—would have to be accounted for even within its fabulously cloistered interiors. (When Reynolds asks at one point "what precisely is the nature of my game" he could be ghostwriting "Sympathy for the Devil" for Mick Jagger a half-decade in advance.) The comparative lack of temporal signifiers to the semiotic deluge of *Inherent Vice*'s Summer of '69 could be a sign of Anderson's relative tentativeness about tackling England as a backdrop, although as far as its actual treatment of time goes—both in terms of on-screen duration and shot length as well as a more abstract, underlying theme—*Phantom Thread* is as bold as any of the other "historical" films.

Within Anderson's filmography, though, the best comparison may be one made inside the lines of genre: To *Punch-Drunk Love*, the director's other "pure" romantic comedy and in some ways *Phantom Thread*'s kooky American twin. Reynolds's introduction as a great designer beholden to European royals and aristocrats frames the House of Woodcock as something monumental even as it is very clearly also an edifice to self-importance. Barry's entrepreneurship is wholly unprepossessing, and his creations aren't remotely built to last; no sooner has he introduced the idea of a novelty toilet plunger than we see one shatter in a haze of fiberglass, an accident that nevertheless confers a relatable, even lovable, sense of humility on the character and his ambitions (the same goes for his pudding-coupon scheme, with its unmistakable subtext of chiseling away at the imperious remove of front-running brand-name items).

Reynolds is also a very different kind of bachelor, punctuating his self-indulgent solitude with ritualistic flings stage-managed by his sister Cyril (Lesley Manville). Cyril's (omni)presence in her brother's life as a business and domestic partner provides an interesting rhyme with Barry's sibling scenario; in lieu of a teeming, undifferentiated mass of shrill, controlling, and accusatory femininity, Cyril's decisive, sexless, deceptively self-effacing presence keeps Reynolds and the House of Woodcock upright. The character also has the trappings of a Madam, not only in terms of Reynolds's lovers but also monitoring the dozens of nimble hands doing his dirty work upstairs. (Enough can not be written about the excellence of Manville's acting: "One of the greatest things an actor can do is make it worthwhile to watch their character think," writes the *Ringer*'s Kameron Austin Collins in an appreciation of the performance). Where in *Punch-Drunk Love*, Elizabeth Egan (Mary Lynn Rajskub) tries to set Barry up with her co-worker (who turns out to be Lena), Cyril's job is to nip fruitless relationships in the bud. In both films, though the ultimate outcome is the same: A mysterious woman in red appears to impose risky, necessary, and cathartic changes on an otherwise static situation.

← **Opposite** The imposing vertical space of the House of Woodcock is defined by stratifications of class and labor; we see the seamstresses enter through the back door on the ground level before ascending to the floors occupied by Cyril and Reynolds— class relations given visual expression through architecture.

↗ **Top; bottom** Reynolds Woodcock's desire for cleanliness and order begins with his own self-care regimen, which renders him as a fastidious, feminized male protagonist. The swift, precise depiction of his morning ablutions compresses a wealth of character development into just a few motions and gestures; combined with Jonny Greenwood's score, the scene plays like a short overture for the film to come.

211

Krieps's endlessly resourceful, almost chameleonic interpretation of Alma as a hardened survivor who alternately schemes and improvises her way into Reynolds's heart and confidence is far removed from Watson's saintly one-note acting as Lena; still, both performers are perfectly attuned to their particular movie's tone and point of view. What makes *Punch-Drunk Love* work (and ties it most closely to *The Master*) is its commitment to seeing the world through the eyes of its protagonist, to the point where certain sequences either only exist or play out the way they do because of Barry's psychology—his fears and desires, his wants and needs. Even the scene where we see Lena—or at least her red dress—stalking Barry in the supermarket can be read as much as his (unconscious) projection of his wish for companionship into the world around him as some kind of "stalker" backstory for Lena herself. But Alma exists well outside of Reynolds's perceptions: In fact, Anderson's reversal of the male-identified storytelling that drove his first seven features occurs in *Phantom Thread*'s very first scene, which has Alma describing Reynolds to an unseen interlocutor, giving her not only an unprecedented primacy within the film's narrative but also real authority in orienting and guiding us towards its inner meanings.

With this in mind, the first ten minutes of *Phantom Thread* comprise a game of chicken between satire and severity; the inverse, perhaps, of *Punch-Drunk Love*'s comparatively guileless mash-up of slapstick and sincerity. Where in *Punch-Drunk Love*, *There Will Be Blood*, and *The Master*, Anderson's onscreen worlds were established via dissonant music and sound design, the pristine piano lines of Jonny Greenwood's score, more classical in composition and orchestration than its predecessors, work to establish a sense of order: Everything in its right place. The fastidiousness that begins with Reynolds himself extends to his environment, and the House of Woodcock (really a house in London's Fitzroy Square) is as much of a psychic space as Daniel Plainview's towering derrick or Barry Egan's catastrophic workshop. It also serves as a microcosm of an external social reality. After watching Reynolds tend to his appearance and Cyril opening up the different rooms, we see their employees gathered by the back entrance; after they enter, their organized, swarming movements up the building's winding staircases mirror the enlisted men entering the military hospital, with a similarly dutiful sense of purpose, a minor army of artisans heading into the breach. Without the framing device of Alma's conversation, the clockwork perfection of this prologue could be taken as objectively seductive instead of as a vision of what Alma wants—and what she will in the process of her wanting, disrupt to the point of potential destruction.

"[*Phantom Thread*'s] view of how fashion is made feels dessicated and airless, as if beautiful clothes can come into being only under a dome of oppression and anxiety," writes

← **Left** "What, precisely, is the nature of my game?" Reynolds quizzes Alma during an argument, unintentionally and anachronistically anticipating the query at the heart of the Rolling Stones's classic 1968 song. The Stones's anarchic rock and roll is not quite on the horizon in *Phantom Thread* but Reynolds's anxieties about the future can be linked to impending shifts in English life and culture.

↘ **Top; bottom** Reynolds and Alma's "meet-cute" at a country restaurant is an intricate weave of stolen glances and non verbal signals, with the young waitress at once flustered (*center*) and seductive in her encounter with "the hungry boy," whose comparative confidence and self-satisfaction are evident.

Stephanie Zacharek, an observation that takes several aspects of the film at face value. If Reynolds's empire is defined by oppression and anxiety—the flip side of its serene, focused workflow—it's because these are the inherent vices of its proprietors; to think that the movie ascribes them real virtue is a misreading. If the hypnotic monotony of the House of Woodcock, synced to Greenwood's coruscating score induces a trance state, it's a morbid sort of daydream—a perfumed labyrinth. "There is a smell of death about this house," Reynolds admits late in the film, missing that the source of the stench is his own unforgiving perfectionism, his need to have things just so. Not only that, but the question of whether the clothes in *Phantom Thread* are actually beautiful—to say nothing of the difficulty of defining "beauty" or reconciling it with the homely realities of everyday life—is not nearly so closed as Zacharek suggests. When a young fan gushes to Reynolds that she wishes to be buried in one of his dresses, it's a compliment wrapped, however accidentally, around a critique—they're not for the living.

Death is a subject of great fascination for Reynolds, who fantasizes that the dearly departed are watching him from the afterlife. Discussing his late mother over dinner with Cyril, Reynolds says that he has "the strongest sense that she's near us," an ominous portent laced with goofy humour. The great man is a mama's boy—one whose whose apron strings extend to the crypt.

Mother figures have typically been of limited significance in Anderson's cinema, often existing only in the past tense; think of *Hard Eight*, whose plot is kick-started by John's need to pay for his mother's funeral (an event that, like the woman it commemorates, is never referred to again). Daniel Plainview and Freddie Quell both speak of their mother

without us ever seeing her (and Freddie's mother sounds to have been damaged to the point of estrangement). In *Magnolia*, Frank's codified, profitous misogyny can be understood as a reaction against his father's abandonment of their household (including his mother). The hateful, masculinity-challenging rant by Eddie's mother at the outset of *Boogie Nights* (one of Anderson's most awkward-ever bits of dramaturgy and Exhibit A for anyone looking to accuse him of hardwired misogyny) is offset by the gentle, incestuous surrogacy of Amber Waves (the same way that the quasi-maternal protectiveness of Barry's sister gets its idealized mirror image via Lena).

With Anderson, it's usually Daddy issues that are front and center (for male and female characters both) and duly sentimentalized, while mothers, when relevant, are sexualized, a tendency that carries through in *Phantom Thread*. Reynolds doesn't just wax nostalgic about "mama" to Cyril (on to whom a certain maternal burden has clearly been offloaded) but also during his first date with Alma, during which he tells her that he keeps a lock of his mother's hair with him at all times. (The whisper of morbidity speaks for itself.) She quickly apprehends that the older man's fixation on this absent parent (without even a mention of his father) constitutes her opportunity. If Reynolds is a Bluebeard, he's a neutered one who poses no real threat and lacks the stomach for overt cruelty; he requires Cyril to "do away" with his partners in the same way that he leans

on the female seamstresses of the House of Woodcock to generate the raw material he can then "personalize."

Reynolds's claims that he doesn't want to be married—"it would make me deceitful" he says vaguely—aren't so much dishonest as at odds with a subconscious desire to be mothered. To return to that ambivalent shot of him in the wake of seeing Alma for the first time, it's as if he's terrified that he might have to finally swap out his morbid, sexless attachment to mother (and her bloodline proxy, Cyril) for somebody more alive—a blushing bride, perhaps. (The hot red of Alma's face signifies beyond embarrassment—it's also the color of rage and passion.) Hence his attempts, going forward to reduce Alma to a muse, helpmate and lover rather than submit to a truer intimacy. The odd confluence of release dates in the winter of 2017 between Anderson's film and Darren Aronofsky's ambitious horror pastiche *mother!* led some critics to perceive a clear parallel in their respective allegories about artists and muses. In the Indian publication *First Post*, Anupam Kant Verma writes that "both films examine the relationship between a self-absorbed artist—a poet in *mother!* and a fashion designer in *Phantom Thread*—and the woman who inspires his work." In *mother!* the (nameless) muse is played by Jennifer Lawrence, an Oscar-winning movie star whose celebrity is used ironically by Aronofsky to place the subordination of her character in sharp relief; in *Phantom Thread*, Anderson's use of a largely unknown actress generates a very different sort of tension.

In an interview with *IndieWire*, Krieps (who was thirty-four at the time of production) admitted that she thought her audition tape was for a student film and didn't realize she'd be acting opposite Day-Lewis until after she had been cast. The film was Krieps's English-language debut after four years of German and Belgin productions, including 2014's *The Chambermaid Lynn*, which is where Anderson saw her for the first time; the resulting dynamic between a relatively fledgling performer and a Method-acting titan recalled a less bludgeoning yet equally thrilling clash of styles and stature to Day-Lewis's scenes with Paul Dano in *There Will Be Blood*. Because *There Will Be Blood* is Daniel's story, Eli is at best, a significant irritant: He gets his own set-piece with the exorcism at the Church but only because Daniel is sizing him up. Day-Lewis is similarly outsized as Reynolds Woodcock, playing on a screen persona that includes not only *There Will Be Blood*'s conqueror, but also a brainy continental lover in *The Unbearable Lightness of Being* (1988) and passionate, romantic heroes in *The Last of the Mohicans* (1992) and *The Age of Innocence* (1993). These were roles in which the actor's trim handsomeness and stage-trained elocution were played mostly straight, but Reynolds is a marvelous comic creation, by turns louche and fusty, with a bit of James Mason's weary gravitas (a mix, perhaps, of the imperious pater in *Bigger Than Life* [1956] and the lusty nebbish in *Lolita* [1962]). And yet, for every wonderfully elongated pose Day-Lewis comes up with, Krieps matches him, by turns shaky, gawky, volatile, and intractable; depending on the angle or the lighting she looks like a half-dozen different women, including any or all of *The Master*'s tall, red-haired objects of desire.

The seeming inequality between Day-Lewis and Krieps also evokes the casting coup of *Rebecca* (1940), a film whose Gothic shadow falls over *Phantom Thread*, beginning with the British location and extending to the basic contours of its narrative. In Hitchcock's Oscar-winning adaptation of Daphne du Maurier's 1938 novel, Laurence Olivier played the mysterious widower Maxim de Winter, whose devotion to his late wife Rebecca becomes devastatingly apparent in the erratic and demanding way he treats his new (and unnamed) bride; in the film, the "Second Mrs. DeWinter" is played by Joan Fontaine, who at age twenty-two beat out hundreds of more established actresses for the role. The parallels between Maxim/Reynolds and the Second Mrs. De Winter/Alma are plain as day, with Cyril serving as a stand-in for the villainous Mrs. Danvers (Dame Judith Anderson), and the House of Woodcock as a version of Du Maurier's legendary Manderley, a spooky, sprawling country mansion whose legacy, like that of Rebecca, bears down on its newest inhabitant to the point of madness.

"I love Hitchcock's *Rebecca* so much," Anderson told *Rolling Stone*. "But I watch it and about halfway through, I always find myself wishing that Joan Fontaine would just say, 'Right,

I have had enough of your shit. I think I have had more than my fair share of your bullshit, so let me just get the fuck out of here . . . the question becomes: Why is she staying with this guy? Because she loves him and they are connected in some profound way. That idea intrigued me."

For all of his dashing particulars—his big house, fast car, and half-superstitious fetish for secrecy—Reynolds is not terribly mysterious. Rather, he's a creature of habit, and his reasons for bringing Alma into his orbit are perfectly legible from the start. At the Hotel Victoria, he's quite content to have Alma serve him and even poke gentle fun at his outsized appetites ("for the hungry boy" she scribbles on the bill for his enormous breakfast). He's also quick to channel his attraction into a familiar dynamic: When he brings Alma to his country house (shades of Manderley), he quickly establishes control through a combination of manipulation and flattery, asking her to stand as a model for a new

↑ *Above* Alma's compart-mentalized life in the House of Woodcock—lover, helper, model, muse—means she's simultaneously self-effacing and on display. Appearing in a splashy photo shoot in Reynolds's dresses, she becomes a prop, wearing her upward mobility on her sleeves but, more crucially, not yet looking (or feeling) at home—the shot emphasizes the staged, performative context for her elegant appearance.

→ *Opposite* Reynolds's dresses are beautiful but often impractical verging on hazardous. The anxious socialite Barbara Rose finds it difficult to breathe in her bespoke gown, whose high neck serves to stifle and choke her; her complaints are rebuffed by Reynolds, who cares more about his design than the effect of the garment on its wearer.

dress. In this set-up, Alma is forced to be static, immobile, demure and deferential—the center of attention and a mute, malleable witness to his genius. It also permits Cyril to arrive and, no less than her brother, "measure" the new girl and submit her to set of cryptic comments reminiscent of Mrs. Danvers's psychological gamesmanship in *Rebecca* ("he likes a little belly," Cyril says by way of acknowledging Alma's build).

On one level, Alma's willingness to be reduced to a prop—and, gradually, another dutiful female helpmate in the House of Woodcock, waiting on wealthy female clients while Reynolds fawns and is fawned over—is a byproduct of her infatuation (or perhaps her research). Fontaine's character in *Rebecca* remains cowed and claustrophobic for nearly the entire duration of the movie; Anderson has woven his heroine out of stronger stuff. "If you wish to have a staring contest with me, you will lose" she informs Reynolds during their first date, repudiating the Svengali-ish power Reynolds

holds even as she still partially submits to it; later, while Reynolds is taking her measurements and admonishes her to "stand normally," she forces him to clarify that he meant "straight"—which is to say, not normally/naturally. "You didn't say that," she snaps impatiently, pushing back. "Maybe one day you will change your taste, Alma," Reynolds chides her during another fitting. "Maybe I like my own taste" she retorts, and so on, fully determined to have the last word.

Alma's refusal to fully submit to Reynolds's "taste" and, in time, to impose her own will on him, turning him into a dependent by nefarious means of poisoning, encodes *Phantom Thread* as a fairy tale—call it *Bluebeard's New Wife*—and pulls it forward in history past its 1950s setting into a contemporary parable about the perils of isolated male genius, or the adjacent condition known as "toxic masculinity," the potent antidote to which turns out to be more toxicity. (Critic Noah Berlatsky's critique of the movie as a mistimed, post-#MeToo celebration of Reynolds's sexist perfectionism says more about his own performative misreading of the material than anything else.) At the same time, it would be a stretch to assert that Alma's actions in the film are particularly heroic or representative of some larger idea gendered vengeance; if anything, the strength of Krieps's performance (which is embedded in Anderson's conception) is the mix of romance and opportunism.

"Nobody can stand as long as I can," Alma boasts at one point via voiceover, a line with multiple meanings: Her durability as a model; her potency as a muse; her resilience as partner. It also recasts her stumble at the Victoria Hotel as possibly suspicious. Did she fall in love or take a calculated pratfall? "[Alma's] seeming isolation in the country town where she works as a waitress suggests that she's not a traveller of choice but a refugee," writes Richard Brody, rightly recognizing the character not simply as an outsider, but—particularly in the film's post World War II context—a survivor. In the *Quietus*, David Hering infers a stronger parallel between *The Master* and *Phantom Thread*, writing that "in both films an ingénue of sorts, profoundly affected by the war, falls under the spell of a strong charismatic individual, setting the stage for an ideological sado-masochistic power struggle . . . are we to understand that she is a Jewish refugee? And are we to hear in her surname—"Elson"—an echo of that awful destination of so many European Jews during the Holocaust?"

Herring also proposes that Reynolds's lack of curiosity about Alma's past indicates his insulation from the realities of wartime—and from any real sense of threat to wealth or privilege. For instance, his contempt for the sallow, excessive Barbara Rose (Harriet Sansom Harris) is rooted in snobbery whereas Alma seems angered more by intimations that her new husband may have been a Nazi collaborator—a detail pointing to possible Jewish heritage. To interpret *Phantom Thread* as an elaborate allegory for the politics of postwar assimilation and Anglo-European relations is a stretch, and yet the reading feels pertinent to its centerpiece sequence, a spectacularly acted dinnertime argument that crystallizes

The pristine white of Reynolds's new commission gets spoiled when he collapses onto it, reeling from the poison administered by Alma. Made feeble and ill, he's forced to confront his handiwork from a position of weakness and wonder if it's any good, a humbling that will only deepen as his body further deteriorates from the effects of the mushrooms.

Reynolds's impatience with his new lover's flouting of house protocols (against Cyril's advice, she dismisses the staff and cooks him a private dinner, claiming a desire for some time for the two of them) and also exposes—quite terrifyingly—the vulnerability of her position as an outsider. Here, Anderson raises his game as a writer of loaded, hilarious dialogue, as when Reynolds praises his own "gallantry" in eating asparagus as per Alma's recipe (she cooks it with butter instead of oil and salt) and dredges up plausible, if exaggerated anxieties on both sides of the table. "Are you a special agent sent here to ruin my evening and possibly my entire life?" fumes Reynolds before adopting the language of espionage or combat. "Is this my house, or did somebody drop me on foreign soil . . . do you have a gun, are you here to kill me?"

His childishness is undeniable, and yet Alma has to take it seriously. "All your rules and your walls and your doors and your people, and money and clothes...everything;" even as she decries the House of Woodcock and the "games" played therein, she knows—as does Reynolds—that she has nowhere else to go. "If you don't wish to share that life as apparently it's so disagreeable to you in every respect, why don't you just fuck right off to where you came from?" Alma *does* want to share Reynolds's life, and its copious spoils: Whether her solution renders her sympathetic or merely cunning is a matter of spectatorial perspective.

The answer is dependent on how much sympathy we have for Reynolds, whose elevated position and apparent greatness is constantly being challenged by the details of the film's script: The way his allegedly masterful dresses pinch and constrict their wearers to the point of suffocation (as when the wealthy, alcoholic socialite Barbara Rose passes out at her wedding); the disparity between the designer's gluttony and his expectations for his models' physiques.

Manuela Lazic smartly draws a bead on these and other hypocrisies in her essay "Alma Matters: Modelling and Being in *Phantom Thread*," noting that "[Alma's] secret private dinner with Reynolds is a catastrophe because of a double standard: The designer isn't averse to surprises when he can spring them on others . . . Reynolds is always the exception to his own rule." She also calls attention to the "straight lines" of Reynolds's designs, shown in close-ups, that replicate similar inserts in *There Will Be Blood* when Daniel is designing his derrick. Both delegate to others, but Daniel is also shown literally getting down in the muck with his colleagues—he gets his hands dirty. In one of *Phantom Thread*'s funniest moments, Reynolds swoons under the influence of the mushroom-laced potion served to him by Alma and gets a speck of shoe polish on his snow-white commission for a Belgian princess: One damned spot is enough to send him retching into the bathroom. He may not be to the manor-born—that he

WE STAINED THE PRINCESS' WEDDING DRESS!

Step 1. Drink poisoned tea and collapse upon the dress.

We thought all was lost...
The dress had to be on the train to Belgium by 9AM! Then we followed these *four easy steps*, and like magic, the dress was ready in the morning!

Step 2. Ignore the doctor's orders.

Step 3. Remove any secret messages.

never cursed

Step 4. Admire your finished dress! It's not very good, is it? Cut out the stain and start again.

learned his trade from his twice-married mother indicates a hardscrabble upbringing—but he acts the part, including an unbecoming petulance when things don't go his way. As the film opens, the House of Woodcock is sagging under the weight of its own legacy and also an unwillingness— emanating from the top-down—to change with the times. "*Chic!* Whoever invented that ought to be spanked in public," he rages, ostensibly carrying a torch for the eternal verities of ladies' fashion but revealing himself, in work as well as in his domestic life, as a stubborn holdout who has to be argued—or bullied—into altering his view even an inch.

Crucially, Alma is not trying to fix Reynolds's business, or to usurp his role as its figurehead and resident genius, although her presence does have an effect on prospective clients for whom chaste flirtation with the designer is part of the package. Nor is she really hoping to supplant Cyril, whose initial skepticism gives way to respect and even affection in the film's most perfectly calibrated subplot. ("I've grown quite fond of her," she tells her brother). In a more overtly feminist film—one truly trying to score points off of the past with a politically correct audience—Alma's surreptitious campaign against Reynolds's immune system and constitution would result in her taking command of the House of Woodcock and reversing (or at least leveling out) the terms of labor; it would reveal Reynolds as the Emperor's New Clothes. Alma doesn't want to lead, just to stay, and, more to the point, to be "Mrs. Woodcock" in both senses of the word—to be a hybrid wife and mother. Her ploy is a form of radical submission that places her in subservient roles that nevertheless add up to a large amount of power. When Reynolds starts vomiting and defecating, Alma is not repulsed but exhilarated: As Shelley Duvall sang, "he needs her."

The scatalogical humor of *Phantom Thread*'s second half is strategically grotesque, serving as a picaresque-style leveller, not just for Alma against Reynolds—whose gluttony as a "hungry boy" comes home to roost via intestinal discomfort— but for the film versus its own corseted milieu. (Alma's methodology mirrors Reynolds's own: The mushroom shavings she drops into her lover's tea are as much her hidden artistic signature as the items he sews into the linings of his

Rescued from ruin by Cyril and her staff, the wedding dress looms besides Reynolds and Alma as they reconcile (*left*), eventually disappearing from frame (*center*) at the same time that he proposes marriage. The surprisingly stripped-down nature of their nuptials (*right*)—with Alma wearing a modest dress—undermines our expectation of what a master designer's wedding might look like.

garments.) Anderson delights in juxtaposing high fashion with low comedy, whether in the extended and cruel detour where Reynolds and Alma retrieve a dress from the near-comatose Barbara Rose (who, passed out prematurely in her honeymoon suite, is at once an abject and pitiable figure), or the cross-cutting between Reynolds's sweaty exertions in bed and his staff primly repairing the ruined garment in his stead—the material can be healed while the man remains a mess. "It's not very good, is it?" Reynolds mumbles to himself about the Princess's dress just before falling ill, a terrifically ambiguous line that could be written off to delirium or else as evidence that in his vulnerable state, he's more able to properly assess his work and its flaws—to see rather than repress the imperfections (and ugliness) of reality.

When Reynolds, in the full grip of his fever, hallucinates a vision of his late mother watching him from the back of the room clad in an elaborate wedding dress that hangs on her like a funeral shroud, it's as severely poetic an image as Anderson has ever conjured up: A stern, immobile ghost out of something by Luis Buñuel or Manoel de Oliveira. But the severity is also a kind of joke, because what's truly being conveyed is something modest, humorous and universal: The infantilizing effects of illness, and the need—innately relatable but rendered punitively humorous in the context of Reynolds's character—to be mothered in moments of vulnerability. When Alma enters the room and crosses in front of the apparition in Reynolds's field of view, she's sutured into his mind's eye as a replacement figure; in the next shot, the ghost disappears, setting her up to be—to use the language of *Rebecca*—the "First Mrs. Woodcock" (a literary echo Anderson inscribes himself by having a visiting doctor address both Alma and Cyril as "Mrs. Woodcock" and having them answer, eerily and humorously, in unison).

To be "Mrs. Woodcock" is Alma's endgame, and *Phantom Thread* grants her a premature victory. No sooner does Reynolds awake from his brief, agonizing sojourn at death's door than he offers marriage, a gesture made wickedly comic by that vision of his mother, whose appearance he takes as a confirmation of his earlier superstition (as well as a blessing from the beyond) and also the way Anderson presses in on the proposal with a long zoom that gradually pushes the miraculously-repaired wedding dress out of frame: For once, Reynolds will focus on his own nuptials. (He even kisses the sleeping Alma's feet to wake her). The weird speed with which the film depicts the wedding and its fallout seemingly undermines Alma's triumph, however; no sooner have the pair undertaken an alpine honeymoon than all the annoyances of their earlier domestic life reassert themselves—she chews loudly; he's a workaholic shut-in—compounded by new and frightening notes of possessiveness and jealousy. Showing up together at a Christmas party gilded around the edges like a Klimt painting, they resemble Tom Cruise and Nicole Kidman at the outset of *Eyes Wide Shut*—a couple perched on the verge of disaster or dissolution.

Phantom Thread doesn't take them there; like Kubrick, Anderson is interested in examining the archetypal architecture of marriage mostly in order to affirm it, albeit through a series of baroque negotiations. The sexual paranoia of *Eyes Wide Shut*—the fear that matrimony is a trap designed to keep one from experiencing the wider, more clandestine world of sensual pleasures beyond the marriage bed—finds its expression in the notorious masked orgy, which *Phantom Thread* answers via a surreal New Year's Eve party attended by Alma—an escape from Reynolds, whose refusal to take her dancing testifies to either to a romance in paralysis or else a stubborn possessiveness. In lieu of pushing representational envelopes à la Kubrick, who used his final movie to up the ante in terms of NC-17–level nudity, Anderson opts for a different, more benign kind of fairy-tale stylization: His masked revelers are not sexualized, but the mix of costume designs (animals, monsters, other mythical creatures) impart a sense of the carnivalesque, while a giant artificial rocket ship—a prop out of fifties B-movie sci-fi—gestures towards the future, rendering the countdown to midnight as a prelude to blast-off. Arriving at the party, Reynolds keeps his distance from the melee, stalking the balcony above the dance floor, determined to keep his distance; eventually, he descends (a suggestive trajectory) to retrieve Alma and bring her home.

The New Year's Eve scene in *Phantom Thread* is modeled on the revels in David Lean's 1949 film *The Passionate Friends*, from which it borrows the key location of the Royal Albert Hall. Stalking through the mezzanine, Reynolds can only observe the festivities, with their carnivalesque tone and intimations of the future (via the artificial rocketship), from a distance. It's not until he descends to the dance floor that he can retrieve Alma and show he's willing to exist—at least a little bit—in the world outside the House of Woodcock.

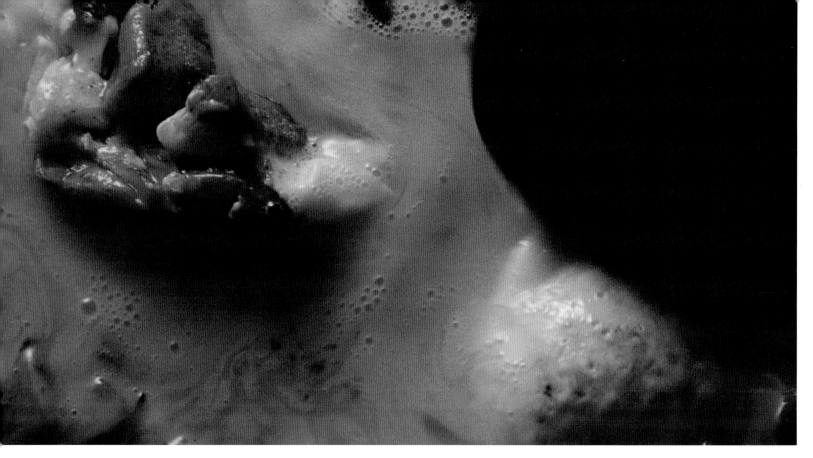

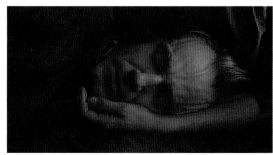

↑ Anderson first met Stanley
Kubrick on the set of *Eyes Wide
Shut* (1000), and *Phantom Thread*'s
interrogation of marriage and
monogamy—as well as its subtexts
about class and wealth—can
be seen as a continuation of
Kubrick's project.

That Reynolds won't join the party indicates a hesitance not just to move beyond his comfort zone, but also, more abstractly, a fear of the future—of time's forward movement and its implications. But he will give chase, and that level of devotion to Alma is enough for the movie to reroute back into the realm of happily ever after, with the perverse flourish that Reynolds not only accepts Alma's methodology for keeping him domesticated—occasional poisoned meals to make him vulnerable and pliant—but welcomes them: "kiss me, my girl, before I'm sick." The late scene where Reynolds watches Alma prepare him a diabolical omelette is pressurized in a Hitchcockian fashion (with glints, maybe, of Cary Grant preparing the glass of milk in *Suspicion* [1941]) before exploding into an absurd, Buñuelian humor; the comedy derives from the complete unveiling of Alama's motives and Reynolds's smiling, masochistic assent.

"You might wish that you were going to die, but you're not going to," Alma whispers, recalling Barry and Lena's weaponized pillow talk in *Punch-Drunk Love*—the fine line between infatuation and the wish to obliterate. But the line also cuts another way: This set-up is about how the previously death-fixated Reynolds is going to live. Bluebeard the serial murderer kills to keep from coming to terms with commitment—the skeletons in his closet testify to his fear of intimacy, his victims sacrificed on the altar of his vanity and their own curiosity. That Anderson's film gives Bluebeard a compassionate comeuppance—a life sentence—could have to do with the director's claims of winking self-portraiture: He's not willing to go so far with his onscreen avatar. Yet it's not vanity or self-deception that comes through in *Phantom Thread* so much as ideas, curious and constructively antithetical to great-man narratives of literature or cinema, of provisionality, compromise, and sacrifice.

For Alma, these concessions are hardwired, and leaving aside the erotic menace of her rhetoric ("I want you flat on your back, helpless, tender, open, with only me to help"), her terms are not really very demanding, requiring only intermittent vulnerability on her husband's part—for Mr. Woodcock to be a bit flaccid now and then before "becoming strong" once again. What she gets out of the bargain is an enviable and elevated level of security, marrying into what is essentially secular royalty, with the tacit agreement to produce an heir. *Phantom Thread* doesn't denigrate her ambitions but nor does it simply celebrate them as a fable of upward mobility. This fairy tale has a piquant aftertaste, with sadomasochism paving the way to happily ever after. The film's own ephemeral, online afterlife as Anderson's most-memed movie, with numerous screencaps and GIFs proliferating on Tumblr and Twitter, speaks to the sly knowingness that it projects (and has been received with) as a depiction of aspirational domesticity, with Day-Lewis and Krieps as only slightly less glamorous stand-ins for the

(continued on page 232)

← **Opposite** The perverse
humor of the film's ending
pays off its fairy-tale motifs,
with Alma playing the dual
role of witch and fairy god-
mother in poisoning (*top*) and
nursing (*bottom*) Reynolds,
a sadomasochistic arrangement
to which he eagerly acedes
("I'm getting hungry") (*center*).

229

"Should auld acquaintance be forgot?" The refrain of Robert Burns's New Year's Eve perennial proffers a question that is meant to be answered in the negative. The poem's meaning lies in its gentle insistence on a remembrance of things past, even when they're tinged with pain. Early on in David Lean's *The Passionate Friends*, we see Mary (Ann Todd) singing along to the song in a private box at a party ushering in 1939; she's there with her husband Howard (Claude Rains) but her thoughts are with Steven (Trevor Howard), who is milling about on the dance floor below her with his partner. Nine years ago, Mary and Steven were a couple, before a quarrel over the existential nature of love—of passion versus practicality—drove them apart. Now, Mary lives comfortably and even freely within her marriage, but her days are steeped in regret over the old acquaintance who's become a stranger.

Before he was entrenched in the collective cinematic consciousness as a maker of widescreen epics, Lean was a miniaturist of the human heart. Both *The Passionate Friends* and 1950's more widely known *Brief Encounter* are masterpieces about the perils of intimacy, focusing on characters trying not to lose themselves while holding on to the ones they love. *The Passionate Friends* is very much Mary's story, with the men serving as representations of different kinds of romantic attachment: The impulsive, scarily all-consuming excitement of her relationship with Steven is contrasted by the comparatively staid—and less perilous—dynamic she has with the older, more prosperous Howard. Because the movie is framed as a flashback, we know early on what choice she made, and why; the suspense is generated across its criss-crossing structure by the possibility that Steven's (in)opportune return into her orbit during a trip to Switzerland will break up her marriage, rendering Howard (sensitively played by Rains towards the end of his career) as, potentially an impediment to her happiness or a tragic cuckold, with the possibility that he might be both left very much open.

The Swiss holiday backdrop of *The Passionate Friends* reappears in *Phantom Thread* when Reynolds and Alma go on honeymoon, one of several affectionate nods to Lean's film overshadowed by more obvious homages to *Rebecca*. In an interview with *Film Inquiry*, Anderson explained that Jonny Greenwood's piano accompaniment was based on the work of the English composer Richard Addinsell, whose lush, swelling compositions give voice to Mary's pathos. The most striking similarity, however, lies in *Phantom Thread*'s use of the Royal Albert Hall as a filming location for its own New Year's Eve party, which, while more baroquely stylized than the one in Lean's sequence, is similarly conceived as a two-tiered revel. Reynolds skulks quietly above the fray like Howard, looking on with envy, reticence and possibly contempt at the celebrants below as Alma dances up a storm before the stroke of midnight. In both films, the date and context of the party are symbolic, calling attention to the passage of time and, with it, the changeability of people and relationships, for better and for worse.

In *Phantom Thread*, Reynolds and Alma's relationship is never really threatened by a third party, despite faint whispers of infidelity during their honeymoon—there is no triangle, only a battle of wills and wits between two well-matched opponents. And yet on some level, Anderson's film deals with the same underlying dilemma as *The Passionate Friends*, which is the leveraging of excitement against dependability, and the attendant fear that in any monogamous relationship, the latter will gradually subsume the former. At what point do longtime lovers become just "old acquaintances"? (Or, to paraphrase Reynolds's term for his sister and surrogate spouse Cyril, "old so and sos"?) And how long after that will they start to either pine for people out of their past or else go chasing some new future with somebody else?

Lean's movie concludes in glorious rush of melodrama with Mary being "saved" by Howard, whose heart she had broken through the appearance (ultimately refuted) of infidelity. Holstering his anger, he saves her from jumping to her death at a train station, preserving a marriage of convenience that has deepened into something like love, a transition which gives the film's title a very different meaning and concludes the proceedings in a rush of sublime, complicated emotion. Near the end of *Phantom Thread*, Reynolds descends to the floor of the Royal Albert Hall to take Alma by the hand and coax her home, a gesture of control that's also an act of contrition, submission and commitment. That Alma ultimately ends up saving herself—and her husband—by finding a way to turn their cozy, homely mutual dependency into a locus of passion furnishes *Phantom Thread* with a happy ending whose ironic tint does not cancel out its own surge of feeling.

audience than Nicole Kidman and Tom Cruise. "I do love you, and there's something very important that we need to do as soon as possible," purrs Kidman's Alice Harford, setting up her film's epithetic-orgasmic punchline. "Right now we're here . . . and I'm getting hungry" growls Reynolds as *Phantom Thread* ends, essentially repeating the entreaty—and the joke—with his desirous eyes wide shut.

Alma's concluding monologue returns us to the space of the New Year's Eve party, the hall suddenly deserted, balloons strewn on the ground as the band plays on for Reynolds and Alma, locked in a slow-dance embrace. It's a shot in debt to Kubrick's many ballrooms (from *Killer's Kiss* [1955] to *Eyes Wide Shut*) and it functions as something more than a flashback; inserted carefully into the slow, stately final montage, it goes beyond the woozy reverie of *Rebecca* ("last night I dreamed I went to Manderley again") and seems to take leave of reality entirely, recalling the synaptic leaps holding together *The Master*, just as Alma comes to adopt—oddly and disconcertingly—the language of Lancaster Dodd and the Cause. (Given the film's setting and timeline, it's possible to imagine, in another part of the country, Freddie Quell getting laid.) "If he wasn't here tomorrow, no matter," she muses, ostensibly to the person she's been speaking to for the movie's duration but directly to us. "I know he'd be waiting for me in the aftermath, or some safe celestial place, in this life and the next and the next one after."

There is a mix of grandiloquence and humility in Alma's words—an undying belief in a great love that transcends time, and a willingness to subordinate herself to its demands at the expense of all else. What she's describing, ultimately, is something that will outlast itself, something truly enduring beyond the House of Woodcock and its labels, or anything that Reynolds could make by himself; something to withstand that which is transitory and merely chic. At the end of *There Will Be Blood*, Daniel Plainview sits alone amidst that which he has made and destroyed, "I'm finished" invoked as a punchline: Having reached the sea, there's nowhere else for him to go. Reynolds Woodcock isn't finished, but still hungry. He is last seen measuring Alma for a dress in an image that is not only polyvalent in its impression of power—the artist kneeling at the muse's feet, the pair "each others' master in submission," as per Lazic's essay—but also thoroughly unstuck in time, a frieze out of the past, the present, or the future, or maybe uniting all three in one temporality: The meet-cute evolved into routine and elevated into mythology; complicity and collaboration; Bluebeard and his wife; wearing the dress as wearing the pants; the comedy of remarriage in a single frame.

↑ *Above* Happy New Year: Huddled together on the dance floor, Reynolds and Alma become a vision of mutual need, cast in beatific light that could represent a new, loving beginning or else paints the whole image as a fantasy—Alma's yearning for a lifetime (or several) of commitment.

→ *Opposite* "Nobody can stand for as long as I can" asserts Alma and *Phantom Thread*'s closing image elevates her steadfastness into the realm of myth: She's Reynolds's muse, but she also towers above him, embodying the complex power dynamics at the heart of the film's conception.

Music Videography
Junun

Junun opens in a state of anticipation, with a roomful of musicians preparing for a performance, slowly and shaking off the torpor of a hot Jodhpur afternoon. Together, they comprise an eclectic, brass and woodwind ensemble made up primarily of traditional Qawwali singers and instrumentalists, inheritors of a devotional tradition dating back to the thirteenth century; they are joined by a pair of western interlopers, Israeli composer Shye Ben Tzur and English rock guitarist Jonny Greenwood of Radiohead fame. After an introductory drumroll, the group locks into a driving, circular melody that seems to cue the camera's curlicues; as the arrangement grows ever more crowded and complex, it's as if the sound and image are rotating together, a relaxed, languorous synchronization that feels organic to the moment rather than carefully arranged—the filmmaker as attentive, receptive audience member rather than all-controlling auteur.

By design a minor entry into its director's filmography (it runs at a trim fifty-four minutes), *Junun* nevertheless resonates with a sense of gentle epiphany. "Have a great time," reads a hand-lettered sign held up to the camera shortly after the introductory overture, a superficially uncomplicated exhortation that can also be taken as a vital mantra. Shot in February 2015 after the release of *Inherent Vice*—a movie steeped in paranoia and produced under the anxiety of influence that goes along with being a literary adaptation—*Junun* represented a geographic and generic departure for Anderson, taking him away from the United States and towards the intersection of documentary and travelogue. The project found its genesis in an invitation extended by Greenwood, whose plans to record with Tzur were already in place. In terms of their collaboration, Anderson was along for the ride as an observer, operating his own camera. "Everything became like a travel brochure where you can't even believe what's coming to you," he told *IndieWire*, casting himself deliberately in artistic terms as a tourist rather than an interpreter or creator.

The result of this physically hands-on, conceptually hands-off venture is a film awash in curiosity and delight, both towards the unfolding marriage of musical styles and traditions (with Tzur asserting himself as a lead vocalist while Greenwood sheds any and all rock star pretense to simply strum along) and the surrounding environment, especially the seven-hundred-year-old mountainside fort that serves as the group's main base of operations. Untethered by the problems or logistics of traditional film direction, Anderson takes the opportunity to explore the space, drawn more often than not towards the structure's more elevated levels, from which panoramic views of the city's rooftops can be captured, as well as images of birds in flight that, in concert

with the film's barely sheathed themes of exuberance and liberation, become richly if only incidentally symbolic of some larger freedom.

There are ways to reconcile *Junun* with Anderson's dramatic features, not only through the fluidity of its camerawork (which anticipates the director taking his own director of photography credit on *Phantom Thread*) and its earnest grasping towards harmony (as realized in the final, perfectly syncopated musical notes of *Punch-Drunk Love*) but also more generally as an affectionate if enigmatic group portrait, somewhere between the filmmaking family of *Boogie Nights* and the recessive, obsessive sect of *The Master*. The lack of any detailed contextualizing information about Tzur, Greenwood, or the members and history of the "Rajasthan Express"—nor any real explanations about the music's style or relative popularity or importance in the twenty-first century—links the film formally to a direct-cinema tradition. And yet it's not as if Anderson's approach is deliberately mystifying. In lieu of mythologizing the musicians in his company, he observes them as a respectful, welcome guest, counting on their work's ability to speak—wordlessly—for itself. "[Jonathan] Demme had said something like 'pure cinema is someone playing music,'" Anderson elaborated, invoking the late filmmaker's great 1984 concert movie *Stop Making Sense* as an inspiration alongside Ahmed El Maânouni's freeform audiovisual experiment *Trances* (1981) about the Morroccan band Nass El Ghiwane; as in those films, the joy of collaboration is front-and-center. Even as intriguing individual figures emerge (or, in the case of Greenwood, lurk quietly around the edges of the action) Anderson resists the urge to emphasize or profile any one of them; his interest is in the collective.

Late in the film, we see the musicians being introduced for an impromptu set at a local festival by the Maharaja Gaj Singh, who praises a "very amazing coming together of vast varieties of musicians." His glowing remarks set the stage for something big and crowd-pleasing, but Anderson cuts back to the interior of the fort, far from the stage, where a crouching Greenwood asks his compatriots if they want to try one. They do, and then just as we've grown acclimatized to the idea of a rehearsal rendition, some more concert footage is interspersed, in effect erasing the boundaries between private and public performance as well as professionalism and pleasure and finally melding past and present into a single, ecstatic temporality: A great time. ✦

Selected Music Videography

Fiona Apple
1. *Fast as You Can* 1999

The most striking effect in "Fast as You Can" arrives during the song's bridge, which serves as a slow yet nervy idyll in between a set of hurtling verses and choruses. Here, Fiona Apple—at the time an ascendant alternative rock icon acclaimed for subverting expectations in both her craft and self-presentation—is seen emoting into a smudged camera lens that obscures and distorts her features to the point where she's forced to wipe it down (see 1. overleaf). A moment after achieving perfect clarity, she smears the screen with her hand, as if reasserting murkiness and mystery on her own terms.

Anderson's use of an old-fashioned iris effect towards the end of the video quotes the early-cinema aesthetic on display in prologue of *Magnolia* and points ahead towards the technique's use in *Punch-Drunk Love*. But for all its swiftness and intricacy—and the extenuating circumstances of Anderson and Apple's personal relationship at the time of filming—"Fast as You Can" is primarily an exercise in directorial self-effacement: His style serves her stardom.

Aimee Mann
2. *Save Me* 1999

As it would be tricky to try to separate Aimee Mann's "Save Me" for the film for which it was written and acts as an emotional anchor, Anderson opts for a bravura form of integration, inserting the singer into the *Magnolia*'s various environments and having her serenade its entire cast—a clever variation on the sequence featuring these same actors lip-synching separately but in unison to "Wise Up."

We see Mann sitting watch over the dying Earl Partridge, facing down Stanley Spector on the set of *What Do Kids Know?* (see 2. overleaf) and silently judging Frank T.J. Mackey. In each case she's not an active participant in the action but a concerned witness, a position that could be interpreted as a form of surrogacy for the director or the audience, or else a simple, powerful acknowledgment of how deeply her music—and specifically her literal and figurative voice—functions as its own character within *Magnolia*'s ensemble.

Joanna Newsom
3. *Sapikonikan* 2015
4. *Divers* 2015

Newsom's casting in *Inherent Vice* as Sortilège continued a tradition of Anderson using idiosynctatic musicians as narrator-figures in his work (following Aimee Mann in *Magnolia*); his videos for the first two singles off of her acclaimed 2015 album *Divers* are a set of mismatched twins.

In "Sapokanikan," Newsom serves—like the Haim sisters—as a kind of sprightly tour guide, beckoning the camera to follow her on a nocturnal winter walk through New York (with a couple of stray cuts to day time); smiling widely and mugging to the camera, she could be a featured player in the opening credits to *Saturday Night Live*. In terms of narrative, nothing happens, although the late appearance of a firetruck in the background dramatically alters the clip's lighting screen imparting a red-tinged sense of menace and intensity (see 3. overleaf).

For *Divers*'s title track, Anderson perceives the singer through a glass, darkly; looming like a goddess over a stylized mountain range, Newsom gradually becomes cloaked in swirling, cloud-like formations created by colored pigments released into water (see 4. overleaf). The technique is courtesy of New York–based artist Kim Keever, whose studio was used for the shoot; the result is a defiantly tactile, strongly analog fantasia that honors Newsom and her song's sweetly ephemeral aesthetic while holding the line against CGI.

Radiohead

5. *Daydreaming* 2016

There's a nod to the cryptic punchline of the *Bends*-era video "Just" at the end of Anderson's short film for "Daydreaming"—the second single off of the group's 2016 album *A Moon-Shaped Pool*—where Thom Yorke, who does not otherwise lip-synch in the video, mouths something unintelligible beneath the shimmering surfaces of the music. But if "Daydreaming" is an exercise in self-citation, it's to Anderson's own filmography more than Radiohead's collected clips.

The opening frame, which shows Yorke wandering through a tunnel, followed (or is it pursued?) by other "daydreamers," quotes Barry Egan's adventure at the airport in *Punch-Drunk Love*, a film whose recurring motif of corridors of portals is duplicated here, while the snaky camera movements evoke the kinetic, backstage tracking shots in *Magnolia* as young Stanley Spector is dragged to a taping of the game show *What Do Kids Know?* The PTA production that looms the largest over "Daydreaming," however, is *The Master*: When Yorke pushes through one darkened archway and emerges onto the beach, it's as if he's transformed into Freddie Quell, blinking in the sunshine in a fugue state (see 5. overleaf).

Beyond the director's self-reflexive playfulness, "Daydreaming"'s ephemeral vibe resists heavy-duty analysis. Still, Yorke's typically gnomic lyrics may offer a way in. "Dreamers they never learn / beyond the point of no return," describes a life drifting serenely out of control—the same dilemma facing Freddy Quell.

At the end of the video, Yorke arrives at his destination: An underground cave where he cozies up to the fire and settles in for the night. The suggestion of a return to the elements— a full-on regression and retreat from the modern world—is creepy even as it returns Anderson to his visual sweet spot, a screen filling close-up that turns Yorke's face into a landscape as vivid as any of the backdrops glimpsed earlier. Yorke's wry, weirdly cozy expression here goes into the director's pantheon of unforgettable close-ups.

Thom Yorke

6. *Anima* 2019

Billed as a "one-reeler"— a pretentious way to say that it lasts for fifteen minutes—"Anima" picks up where "Daydreaming" left off, with Yorke at the center of a dreamscape: In the first scene, shot on the Prague subway, he's shown nodding in and out of consciousness while his fellow passengers sleepwalk their way through spastic group dance choreography. Yorke joins the fray and his herky-jerky physicality (see 6. overleaf) remains compelling as space and gravity seem to bend around him: He ends up trapped on a tilting gray slab that catches angular shadows like a backdrop from a German Expressionist movie.

From there, the video switches locations to France, where our hero moves trippingly through narrow streets with a stunning partner (Dajana Roncione), his isolation at an end. The whole journey has the outlines of a yearning, aspirational fantasy, and the video's refusal to clarify the nature of Yorke's happiness—if it's experience, projection, or somewhere in between—places it on the same continuum of emotional ambivalence as *The Master* and *Phantom Thread*.

Haim

7. *Little of Your Love* 2017
8. *Hallelujah* 2019
9. *Summer Girl* 2019

The clips Anderson has directed for the Los Angeles-based pop group Haim—composed of siblings Danielle, Este and Alana—are united by a joyful sense of mobility: They're built out of long takes whose complexities are more playful than magisterial: The style is impressive even as it's meant to seem tossed-off, as if the filmmaker was just following his friends around town.

In "Little of Your Love," Danielle, clad in a Stevie Nicks T-shirt, strides into a country-western bar and immediately falls in with the line-dancing patrons (see 7. overleaf), including her sisters; as the trio trade verses and harmonies, the camera keeps fluidly switching its attention between them.

"Hallelujah" unfolds on a darkened stage where the girls have seemingly been granted magic powers (see 8. overleaf), using small physical gestures to cue lights, open curtains and reshuffle objects as they move through a lilting, Fleetwood Mac-style ballad.

The Lou Reed-inspired "Summer Girl" features a saxophonist tailing Danielle (see 9. overleaf) through LA ("Walk beside me, not behind me" she implores), a journey that includes a shift working the box-office at the New Beverly Cinema. In each video, the placid effect recalls the shopgirl's rapt choreography in *The Master*, suggesting a camera mesmerized by its subject, albeit with less severity.

JOANNE SELLAR

Born in the UK, Sellar worked on several independent horror films including Richard Stanley's *Hardware* (1990) before she and her husband Daniel Lupi became producers on *Boogie Nights*. She has subsequently produced all of Anderson's features, earning Academy Award nominations in the Best Picture category for *There Will Be Blood* and *Phantom Thread*.

Do you remember when you first saw *Hard Eight*? Well, I can tell you how it all happened . . . Robert Jones, who was one of the producers on *Hard Eight*, was a friend of mine from England. He was looking for a line producer for *Hard Eight*. My boyfriend at the time (now husband), Daniel Lupi, was a production manager, so he reached out to Daniel and he worked on that film. Daniel and Paul really got along, and I got to meet Paul at that time. Paul was looking for a producer for *Boogie Nights*—to coproduce with John Lyons, who was already on it—and so he gave me a copy of the script. And that's when I read it and like freaked out, because it was like, amazing this script. I was about to go back to London to do a job, but then I obviously stayed.

It's a big shift for you at that point, right? You'd previously done a lot in genre and horror; *Boogie Nights* **is obviously quite different to that. It's an extremely culturally specific American production.** Yeah, I mean I was living in LA at that point because I came over to America to produce a film called *Dark Blood*, which was the film that River Phoenix died on. Then I stayed and did a film called *Lord of Illusions* and that's when I met Paul. So, I was living in LA but didn't really know the [San Fernando] Valley at that time and only had a romantic vision of Reseda Boulevard through the Tom Petty song,

Did you feel that the experience of *Hard Eight*, **where there was all of this stress over the edit and different cuts of the film, was something that Paul wore very openly?** Yes, he was very, very on guard—and non-trusting of the producers in general—after what happened on that film. It took quite a long time for me to gain his trust. However, once he realized that my motives were only to get his vision on the screen, that's when he totally trusted me. He's an extremely loyal person.

Sometimes directors don't work with the same producers, or sometimes by its nature it's somewhat adversarial. But it sounds like this is a tremendously deep creative relationship. Definitely. I mean, Paul will talk about ideas or something that he's working on and maybe hasn't started writing. As you can tell from his work, he's a one picture guy. He's not developing different projects at the same time. He's doing his one thing and that's all he can really think about. He'll show me stuff in its very early stages and I'll read it and give him opinions and we'll just talk about it. It's the same with casting and locations, or whatever it might be. It's a very organic process. I'm also very involved in the whole process with the studio, the distribution and the marketing—and Paul has a really big say in all of that.

This idea of vision and singularity and young directors, New Line was very much at the forefront of that in the nineties. You were present for *Boogie Nights* **and** *Magnolia*: **What did those films seem to mean coming together**

in that period? Well, at the time Mike De Luca was Head of Film Production at New Line. He's a huge cinephile, and unlike a lot of executives, he felt like a real film person. He totally got *Boogie Nights* and was just like, "We've got to make this movie." I don't think it would have been made if Mike hadn't been at that studio. In fact, I know it wouldn't have been. I think he really had to convince folk to make that movie. Originally we had a different cast and everything. And when you read that movie, it was so electric off the page. You felt like you had to get this movie made. There was an energy to it.

What did *Magnolia* **read like off the page to you? I've always wondered how a movie like that is ever realized financially or gets made, because it's so unusual.** Coming off *Boogie Nights* there was obviously a huge buzz about Paul. He had established himself. And again, it was Mike at the studio. But really what triggered that whole thing coming together as quickly as it did—because it was obviously a bigger budget than *Boogie Nights*—was Tom Cruise saying yes. He said, I can give you this slot in my calendar so we had to make it then.

Did you get a sense that the nature of what the movie was had changed because suddenly a star was attached? The nature of the movie didn't change at all. Tom was dropping everything and coming to make a film for Paul. It was very much a Paul movie with Tom Cruise in it.

With *Magnolia*, **was there a feeling that Paul was working with a different part of himself?** Definitely. His own father died from lung cancer, and I think a lot of that was in the movie. There was a lot of stuff going on in his personal life that translated to the screen.

This was a film with a certain amount of stress about what to leave in and what to leave out. As the producer, just in terms of putting the movie into the world, was that a fraught period? Yes, to a certain degree. We had a very rushed post-production schedule. It was kind of ironic, considering that it was obviously this huge movie both in length and content. We could've done with a lot more time. A lot of people hadn't seen *Hard Eight*, so it was almost considered his second movie. And it was the first movie where he didn't have to have test screenings. We'd gone through this whole thing with *Boogie Nights* . . . I think we had five or six test screenings, and each one just got worse and worse! So yeah, it was a huge amount of pressure.

Is it a film that you've revisited recently? It's actually my personal favorite of Paul's movies. I haven't watched it that recently, but it really speaks to me. It's hard when you produce the films because you're not quite watching it with the same eyes as everybody else.

Rewatching *Magnolia*, there are things about it that are just off the charts that I'd forgotten about. I think it has really stood the test of time. Yeah. A few years ago I taught a course at Chapman Film School, and I showed the students all of Paul's films. It has held up really well, I think. There's something about that film that is so poignant and really moving.

Punch-Drunk Love is an interesting parallel with *Magnolia* in the sense that it's a movie made for a star. Was Adam Sandler the thing that Paul first came to you with? Or was it the character before the actor? Well, after *Magnolia* he wanted to make a really short movie. That was the first thing I remember him saying. But yeah, he wrote it for Sandler. He was a huge Sandler fan, and I was just befuddled—I just didn't get the whole Adam Sandler thing at that stage. I mean, the *Saturday Night Live* stuff, yes, but the movies that Adam had done weren't for me. As a British person I didn't really get the humor. But Paul just kept saying, "Oh my God, he's so great!" And he completely made me change my mind about Adam.

Even though it's a very pressurized, tense movie, I get the feeling that it's by a more relaxed artist. There's something about it that seems to be more open. You're completely right. On *Boogie Nights* and *Magnolia*, Paul was super prepared with his style of filmmaking—especially with *Boogie Nights* because he'd lived with it since he'd made the short. When we were putting that together, he knew every shot in his head, and he would have shot lists and everything. The same with *Magnolia*: He was really, really prepared. But on *Punch-Drunk Love*, he went for a much more organic process where he was shooting but not doing shot lists. It was much more from the hip, I would say.

Also, that was the year of the potential actors' strike, so in our schedule we had to release Adam for a few weeks and then we were going to get him back. Even though the strike didn't happen then, we actually had this break, and it gave Paul the opportunity to edit a lot of the film, knowing that he was going to go back and shoot for another three weeks or whatever it was. When we came back, he shot what he still needed to shoot, but he also reshot some of what he'd already shot. He loved that process. It's not a very cost-effective way of doing things, but it gave him this freedom that he experienced before.

My understanding of *There Will Be Blood* is that it was a much cheaper movie than people realize. On screen it's overwhelmingly big, but that's not an economic truth. We made that for about $35 million. It wasn't cheap, but certainly for what it looks like on screen, there was a lot of value there. But we found that film really hard to put together, in terms of getting the financing: It was originally set up at Universal but it fell somewhere between being a Focus film and a Universal film. Fortuitously Paul's old agent, John Lesher, set up Paramount Vantage, and he called and was like, "I can do it over here." So it was brilliant timing, from that point of view. At the same time, he did *No Country for Old Men* and both films were made by Paramount Vantage and Miramax Films.

There Will Be Blood and *No Country for Old Men* have always aligned in my mind. We were both shooting in Marfa, Texas at the same time!

I know what I think *There Will Be Blood* is about, but I've always wondered if it having a contemporary political dimension beyond the period and the character was something that was always woven into the movie? I don't think it was ever talked about, but most probably subconsciously. it was always just there in the ether of how society was at that point.

With *There Will Be Blood* and *The Master*, was there ever talk about dealing more with history? Yeah, I mean, Paul is very much into history, especially World War II—I think from his dad. And, you know, he reads a lot of historical literature: He's definitely always had a real interest in American history.

Even before *Inherent Vice*, do you know if he had been reading Pynchon around the time of *The Master*? Yes. In fact, we actually optioned *Inherent Vice* before we started working on *The Master*. Why do you say that, though?

Because there's aspects of the Pynchon novel, *V.*, in terms of the cult stuff, that slips into *The Master.* Yeah, I wouldn't be surprised if that happened subconsciously. He's been reading Pynchon for years.

How hard was it to get *The Master* financed? That was one of the harder ones to get financed. We were originally going to shoot it the year before, and tried to cobble it together with a bunch of different financiers. We could never get enough money, but we were going to make it and actually shoot it in New York. And it was a different actor—Joaquin wasn't on the scene at that point. And then, to be honest, the script wasn't really ready.

Paul did some readings and he rang me and was like, "It's not feeling right." And I was like, "Well, we shouldn't make it then. You obviously need to do more work on the script." I remember we had to ring all those financiers and say, "Oh, we don't actually need you after all . . ." So we made it a year later and basically what happened in between was that the script became what it became, and Joaquin came on board, and he was amazing. And then we met up with Megan Ellison, who was just launching Annapurna—she was a huge fan of Paul and wanted to finance the entire movie. So she was a gift from heaven at that point.

Was *Inherent Vice* somehow an easier prospect commercially because of the novel? Warner Bros. had always expressed an interest in doing *Inherent Vice*, and after we finished *The Master* they were still there and willing to make it as long as the number was right. The money had to be really low to get it made.

Did you sense an anxiety in Paul about how it had to be faithful to Pynchon's novel? The book was like a Bible to Paul. He stuck to the book, as opposed to something like *Oil!*, which is his only other adaptation, where he took the first hundred pages and made his own thing from there.

Is it true that Pynchon himself is hiding somewhere in the movie? He's not.

He's not?! Unless you spotted him, and I didn't know he was there!

No, no. It's one of those things where it's funnier to think about. Now, for *Phantom Thread*, were you very cognizant of the British stuff? Yes. Paul was very excited, he always wanted to make a film in England—he has a lot of affinity with the place and seems to be attracted to English people. Like Jonny Greenwood and myself and Daniel Day-Lewis. After *There Will Be Blood*, he and Daniel really wanted to work together again, and over the years they kind of concocted this piece. A lot of it was obviously led by Daniel in terms of Britishness. Early on I think they it could either be set in Paris, given the nature of the fashion industry, and I guess New York was considered, but it just felt right to have it in England. That's how it came about, and Daniel was really involved from day one.

Was it evident from the beginning that the film was just supposed to be very funny? Yes and no. Because I obviously know Paul's kind of humor, and there was always a lot of Paul and Daniel's humor in the script. But that got increased a lot through the acting and execution of it. When we were filming it, it didn't feel like that. There were scenes where we knew it could be very funny, but it didn't feel like we were making a comedy. It had a heaviness to it.

The impression I have of *Phantom Thread* is that it did well commercially, and I've noticed it's migrated online and it's become a big thing on social media. Yeah, I've noticed it's become a bit of a meme movie. Commercially, it wasn't as successful as you think. They did an amazing marketing job at Universal and Focus. And it was out there in the world and got really great reviews.

It got a bunch of Oscar nominations . . . I was absolutely shocked about that. Apart from the Costume and Acting nominations we didn't see that coming.

Hardware (1990), directed by
Richard Stanley and produced
by JoAnne Sellar

Lord of Illusions (1995), directed
by Clive Barker and produced
by JoAnne Sellar

DYLAN TICHENOR

Editor
Hard Eight
    (post-production coordinator)
Boogie Nights
Magnolia
There Will Be Blood
Phantom Thread

Few film editors can claim to have worked with as many major contemporary American filmmakers as Dylan Tichenor, who, in addition to his credits for Paul Thomas Anderson on *Boogie Nights*, *Magnolia*, *There Will Be Blood*, and *Phantom Thread*, has cut features for M. Night Shyamalan, Wes Anderson, and Kathryn Bigelow.

I read that your entry into editing was through working with Robert Altman's editor. Is that correct? Yeah, that's where I started my professional career, with Altman and Geraldine Peroni; I did five movies with them.

What was it like to come up working on the films of this incredibly iconic director? I count myself very lucky to be among the many people whom Bob and his producers, and Gerri, were just so open to. Bob did this thing where if you thought you could do it he would let you try. He was very inclusive. I met them because I was a PA in John Sayles's office, and their mutual accountant recommended me to work in Altman's office. Altman's producer, Scotty [Bushnell], saw that I had done editing, and offered me a job on a movie they were going to make. At the time, I was a second AD on a low-budget movie in New York and I got a phone call from her [Bushnell] saying, 'Do you want to come to LA and do a movie with us and be the apprentice editor?' And I said, "Sure!" That was The Player. Then I did several movies with them where I went to second assistant, then first assistant. I was also the dailies projectionist, and the audio transfer technician. I did the temp sound mixes for all the screenings—I just got to learn a whole bunch of stuff.

When they went to make Short Cuts, Bob had me and one of his producers pick and put together all the material that plays back on television in the movie—there was a lot. It was a lot of pulling material and taking it to Bob and saying, "We thought this would be good in this scene," and he would say, "I like that; play that so that when she walks in the door, and puts the keys down, this is what's happening on the TV." And then I got to play it all back on set. So, I was on set, working on a lot of the movies, doing playback. That was a really interesting job because it was sort of like being another character in the movie. It was really challenging, being able to find material, edit it, and then also play it back with the energy of being on set. I really got a lot out of it.

Was there a particular idea of editing with regards to your work with Altman that really imprinted on you? Even before your relationship with Anderson. Bob made movies like a traveling circus: They were always these huge, sprawling, dysfunctional families—in front of the camera and behind the camera—and he would orchestrate that into resonant moments. To me the trick is to have a certain visual and cinematic excitement in the cuts. But what's really important is the emotional resonance that you can achieve by juxtaposing two different events. What is similar about them becomes an object, and what is dissimilar about them becomes an equal object. That's what's really fun about working with picture and sound and those being your elements to tell a story and to make emotions happen. You know, parallel action is one thing, and you can have that in a number of different ways, but when you have parallel storylines, to the degree to which Bob did

and later Paul, it really opens up a lot of avenues to synthesize some really numinous moments.

What Bob was all about—and what Paul is all about—is elucidating the human condition: "Here's what I see. This is what it feels like to me—what does it feel like to you?" I think that that is the baseline of their art in a lot of ways, and they both deal with dysfunctional families and powerful men. There's a lot of similar things going on. For me personally, it resonated a lot, because I come from a big family. I come from an early divorce; I had two sides of my family that were both very big and colorful, and a number of brothers and sisters and a number of step brothers and sisters and extended family. I was just used to having people around and voices talking, and my father and my whole family played music all the time in my house. So that type of filmmaking always drew me in.

I was interested reading about Hard Eight, how you weren't involved in the making of it on the ground or even in the initial recut of it? You're credited as a post-production supervisor. I'll tell you the four-line story of that. My girlfriend at that time was Jennifer Jason Leigh, who knew John C. Reilly very well—they had done a movie together. And we were invited to a screening of a movie that John was in called Sydney, that his friend Paul had directed. We saw it and I was like, "Wow, what a great movie." I met Paul at Gwyneth [Paltrow's] house afterwards, and I said, "I really loved the movie, man. If you ever need any help, give me a call." Two weeks later, I got a call from Paul saying, "I need help." What had happened was, the cut we saw was his cut that he had worked on after the studio had taken it away from him, recut it and redone the music. So he then submitted his cut to Cannes (he had saved a workprint of it), and they liked the movie, and so Paul said to the studio, "Look, my cut got into Cannes . . ." That was a big fight, but they ultimately gave him the movie back.

That was the point I came into it. He had about six weeks to get this movie finished for Cannes, so Barbara [Tulliver, the editor] came out and recut it and I basically just did everything else, which was find the sound guy; get the sound job done; get the music done; do the titles on my very early Macintosh PowerBook. Paul had taken a loan to pay for it all, so we did it as down and dirty as we could, but still with class. That was when Paul and I started working together, we basically spent a lot of most days together and learned that our love of film and our opinions about filmmaking were copacetic. We really just got along. I mean, we come from two thoroughly different backgrounds, but we met in the middle on film, and started a lifelong, ongoing friendship.

He must have been very interested in the Altman stuff. He must have been, but at the time I really didn't know that. We certainly talked about Altman, but I didn't know that that was a huge thing for him. But over the years, it became obvious and then he got very close with Bob.

It's not hard to see an expansion of scope from something like Hard Eight to Boogie Nights. Hard Eight is a character study, but Boogie Nights announces its intentions to be this incredibly sprawling, intricately structured movie. Yeah, well, a lot of it is in the script. You know, he laid out what he was trying to do. Now that doesn't take into account how you cut scenes and things like that, but it was very clear what vibe he was after. And we were both big Scorsese fans, and Jonathan Demme, so I understood what he was getting at. One thing that we did do on that, and we've done it since and maybe it's even progressed, was we sat down over the course of a few hours and went through the script page by page. I would say, "How are you going to shoot this? What's this?" I would get what his plan was, and he would get what my concerns were. I certainly came out of it much clearer. I've gotten even more involved actually, where I read early drafts over with him, and that helps tremendously. I think he was happy to have somebody who totally got what he was talking about, and I was happy to have somebody who was so excited about film—he was just going balls out with the ideas.

There's a lot of fun in that movie where you're trying to mimic the editing textures of other eras: You've got the editing within the porn films; you've got the editing within Amber's documentary. That was super fun actually. Amber's doc, we shot that on 8mm, I believe, and mostly 16mm. I cut it as a separate little project; edited it the way I thought Amber would do it—put a big pink title on it. And I would do stuff like cut in the middle—I remember there was this bit with John Reilly where I said to myself, "Well, if it were me, I'd cut here because this has been going on long enough, but I'm sure Amber wants to keep this next part."

So I did a splice, knowing that that wasn't going to be where we cut, and we added splicing tape and you see it go through as you're watching. The films within the film, a lot of them in the beginning are one cut, sort of single take. But then as we get into the dark period, where violence creeps into the films, we were mimicking a specific film—the one where Melora Walters comes in and walks up to the bar that Luis Guzmán is tending. I cut it as close to how they cut it as possible. And I think it was the same thing that Julianne [Moore] did with the acting—analyzing: "What about this is bad? Why is this bad?" I think it's very effective. I really love that it's off just a little bit, and has that very honest vibe because of it.

With Magnolia, how were you able to create a sense of momentum without being mechanical about it, without going: Story one, story two, story three, story four. As an editor, is that exhilarating or is it terrifying? It's both. I think that's what makes things exhilarating, when they're slightly terrifying. Magnolia was a great challenge that way. Certainly a lot of it was worked out, but the specifics of it are where the rubber meets the road, and we just tried to make the individual sections sing. It's this thing of having these streams that come together like a river. For Paul, it was always nine stories that were really one story. It's all about the same thing. And the idea with how to edit that is, how do we make this all one story? How is this storyline illuminating what's going on with these other characters? And at what point do we decide to bring them together, or hold them apart? The one thing that brings them all together is the frogs, so we had to steer them in that direction as well. I don't think there was any kind of hard rule, and much of it was indicated in the script. We made it work the best we could.

Do you stand by the view that he could have made it shorter? Oh, for sure! Definitely. I mean, I had stuff picked out to cut out that Paul was not ready to entertain. But, you know, this movie was so personal. And it was a one-hundred-day shoot—a lot of footage and a lot to wrangle. We could have used another couple of months on editing. Had we had that time, I'm convinced more would have come out because that's really what it takes—once a director sees the idea that they had in their head or what they were hoping to achieve on the screen, then it can be objectified. And I can say, "Alright, actually, in the overall picture, I think we need to do without this."

But if you take it away just as a director gets to the end of phase one, of just seeing it come together in a way they imagined it, they haven't gotten to phase two yet, which is, "Alright, for the good of the overall picture, this needs to go." It's just a matter of time sometimes, you don't want to be so ruthless from the get-go that you may miss some very key and resonant moments, whether that be a look, or a whole scene or whatever it is. Often what ends up happening is, "Alright, I'm glad we cut this, we can't have it all. But what we can do is use this little exchange right here in this other place, or just keep this little bit of it, and that does as much as we need."

But that takes time and a little bit of objectivity, and, you know, it's a living thing. When you go back and think about stuff, there's always other ways you would have done something. I look at stuff from twenty years ago and think, "Gosh, I should have done that differently." But we're human beings working in a medium and so things are not perfect, even masterpieces that are considered masterpieces two years after they come out— twenty-five years after they come out—there are things that you can look at and say, "Well, that could have been a little different, short, better." That's what it means to be human. It's not about perfection.

Moving on to *There Will Be Blood*, **the running time is not necessarily hugely shorter. It's an epic, but it's defined by a spaciousness. It takes its time. It's not balancing a bunch of parallel stuff.** Yeah, it is essentially one straight line. I think the challenge there, obviously, is pace. Also the sympatheticness of Daniel's character; exactly what the story is; when it comes down to plot, what's going on exactly? Those are all challenges. We had always talked about *There Will Be Blood*—and to a certain degree *Phantom Thread* as well—as a horror movie. As sort of

a gothic horror movie. And in attempting to keep the tension, Paul used to do these long Steadicam shots or dolly shots where you really live in it and the reveal comes in-camera a lot of the time. That can be a challenging way to work in itself because the pace is basically dictated in a certain way, and you're also trying to control it whatever way you can. I worked hard to keep the revelation of a cut meaningful in that movie. When we cut, it opens a blind and you go, "Oh, I see this new bit."

When the cuts happen, they're so powerful, almost kind of electric or explosive. One cut I want to talk about is that ellipsis very late in the film, from the children on the porch. I don't know if I've ever been hit by a cut like that on a first viewing. Oh, great. I'm glad it works so well.

Did it feel like a momentous thing within the movie to make that kind of time leap? That cut was. . . yeah, it's just delightful. Your mouth opens a little bit. You go, "Whoa, what's this now?" And it was like that for us too, for sure. We actually had conversations about how we made people live in pseudo real-time in so much of this movie, that we owe them some dynamic jumps and tried to build a few of those. That's certainly a big one.

There's a cut in *Phantom Thread* **which reminds me of** *There Will Be Blood*. **In Alma's monologue at the end, you cut to the two of them dancing at the New Year's Eve party, in the empty hall. It's kind of a leap of outside of what we've seen, or maybe something that she's imagining.** Yeah, it's a bit exegetic because they never danced—we talked about it and I was a big arguer for it. With Paul's movies in general, because they get so voluminous, it's like, let's get ourselves to the place where we don't have to be totally beholden to walls of narrative and reality—this is about feelings and emotions. So maybe that's a wish that she had or maybe it's in her imagination. A lot of times with movies, part of what you're doing is, "I want the audience to have the image of this in their mind; how do I get them to have that?" That's almost the essence of filmmaking. I want them to go forward with that image—however I have to justify it. Sometimes it comes down to that.

Those leaps that you're talking about—outside of reality, outside of plausibility—now seem to be part of the DNA of Anderson's movies, but it wasn't quite the same for the first three. Well, I think that's largely Paul's growth as an artist. He was much more granular with his conceptions early on and as he got more comfortable as a filmmaker, he shot from the hip more, in conceiving and in executing. People who don't know him or haven't worked with him have an idea that he's a very controlling person and, truthfully, he's not at all. He has very distinct ideas, but he is very collaborative with everyone. I think that as he relaxes a little bit, he doesn't need to have everything spelled out because, like Altman, what he's interested in is the mistakes and the unexpected bubbling up of life in front of the camera. Sometimes in editing rooms there's convincing that goes both ways, the bravery that happens in making some of these leaps is born out

of necessity. Often it's, "We have a problem. This is too long. This doesn't make sense. This is counter to the rest of the story we're telling. What do we do with it?" And when you get down to, "Just cut it out," sometimes some electrifying things happen. But it takes a lot of bravery. Sometimes it takes some reinvention. And in all these movies, we've had moments of that, without doubt.

Can you talk about the cutting in *Phantom Thread*, **specifically to the idea of comedy. To me it's closer to Blake Edwards than to some of the things people compared it to, like Hitchcock.** Blake Edwards is a great reference and I certainly brought that up and Paul—we're both huge Blake Edwards fans. You know, this was always largely a comedy to Paul, even though in the early stages it was pretty dark sounding. And we talked about Hitchcock, and relationships and poisonings and things like that. That didn't mean it wasn't funny though. We were actually quite worried about the humor for a while, and we tried very hard to highlight a lot of it. Certain moments could have been played totally differently. Daniel, you know, if you take it one way, is very heavy, serious and oppressive. If you take it another way, it's downright hilarious. That all depends on whether you give him four frames after a line or forty-four frames after a line. It's great fun to be able to work with material like that.

One thing I remember cutting is when they're having breakfast on the balcony, when he's finally acquiesced and discovered that he loves her. Then after they marry he goes right back into being annoyed by her little habits and loud eating. That was one of the most fun things to cut because I cut it very quickly. I don't mean because the cutting itself is quick, I mean I threw it together. Paul and I were watching like, "Oh yeah, that's going in." It just made us laugh because Daniel is funny, and Vicky is the perfect straight person. We worked hard at teasing out the humor, because at the end of the day it isn't meant to be some sort of cold life lesson. It's meant to be, you know, turning things on its head a little bit. What if poisoning your lover is the most sincere form of devotion?

I would imagine with someone like Lesley Manville, she almost creates her own edits in the way that she delivers dialogue. Lesley's just a Greek goddess of comedy acting. We had many in that movie, frankly. But Lesley's just amazing, her timing and her inclination—it's just a joy to deal with stuff like that. It's like having the perfect weapon. You know, "I need this moment to do this. What do I have at my disposal? Well, I have Lesley Manville's perfect reading and perfect eye-bat and lip curl. Well, great. Job done!" That was often the motto in the cutting room: When in doubt, cut to Lesley.

The Return of the Pink Panther,
director Blake Edwards
on set, 1975

ROBERT ELSWIT

Cinematographer
Hard Eight
Boogie Nights
Magnolia
Punch-Drunk Love
There Will Be Blood
Inherent Vice

After beginning his career as a visual effects character operator, Robert Elswit shot several films by Curtis Hanson before collaborating with Paul Thomas Anderson on *Hard Eight*. Elswit has lensed six of Anderson's eight features, including *Boogie Nights*, *Magnolia*, and *Punch-Drunk Love*; in 2008, he won the Academy Award for Best Cinematography for *There Will Be Blood*.

What was your first encounter with Paul?
About a year before we did *Hard Eight*, John Lyons, who was a casting director at the time, called me up—he had offices in Culver City, in what used to be the David O. Selznick building. I went over there and just talked to Paul. The guy was only twenty years younger than me, but his whole frame of reference, was films from the thirties and forties and fifties, which was extraordinary and kind of mirrored my own. He loved old movies. I learned later that it was because his father, Ernie, showed him old movies. His world of films grew out of, I think, looking at those older films and seeing them on TV too.

We had a lot in common; we had certain directors and certain actors and certain movies that we just completely agreed on. So we just had kind of a general conversation and he gave me the script for *Hard Eight* and I read it and thought it was a great idea. So anyway, then I went off with [director] Curtis [Hanson] and did *The River Wild*, which was a Universal movie with Meryl Streep and John C. Reilly. And I came back and I was actually having lunch or something in Santa Monica and there's Paul with Gwyneth Paltrow, Philip Baker Hall and John C. Reilly. They're sitting in a booth and he looks over and we see each other and I come over, I introduce Curtis and Paul says, "You know, we're making *Hard Eight*—we're going to Reno, I've got it all figured out and I was just about to call you. We're gonna do it." And that's what happened.

Hard Eight **is well-received, and your relationship with Paul is such that you work on the next film. In your discussions around** *Boogie Nights*, **was it evident that this was going to be more conceptually challenging in terms of camera movement?** Yeah, all the energy of Dirk Diggler and how he makes his way through that story, Paul really wanted to jump-cut, have fast, high-speed push-ins, etc. With shooting photochemically, you can do a lot of that stuff in camera: You can go from twenty-four [frames-per-second] to slow-motion, twenty-four to twelve; you can do all these things that you don't have to do on the set, you can fuck with it later.

I remember Paul, [producers] Daniel Lupi, JoAnne Sellar and I were standing on this corner trying to figure out how to do the opening sequence, and across the street was kind of a lit-up, billboard-y sort of thing on top of the skating rink. The original plan was, "Well, let's go shoot that!" We wanted it for the very beginning; we wanted something that was bizarre, that wasn't a literal reality of what was going to happen in the rest of the movie. But we walked down the street and there was a defunct theater, the Reseda Theater, about a block-and-a-half away. And I don't know if it occurred to Paul or me at the same time, but we just kind of looked up and went, "Oh, come on, this is what we have to do." And for Daniel it meant, "Where do I find the money to take this boarded-up theater, redo all the neon?" It wasn't a lot, but for that movie it was a lot.

And we bought it. All the neon was redone, we redid the marquee, and figured out a way to move across the marquee with a crane. So that's how the Reseda Theater came back to life.

It's a film that very strategically offers an incredible sense of mobility and access and freedom, which of course works on an historical level and on a thematic level and on a character level. You just kind of feel carried along, as if there's nowhere the camera can't be. Yeah, it's supposed to feel energetic and alive in that way. The pool scene is stolen from *I Am Cuba*, but I can't remember the movie we watched which has this long elaborate opening set-piece, where the characters jump in a pool. In our movie it's a series of scenes with characters you actually know, and you're seeing whatever little conflicts are going on in their lives and their struggles, and you're watching this girl walk in there. You follow everybody and you jump in the pool and you see Mark Wahlberg and John C. Reilly. It's kind of a storytelling bridge. Everybody thinks there's a cut when we go in the water, but there isn't. We—the grip, Joey Dianda, and I—are actually holding a camera on an underwater mount, and we jump in the water and both of us lift the camera out of the water so we can see just slightly above the water and continue the shot. There's no monitor, I think there was some kind of viewfinder . . . We could sort of see. But Joey and I—he's one side and I'm on the other—we're carrying this thing and trying to coordinate our movements so we're not bouncing it too much. So it kind of looks like a hand-held shot, and then we jump in the water. Let me tell you, it was wacky.

Could you talk about the challenges that a director's impulse presents for you as a cinematographer? Paul is always looking for life to break out. One of the true gifts he has is that he loves what actors go through to get where they are, and he makes them feel protected. They feel like no matter how weird or neurotic or strange they are, he's going to react in a positive way—even if he wants to go somewhere else. They know that the best of what they're capable of doing is going to end up on the screen, and they're willing because of that to take chances to do things that they might not do for any other director. But he *wants* things to go wrong, he wants something to break, he wants someone to fall down. He wants things to surprise him.

We've always had a pretty good idea, on those two movies and certainly on *Magnolia*, of what we were gonna do. The prep on those movies was pretty extensive—I can't just show up and go, "Let's do this." We've actually gone to these locations and had a really thorough conversation about what the set-ups might be. He really trusts his own instincts. He's not worried about time. The most important part is that he feels like whatever he's doing is, it makes emotional sense to him.

Boogie Nights's **success is such that** *Magnolia* **gets to be this huge, inflated thing. There's just so much in it.** A lot of people felt that. I remember an executive—whose name I won't mention—was sitting with Paul going, "If this movie was half an hour shorter, we'd all make a lot of money." That's not a charming comment to make to Paul.

Dovetailing with this larger idea of Los Angeles, *Boogie Nights* **seems to me to be the most "Valley" of the Valley movies.** There's something about the Valley . . . because I grew up in Los Angeles too. I mean, Paul grew up in the Valley and I didn't, I grew up on the west side. So my knowledge of the Valley was fairly limited. I never went there. Occasionally I went to a couple of movie theatres along Ventura Boulevard, but I never went there. There was nothing there unless you lived there and you knew that there were places you went, things you did. To me, the west side Hollywood, Sunset Strip, when I was a teenager and I was in college, everything's over here and nothing's over there. It was like a dead area. To Paul it's sort of a mythical place and actually *Punch-Drunk Love* really makes a point of that. But yeah, *Boogie Nights*, and also—*Magnolia* is about the San Fernando Valley, and everybody who lives there.

Paul grew up with all these actors who were friends of his father who lived in the Valley. And when his father was socializing with his friends they either went to some place in the Valley or they went into Hollywood. But never the west side, never Santa Monica, never anything where I lived. So that was kind of my introduction. When we were scouting locations, we actually went to where Paul lived, because we were trying to find a spot for Melora Walters's character. We went to the actual apartment where Paul lived when he was in college. We knocked on the door and this poor Asian-American kid opens the door and Paul goes, 'I used to live here. Can we come in?' And he actually let us in, and we sort of looked around and I went, 'Well, Okay.' I think we ended up building Melora's apartment. We must have scouted so many places down in the Valley, and then of course on Magnolia Boulevard.

Magnolia **is the movie that feels most reliant on close-ups.** Part of that is because we couldn't keep the entire cast hanging around. The whole thing was scheduled around the actors' availability. It was the most thoroughly thought-through of all the movies we did, everything was very clearly defined in terms of where the actors were gonna be, what their movements were, how they were going to be in relation to the other actors. And it meant a lot of close-ups too. Paul is not doing coverage, he's not shooting four angles of the same scene from four different places and then finding the scene in the editing room. He's going, "Here is the part of the scene I want to play from, here are the bits I want to be closer, here are the bits I don't." And we had all the different weather issues. That's what made it such a challenge technically. It's magic hour, it's raining, it's night, and then the frog thing, and all the stuff that precedes that—that was a challenge. It was the least flexible of any of his movies in terms of how we had to shoot it. I know we all felt the pressure a little bit. And we knew we were gonna lose an actor. These people weren't going to be here in a week and we couldn't bring them back again and figure it out if it wasn't working. And it was, I think, a little bit more frustrating for Paul— I think based on that he decided never to do anything like *Magnolia* again.

Punch-Drunk Love **feels like a turning point movie. It's incredibly refined on a visual level. Like, there's nothing that's going to be sacrificed in terms of the movement and the design. There's nothing that's going to be sacrificed in the name of performance, or spontaneity. There's an erraticness to the characters and an erraticness to what's going on in the plot.** I think a lot of that has to do with sort of the limited number of people that are in it. Emily and Adam working out who they were—who they would be and how they would function—was a joy for Paul because it was either only one of them to talk or both of them. The rest of it kind of fell into place. But the initial planning, the whole idea, grew out of a lot of inspirational moments he sort of talked about in the past.

The design of the film was Mark Bridges; finding the color of that suit. Paul managed to get Raoul Coutard's personal print of *A Woman is a Woman*, which we projected and looked at over and over again. Coutard was one of these icons of New Wave cinema that we all admired, and I'd read many things where he talked about how he shot. In those days it was hard to shoot on location, and the way he solved that problem technically was to shoot inside and look out a window; to be in a real space and pan 360 degrees around the room. He would use this elaborate overhead rig where he would suspend photoflood lights in a kind of giant rectangle the same shape as the actual room he was shooting in. And he covered the ceiling with tinfoil and these photofloods would be aimed into the foil, and that's how the room was lit. Paul was really intrigued by that—and I'm kind of sorry I mentioned it because then I had to do it twice in the movie! It was really a pain.

But the big thing at the beginning was the amount of prep: Finding that suit, finding the interior that would work for Barry's shop, and all the other locations in the Valley. The production designer [William Arnold] and I were like, "It'll all be color, we'll paint the wall outside one color . . ." And Paul instinctively knew that the only colors the movie needed were these marvelous kind of off-pastels, which were Emily Watson's wardrobe and the blue suit. Because we were shooting in these horrible, banal Valley locations. I remember we were sitting there looking at dailies and we had painted walls with these colours, and I thought, "God, he's actually right. There should be no colour in the movie except the costumes, everything should be painted white." He never went to film school, never studied in any sort of serious way pictorial style design, but he knew that in order to tie all these locations together and make you feel like you were in a fairy tale, all these different spaces had to be either white or neutral gray. So we painted

everything white—inside, outside, walls at night, interiors, wherever we had control. Except for Hawaii, which was sort of naturally colorful in other sorts of ways, it just was all white. It unified the movie visually. It made you feel like the world of the movie is this sort of unique, special place.

I've read a lot about the prepping and the location scouting on *There Will Be Blood*. **What I'm interested in more than anything is the handling of light, because it's set in a time and place where interior light is at a minimum and kind of at a premium.** As much as possible, it was an attempt to create a realistic idea of what these interiors would look like if there were oil lamps, if there was no electricity. They would build houses and buildings with huge window spaces to take advantage of the ambient daylight. To try and create that feeling and do all that was important to us.

The thing I had the hardest time convincing Paul of was what to do for late night exteriors— what's it supposed to look like outside at night? Is it moonlight? Is it ambient moonlight? Is it starlight? How do you create the illusion, how do you stand outside the cabin outside at night and see anything? Well, the reality is you can't, there isn't anything. So, if it's a fire, and the fire's lighting the foreground, and it's not a big fire, you can't see anything in the background. There's nothing there: There's no light, there's no illumination, light falls off. So we had these big spaces where I had to somehow show how you light a night exterior. That's one of the big challenges in cinematography. Digital has kind of taken over; it's a little easier because it's faster and you can get away with more, and you can have synced sources, you can actually say it's the moon or something. But it's still the same problem if you're in the middle of a desert, in the middle of the night. Because there might be enough moonlight to see, but there isn't enough moonlight to expose motion picture film.

Paul is very concerned about having it feel real; [*There Will Be Blood*] wasn't *Punch-Drunk Love*. We have to believe that we're actually in the desert, we're in California, we're there at night. So it's finding locations that lend themselves to creating an artificial light without it feeling artificial. That was the hardest thing I had to do. We shot a lot at magic hour, and I remember we were really scrupulous about doing it honestly. And so when they're standing in front of the burning oil derrick, we had the visual effects team turn on essentially a giant propane fire hose behind us, and that's what was lighting the actors.

The one other technical tricky thing was we were inside this tent—there were a couple of scenes where Daniel is sitting at his desk—and we're looking out the window and I don't want it to be a whiteout, I want to be able to see the clouds and the sky. I have to balance the film on the negative so that we see Daniel, we believe he's lit from the windows, but also there's enough light on him that it looks natural, it looks real. I know with Paul I can't cheat. I can't fix walls and windows later. I have to balance everything on the set where we're shooting. Because there is no later. And he's very patient with that, he knows. He's not sitting there tapping his foot, which is good.

In *Inherent Vice* there's a feeling physically of drift and visually of a kind of paleness and haziness which I think is built into the material. It's the softest looking of Paul's movies, I think. *Inherent Vice* was particularly frustrating for Paul because of how much the Valley has changed. Manhattan Beach used to have lots of small, really lovely beach houses where anyone lived. And there were kind of charming old apartment buildings where a lot of flight attendants and pilots lived; it was so close to the airport. I went to parties there all during the seventies and it was. . . not run down, but it was like Venice in Los Angeles. It was like another version of that, and because it's slightly on a hill off the beach, off the boardwalk, it became prime real estate because you could build say a series of condos or apartment houses that all had these spectacular views of the ocean.

Everything that was charming and quaint about those neighborhoods has disappeared. It's all turned into hundreds and hundreds of quite ugly apartment buildings and condos—that's all there is. So there was no way to go there and find the real place where [Thomas] Pynchon had lived. And the few places that we did try to shoot were so cut off from anything else, they're just isolated. And I know Paul would have loved to have shot a real house, he would have loved to have been able to have something on location. We were forced to build the interior of Doc's house on a stage and put bluescreen outside the windows—all the things Paul hates. Lots of directors have no problem, nobody's gonna question that, you do it artfully. You know, the entire sequence in *Inside Llewyn Davis* where they're driving to Chicago is on a soundstage. They're on a set with beautiful background plates and incredible lighting. But Paul would no more want to do that than put a bullet in his head. We'd have to actually drive to Chicago with Paul. That would be the only solution.

Did you like how he shot *Phantom Thread*? Well, I know how he did it because it's the same people I work with, it's the same crew. He just threw a lot of smoke in the room. Which he would never let me do, he never let me smoke a set. Not that I've wanted to—I mean, he wanted it for a scene. But I think he shot tests and he knew enough that he didn't know enough. But with the modern stocks you can do minimal low lighting and you can lower the contrast and shoot all the detail you want, just by adding smoke. I can't imagine I would have done it that way and I probably could have talked him out of it if he wanted to. But yeah, it was a period film, it was okay and had really good locations. I enjoyed the film, I just . . . if I'd shot that movie I would not be happy with it ending up looking like it looked, that's all. But I liked the movie. I actually like it better than anything else I've done or he's done with me or without me. I like it more than *The Master*, I like it more than *Inherent Vice*.

The Hollywood sign in Griffith
Park with the San Fernando

JONNY GREENWOOD

Composer
There Will Be Blood
The Master
Inherent Vice
Phantom Thread

Best known as the lead guitarist and keyboardist for Radiohead, Jonny Greenwood is a multiplatinum-selling and Grammy award–winning musician. He has written four film scores for Anderson, including *There Will Be Blood*, *The Master*, *Inherent Vice*, and *Phantom Thread*, and was the main subject of the director's music documentary *Junun*.

Do you recall the first time you discussed collaborating with Paul on *There Will Be Blood*? I don't think I'd seen any of his films before he approached me. The first I heard from him was that he'd used a fan's bootleg of an orchestral concert, and wanted me to write more. I believe he'd also seen the film *Bodysong*, the first film I wrote music for, and was impressed with the music in that.

For *There Will Be Blood* was there much conversation about the idea of "period" with regards to the score? I remember making the conscious decision to stick to period instruments but use contemporary techniques. I think that's a usefully jarring technique: The string orchestra has a familiar sound quality for that kind of film—getting it to do non-standard things created a nice mismatch which seemed to suit the story.

Did you write to specific sequences during your first collaboration? Some of them were written specifically—"Open Spaces," "Future Markets," "Prospectors Arrive," and a few of the others—but many were just a suite of pieces for him to use, inspired by the story (for the chamber pieces) or the landscape (for the full orchestral ones).

Is it fair to say that there's a bit more melody in the music for *The Master*, and if so, can you talk about the conception of the score? The key for that score was the electric organ—I wanted a bland quasi-church sound to match the bland quasi-religion. Not cheesy, just cold and odd. So I used the test tone of an old Akai sampler—really just a sine wave—and lots of reverb. I wrote music for that, and arrangements for a small orchestra around it.

Does your writing change when you know it's going to be part of a soundtrack that's also period appropriate (i.e., "Get Me Behind Me Satan")? It was more of an issue in *Phantom Thread*, where I was wary of overlap. Actually, overlap is a polite way of putting it—really, I was very concerned about writing fifties style romantic music, knowing that there was going to be much of the real article in that film. So I tried to make it slightly more British, hoping there'd be a contrast with the very American Nelson Riddle. Not sure I managed that, but the cue Alma came closest to sounding natively English, I think.

How did *Junun* come together? I just told Paul that I was heading to India to record an album with some Sufi Muslims in an ancient fort, and he was up for the adventure.

For me, the score for *Inherent Vice* is closer to the kind of composing you do for Radiohead, both in terms of instrumentation and production. What were you aiming for in terms of the sound of that score? *Inherent Vice* was hard to get right. Paul never said this, but my impression was that he wanted the music to underline the fact that the story—and [Thomas] Pynchon's book—despite being a series of jokes, is not just a joke. Otherwise, the emotions are just cartoonish, hence the sincerely romantic music, which isn't meant to be pastiche at all. Or, not to me: Perhaps he likes it because it is. I did go intentionally pastiche for the asylum scene, but other cues are meant to be straight.

The *Phantom Thread* score is so omnipresent in the film; am I wrong to think that it's the movie you've done with Paul that has the most music? I'm not sure. There's a lot, but I remember him having far too much in *There Will Be Blood* and being relieved when he stripped some out.

What was the atmosphere you were hoping to evoke with those surging, recursive piano pieces in *Phantom Thread*? I just wanted it to be, again, sincere—not arch, or pastiche. Which was easy in a way, because I don't have the technique to do pastiche. Really, this was as good as I could arrange it—and at the limits of my piano playing—which is why it's relatively unflowery.

Everyone I've talked to about *Phantom Thread* seems to understand how wickedly funny it is: Is there an element of humor in the music? Well, you should know that whenever you're in the edit with Paul he is—without exception—laughing throughout. And when we perform the scores live, the audience also laughs a lot, I guess because they know the story and what's about to happen. But even in *There Will Be Blood*, there's so much humor there. It's the main reason I love his films, I sometimes think, because I recognise him in that humor. On one level, *Phantom Thread* is him doing a big piss-take of Englishness, and finding it absurd and amusing. This is cut through with sharp, sincere emotional scenes too, of course.

Do you have a favorite music cue in any of the movies? I always like "Alethia" from *The Master*. I feel like it captures the whole odd sea-bourne pseudo-religious oddness of that scene.

What does Paul do as a filmmaker that most engages you? He's the whole package—scripts, cinematography, storytelling, humor, romance, oddness, and genuity. There's no one like him: Perhaps there's people who do the individual skills as well—or better—but no one has the full deck like Paul. I'm glad he's terrible at playing musical instruments; there's a job left for me.

JACK FISK

Production Designer
There Will Be Blood
The Master

A legend of American cinema, Jack Fisk has worked as production designer on all of Terence Malick's feature films, as well as Brian De Palma's *Carrie* and David Lynch's *The Straight Story* and *Mulholland Drive*. Fisk also acted in Lynch's debut *Eraserhead* and has directed several movies of his own, including 1981's *Raggedy Man*. He was nominated for an Academy Award for Best Production Design for *There Will Be Blood* and also worked on *The Master*.

Having worked with David Lynch, Brian De Palma, and Terrence Malick, is Paul Thomas Anderson a director you saw coming? I was working on a film in England when I got a message saying Paul wanted me to work on his next film. I wasn't that familiar with Paul's work, but I started watching his films, and was blown away by how good he was. When I met Paul at the Burbank Airport a couple of months later, it felt very natural—like I had known him for a long time. That was our first meeting and we were off to look for locations for *There Will Be Blood*.

For him, your reputation obviously preceded you. Was his original idea to build a set from the ground up, which you're known for? That may be the case, but I don't remember him saying that specifically, We just started talking about the story. Paul does so much research he was able to give me a hundred or more research photographs that he had pulled together in writing *There Will Be Blood*. After the scout, I went to LA and visited the oil museums and some of the story locations with him, and we began working. Paul had shot his earlier films in California, but he wanted a harshness to the landscape and we found that harshness in West Texas. The first location we went to look at was a 50,000-acre ranch outside of Marfa, Texas, with eighteen miles of train track. That ranch became the main location for the film. We would get to build the set from the ground up because nothing was there even though a few films had been shot in the area.

Like *Giant*? Yeah. That was shot nearby. *Giant* was made outside of Marfa and there were still some telephone poles standing that were once holding up the *Giant* house set, and I stayed in the Elizabeth Taylor suite at the hotel!

Anderson has talked about his need for 360 degrees of visibility, where you can't have anything that betrays that there is any other town nearby. Yeah, I agree with Paul on that. Our main location was in the middle of nowhere. We would drive for thirty minutes every day to get out there, away from the little town of Marfa and through a border check point. The ranch was so large and varied that we were able to find almost every location we needed on it.

And was it liberating to just kind of say, "Now we build a town"? Yeah. It was the greatest. Probably the most fun thing because there was nothing else interfering with our world. Paul and I were like two kids building a fort. We picked a hill for the derrick because it was the tallest hill. That made it more difficult to build, but I liked it because the derrick was going to be ninety feet tall and the hill added another thirty feet. It would be impressive looking at the derrick from the ground level. On an opposing hill, we decided to put the church, so they're competing structures—both reaching up to the sky. The Sunday ranch we put in a little valley, where you could see it from the church and the derrick.

I'm sure it's not what's on your mind while you're doing it, but there's almost something self-allegorizing about that because so much of the first thirty minutes of *There Will Be Blood* is Daniel Plainview staking out that same location, right? I remember the excitement hiking with Paul laying out all of New Boston. You felt like a cross between a child and a god as someone who creates a world or a Daniel Plainview.

The two major structures are so symbolic within the logic of the film and they're so iconic when you watch it. I love the idea that Daniel can keep an eye on the church because his structure is open, but he doesn't face it. There's this transparency between the structures because they're still being built, and you can see what the other guy is doing. That's thanks to the script and the qualities of the location. A lot of the films I do, are made outside, on location, instead of on a soundstage. And it's taking advantage of what is in the area, finding the gifts given and dealing with the challenges. The wood for the church was made out of old fence boards given to us by a rancher. The derrick was built from plans for a 1906 derrick I found in an oil museum in Taft, California, for $2, but the closest lumber yard was six hours away.

What degree of functionality did the final structure have? The derrick worked! If there was oil down there, we could have gone for it. We met a lot of interesting people in Texas. In Odessa, I found an elderly oil man who had a large open field full of old oil equipment. We needed a period pump and a generator and lots of pipe. He had it all and more, in his field. He said, "Take whatever you need." We found good period equipment and put it together with our derrick. He was excited about the film but, I remember him saying, "The last good movie I saw was *Gone with the Wind*!"

The other environment in the film that I'm interested in is Edward Doheny's mansion at the end. What did you have to do to it? Well, we built the bowling alley and brought in period furniture and dressing.

Can you talk about the bowling alley? There's a vaguely surreal aspect to it in the sense that it looks like it's never been used. We moved to California to shoot the best mansion we could find. I was familiar with the Doheny mansion and it used to have a bowling alley in the basement, but it had been destroyed over the years. So, I suggested we build it back and that's what we did.

And it's still there? Yeah, I haven't been there in a long time but I believe it's still there. It was nice to restore that space. Jim Erickson, the set decorator who was working on the film and I dressed up the mansion with all the trappings of a successful oil man.

When Paul came in and saw it dressed he said, "No! No, we've got to do something else!"

He wanted it to look like Daniel was camping by the large fireplace. We discarded some furniture and brought in a pot of beans, sleeping bags, firewood, and camping paraphernalia. Plainview was living in that mansion, but he was living like he was still out in the oil fields, it was wonderful character detail. When you see Daniel Plainview in the bowling alley it is great.

When I initially talked to Paul and asked, "Do you have any ideas about the design of the film?" He said, "No signs." So, we made the film without any signs and most people didn't even realize it.

Without violating the period authenticity, it does take the film out of time and out of place a little bit. I like sets that are timeless, universal. Period films are challenging because you don't want to be weighted down with specific period detail.

I've read profiles of you that stress how physically connected you are to that physical part of the job—the tacks, the nails and the wood. Is that rare with your job at this point? When I started working on films in the seventies, I didn't know what an art director did, so I just started doing everything to cover my backside. But I've always liked to build. For me, creating sets is like sculpture. I want to climb on them and paint them. I've gotten a reputation of being a "hands-on" designer, but film making is more fun when you are involved as much as you can be.

Paul may be one of the few directors that still watches dailies projected with his crew. Watching dailies on his films is a fun group commitment where Paul plays music that Johnny Greenwood has sent to him or he discovered in his research for a scene.

I think it's fascinating how when you put *There Will Be Blood* and *The Master* together, and even to some extent *Inherent Vice*, you get this history of the twentieth century to some extent. He hasn't finished yet. . . . You know, Paul is such a great writer. He ends up with a script but he pretty much writes a novel. I have so much respect for him as a creator because he starts with an idea and creates this whole world. I always just feel like an enabler, sort of helping show it to people. But he loved that film, *The Treasure of the Sierra Madre*. It's one of his favorite films, I've read a couple of times. He wanted me to watch it and I watched it and I go, "I don't like it." Because I was looking at it and thinking about thirties Hollywood. They didn't make great films then. The sets didn't look real. It upset him so much.

I'm sure he got over it. Oh yeah, I explained to him, when I'm making a film, I don't like to watch films because they distract me and I might try to emulate something that they did and I think we're making a much better film than *The Treasure of the Sierra Madre*. And so he kind of accepted that. And then he started talking about *Moby Dick* and I go, "Oh, it's too thick I can't read all that stuff!" So he wrote me a version of *Moby Dick* that's like, five pages long. It was important for him, though. I try not to use film for references.

What were the references for *The Master*? In addition to the script and period research, a lot of that film came from the way I remembered things having grown up in the forties and fifties and the genesis of new religions. We went up to San Francisco because there was a boat there we wanted to shoot. Once in San Francisco, we started looking around for other locations and on Mare Island we found these beautiful houses that were constructed for officers when the Navy was building submarines on the island. They were just great. So we picked one of those homes and it became the main house of the film. It reminded me of houses outside Philadelphia, where I went to art school, and in the script, the house was supposed to be in Philadelphia.

The department store is my favorite space in the whole film. Oh, I love the department store too. You know in the store's wedding section, there's a picture of my mother on the wall that I had blown up, from the day she got married.

In the film? Yeah, Paul made sure he got it in the film. I found an old book from the '40s about designing layouts for department stores, and that became a bible for that set. It had beautiful black and white photographs of decorations, interiors, and lighting. The location we shot in was an old tax office building in downtown LA, it had high ceilings and some great fluorescent light fixtures that we incorporated into our set.

Did you have any bearing on the department store photos that Freddie takes? Well, I did in that I brought in that yellow backdrop.

That's yours? Yeah, Paul said, "You're so lucky!" That made the whole thing.

Those images are so evocative of the idea of a time and place than, as you say, being too specific. Yeah. A lot of that was just choosing the essence. Whether it be space, color, texture, lighting, etc.

Was "realism" a word you were thinking about when making *The Master*? Like Edward Hopper does beautifully in his paintings, I try to distill the visuals to a minimal essence and sometimes that is not realistic, but it tells us more.

Did you have good working relationships with Anderson's cinematographers, Robert Elswit and Mihai Mălaimare Jr.? It is to my benefit to have a good working relationship with the cinematographers I work with, but I especially loved working with Robert, one of our great cinematographers. I believe the films he made with Paul helped prepare Paul to shoot his own films. Paul shot the beautiful *Phantom Thread* and I believe if Paul had more time he'd design his films.

The oil derrick constructed on set during the filming of *There Will Be Blood*

MARK BRIDGES

Costume Designer
Hard Eight
Boogie Nights
Magnolia
Punch-Drunk Love
There Will Be Blood
The Master
Inherent Vice
Phantom Thread

A two-time Academy Award–winner for Best Costume Design—most recently in 2018 for *Phantom Thread*—Mark Bridges has worked on all of Anderson's features to date, as well as multiple films by Noah Baumbach and David O. Russell.

Could you talk about the costuming of Philip Baker Hall's character, Sydney, in *Hard Eight*? Paul wanted a vestige from the era of the Rat Pack; a kind of *Ocean's 11* look when Vegas was so different to the mid-nineties. Throughout the film there's the idea that [Sydney] is kind of a dinosaur, like somehow this world of nightlife and showgirls never changed for him. Paul had a strong feeling about the shape of the collars for Philip. We found that suit at a rental place in LA and it was made out of this wonder-fabric that was appearing in the late fifties and early sixties. Phil would wear it all day and we'd hang it up for the night in his trailer, and we'd come in the next day and all the wrinkles had gone. It's exactly the kind of thing that Sydney would've had, so he always looked sharp and smart. Of course, Paul and I turned out to be a great match because he wanted his films to look real. He knew how he wanted Sydney to look, but he left most of the other characters to me. He does these funny things with close-ups on Gwyneth [Paltrow]'s leggings or boots—I had no idea he would do that, but I think it's a wonderful way to talk about those characters. You take someone like Gwyneth and you put her in a puffy coat with smeared make-up. It's an extraordinarily strong look, but it's really simple.

Five years before Wes Anderson did the exact same thing in *The Royal Tenenbaums*. I remember Paul had a lot of details in his mind from his research in Reno, things that he'd seen: He wanted a woman in a wedding dress with her groom sitting gambling at a slot machine; he'd seen that and loved it. So I got a wedding dress to have on hand and it's in the film—it's like a wonderful, weird bit of this world in Reno, and he picked up on those unusual things. We used to watch dailies on a wrinkly sheet in the production office, and even watching the dailies you knew that we were creating something special. There were long takes that Paul does, and scenes between John [C. Reilly] and Sydney, or John and Gwyneth—it was chilling how great it was, you just felt like you were part of something really cool.

And then there's an expansion of resources that happens with *Boogie Nights* and a different challenge—it's all about fashion and the characters' appearances are coded by what they wear. You know, it's funny, I wouldn't say we had that much more resources for *Boogie Nights*. I mean, we did have more resources, but his producers were always very mindful of money. It was only Paul's second film so we didn't have that much more money to do the costumes. I remember going to St. Louis and spending $12,000 on all kinds of never-been-used seventies clothes that miraculously worked on all of the cast—I even got these red roller skates on which we ended up changing the wheels that actually fit. It was crazy. That was a big saver. We rented; I did a lot of vintage. The creativity stayed the same though. Paul wrote rich, interesting characters, and I was loving the fact that I got to bring them from the

written page and give them a three-dimensional shape, a character and a look that told a story about who they were. And I was loving the fact that period was 1977 to 1984. It was such a fun-filled period in fashion. The research was so fun, and I lifted things that I saw from layouts in *Playboy* for Dirk's first film, or a *Hustler* editorial for Jack, and Rollergirl on the prowl in a limo cruising the San Fernando Valley. Paul had us watch vintage films and vintage porn just to get the feel of the cheap set and the high aspirations. And Paul had some direction for me, but it was things like, "Scotty J should dress like a fourteen-year-old."

So you purposely gave Philip Seymour Hoffman a t-shirt that exposes the tiny little bit of his belly at all times? That's how it worked out. When I do a fitting it's a laboratory. I bring a bunch of things and we work it out, we try things. I mean, some of those shorts that I put on him, I'm surprised that he was ultimately able to have children because they were so small! And then Paul's direction for Jack was, "He should wear something that he could write in all day and just go in that to the disco."

Obviously it's the actor who fills the costume out and brings it to life. But there's so many iconic looks from *Boogie Nights*. Don Cheadle has been excellent in a lot of films, but when I hear his name I just picture the cowboy stuff. It's just such vivid character-based costuming. That's something Paul wrote into the script. Paul actually wrote the script in sections: "A, B, C, D, and E." For no other reason than just to order it—but I took it literally and did different palettes for each section of the film. So "A" is kind of like just pure seventies: Blue, terra-cotta brown. Then "B" is kinda *Good Times* and the colors pump up and there's a lot more fun. It's always good to have a concept to hang on to, it narrows down your choices and it focuses you. But we see these characters over seven years, so they grow up and evolve and their lives change. Hopefully those beats and what they're wearing indicates where they are in life. I mean, when Rollergirl and Amber are snorting coke in that bedroom on a hot afternoon, what they're wearing speaks volumes. What Amber wears to her court appearance says everything you need to know about how it's gonna end. Hopefully those things communicate without trying too hard by those choices.

The contrast between what Amber wears when she's in court, or some of the really tragic stuff that Dirk is trying when he's trying to diversify his persona . . . you can laugh at it because it's a bit of a sight gag, but at all times in the movie the fashion is tied to character and motivation. Yeah, I mean, Paul would turn to me and say, "Oh, didn't I tell you I wanted Amber to look like Blondie on an album cover for her last scene?" And I'm like, "No . . ." And it's funny that the last time we see Amber she's in a white spaghetti-strap vest and they're gonna shoot again. It really is like [Debbie Harry] on the cover of one of her albums. But then also—this was nothing to do with Paul, it's just my own thing because I think it's interesting—because AIDS was starting up, it was gonna shake up that industry . . . like, what happened to Amber and Dirk down the road once the eighties really hit? There was a store in Burbank for years that was called Amber's Dress Shop, and I'm thinking, "Yeah, that's what happened to Amber, she opened a dress shop."

Then *Magnolia* is interesting because it's Paul's longest movie, but it covers the shortest time frame. There's some very distinctive outfits in it. In a lot of ways it's the world that Paul knew growing up. You know, his father had a lot of show business friends. So [Paul] was offering a touchstone for the characters, because they each have an iconic look as they move through the story. I don't really feel comfortable revealing some of Paul's choices, where they came from, but there are people that he knew... things that he experienced in his life. We all create things from our own experiences. But [with *Magnolia*] there wasn't a really clear idea; that's where I come in and we talk about, when there's three kids on a game show, how do you pull out our main kid, graphically, and show how he's old before his time? You know, turtlenecks always make someone look more mature. . . .

In contrast to *Magnolia* you have a movie like *Punch-Drunk Love*, which is very small, it's not a sprawling ensemble. You've got this lead actor who in his way is iconic—certainly not as a fashion icon—but when I think of the movie I think of the suit, it all starts with that. *Punch-Drunk* is essentially a musical. One of the things [Paul and I] were struck by was *An American in Paris* and that incredibly lush Technicolour, and what it does to blue. So we saw the beautiful vibrating blues of early Technicolor and that's Barry's suit uniform. Other Hollywood musical references were inspired by something we wanted to riff on. Paul's strength is being able to move on that and riff in his own unique way.

As Paul has gone on directing I've seen him become more of a musician in clothes. It's like going into a recording studio and remixing things and taking away the horns and bringing up the strings or something. You know, we'll be looking at fashion references for *Phantom Thread*, what was going on in the period, what London was like in that time period, and we'll be listening to music. He's already got music that he wants to use in the film. You put together these visuals, like the Pea-Souper in London in 1954, and you're hearing this music—it's incredibly inspiring.

In *There Will Be Blood*, were you working towards period authenticity or a stylised authenticity? It was all about research, research, research. Early on, Paul had a version of the script and called me and said, "I need to know what my movie's gonna look like." And I put together images in chronological order of people as the story went on: Here's the Sunday family; here's Daniel in 1898; here's what 1911 looks like; here's it by the end. I think we showed Daniel [Day-Lewis] to seal

the deal on Daniel [Plainvew]. We had thousands of photos of the period with us, and early twentieth century California towns. My first fitting with Daniel, which was almost eight hours long, we got a lot done in that time to flesh out who he was and how he was gonna look—I think we even got the iconic hat in that first fitting. My job is to give a three-dimensional look to a character that's on a printed page. It's always interesting to watch someone like Daniel Day-Lewis start to take on a different personality as we try on things.

And was *The Master* similarly rooted in a researched realism? I love doing transitional periods. So that's 1950, and there's elements of the forties in there. . . . Again, how do I tell the story: When he's in World War II, how do we say that time has passed and just give you the flavor? You can taste 1950 there, hopefully. And it is less stylized; I think Paul always wanted it to seem real. But I tend to look for unique things from the period, that you don't usually see. They are from the period, but they're sort of extraordinary examples of the period. Whether it's a riff on a Larry LeGaspi jumpsuit; Larry LeGaspi used to do Labelle and Kiss and stuff, and I made a little number for Rollergirl that is in the dance number. You just look for these pieces from that moment in time. I'm always looking for the weird things.

In the case of *Phantom Thread*, what was it like for you to suddenly be confronted with a narrative about someone who makes clothes? It was on two levels. We had to create that real world, tell Alma's story from rural fisherman's daughter to high-fashion society in London; give exposition of how Reynolds Woodcock is, what the world for the sister is, and what London in the mid-fifties was like. On one level we're always trying to create the world, whether that's Manhattan Beach circa 1970, or a California oil town—we're always doing that.

On *Phantom Thread*, Paul and I had several meetings within the six to eight months prior to shooting with Daniel. You know, sitting down with things that were iconic dresses, and the mother's wedding dress. We would sit and talk about each of them and what they could be. I had images of what real dresses were like, but of course there were legalities as far as copying a designer—they have to be dead for seventy years or something before we could copy a dress. At some point part of Daniel's preparation for Reynolds Woodcock was being involved with the design, what this character would be designing. I'd already started things in London and Daniel came in, we had a big meeting about colour choices and fabric choices. Some of those choices, and what turned out to be the Woodcock look, were really influenced by my taste and what was going on in the fifties in London and in France. And also Reynolds's taste. That guided where some of these dresses came from, for better or for worse. I think it made it more interesting.

My personal thing is that I want everything to look like Lana Turner in *Latin Lovers*. I'm a Hollywood baby so I want it all to be super sparkly and grand, and honestly, having this English high-class sensibility put into these things—a world that Daniel grew up in and a world that he had to unpack—I think added a dimension of richness to

the choices. My colors were probably a bit bolder and a little more photogenic, but something I had to wrap my head around was that the Reynolds Woodcock look was a bit on the way out. I thought it was perfect for the film, and I think that the dimension of Daniel's contribution, as well as my contribution and the practicality of getting the clothes made and on screen, is what we see as the final result.

In terms of the Woodcock dresses and how they look, it's so bound up in what the movie is about. The dresses that he makes strike me as untenable for living. They don't permit breathing, they don't permit anything in the way of movement, they're so constrictive. Which was very true of the period; there was sort of an artifice of clothing. But I think that adds a level of resonance for Reynolds Woodcock. Also, he has these visions of his mother and he learned his craft from his mother. The choices of materials and the way they're worked are kind of old-fashioned, so you see down the road that he's going the way of the dodo a little bit too. I had a complete backstory for who Reynolds was, where his designs came from, and where they were gonna be going.

I love that when Alma gets married she doesn't wear a wedding dress. That's obviously something that's in the script, but can you just talk about what she's wearing for that scene? Well, it's interesting that you say that because it was something I did as an homage to Helen Rose, who was a designer of incredible musicals for the last years of MGM. And it's very much a riff on Grace Kelly's civil ceremony suit that she wore when she married Prince Rainier. Legally we couldn't copy it exactly, but it had a lot of the DNA of that dress, and people are aware of it, certainly costume people. I felt like she wouldn't wear a wedding dress because they were going to have a civil ceremony. I think Daniel picked that oyster color; I picked that sort of sun-tan blush lace colour. So everyone was on board with doing some kind of a riff on a cocktail suit or wedding suit.

Grace Kelly marries Prince Rainier at a civil ceremony at the Royal Palace, Monaco, 1956

VICKY KRIEPS

Born in Luxembourg and trained in Zurich, Switzerland, Vicky Krieps appeared in several European films and Joe Wright's 2011 action thriller *Hanna* before being cast in *Phantom Thread* as Alma Elson.

How much of Paul Thomas Anderson's work had you seen when you were first starting out as an actor? I went to the Cinémathèque in Luxembourg, so I was like a film buff or whatever—something like a "cinephile." I did know his movies, but I didn't know that they were all from the same person. For me a movie was more like a phenomenon that happened. And I didn't go on the internet and look up who the person is and what else he had done. The biggest impact that one of his films had had on me was the love movie—you know, with Adam Sandler?

Punch-Drunk Love? Yes, *Punch-Drunk Love!* I saw that in the cinema and I remember it really hit me. Probably because I wasn't expecting it or whatever. Also because it was so strange in a special way that I've never seen before. Strangely enough, I connected to all of his movies—even *The Master,* which I didn't quite get the whole universe of it, you know, not being American. I kind of knew about Scientology but I think if you're American you feel closer to it. I was also very impressed by *Inherent Vice.* I love Joaquin Phoenix and I loved his character. Interestingly enough, *There Will Be Blood* was the one that I connected to least. Which is very funny, because I think it has a lot to do with Daniel Day-Lewis, the extreme to which he plays his roles, the aggressiveness, you know? It was too much for me, I think. When I watched *There Will Be Blood,* I could see it was a good movie, but emotionally I was closed because it was too violent for me.

When you were beginning to act, how much was filmgoing part of your craft? Were there performers or actors you would seek out? Were there performances that you found yourself deconstructing while watching? Or was going to the movies and watching films separate from what you felt you were trying to do yourself? I think I was too unaware, too unconscious about myself to be able to make these connections. Since the age of eight probably I wanted to play, I think it was a deep inner passion, a wish or a will. But I'm not coming from a family where people act or people are doing this. I think I thought it to be too strange, or even more so too fancy. I saw someone being an actor as someone who comes from Paris or London or New York, but not Luxembourg. You know, I felt like a peasant compared to an actor. I think this is why I didn't allow myself to make this connection.

Now that I look back, I can see that I had a huge connection to some of the performances I've seen. I think the biggest performing shock that I had was *Breaking the Waves.* Because it was something that during the first time, I couldn't detect whether it was true or not. Was I watching a performance or was I watching someone be crazy for real? And the tears were so real, and the crying was real. I couldn't make something concrete about it, but I was completely swept away by that movie.

Maybe that has something to do with why you loved *Punch-Drunk Love* so much too, because Anderson obviously cast Emily Watson in that off the back of *Breaking the Waves.* Yes, exactly. I see a connection. There's also a funny connection between me and Paul that we like to joke about. He saw my movie, which was a very small German movie—no one saw it; I was very sad about it because I thought it was an interesting film. But anyway, he saw it, of all people, and that's how I got into the casting process, because I was not one of the girls you would pick. I was not on these lists, you see. I was an actress and I was doing my thing, but I was not one of the ones you would propose to international people. I was too quiet in my corner. So it's really because he saw my movie, which is my favorite part of the whole story of how I came to be in *Phantom Thread.*

People always told me that you have to go to these parties and shake hands and do all of this game, which I was not interested in. I always told myself, either it's going to work the way I wanted to, or it's not going to work, and then I'll just do something else. Later I said to Paul, "But why did you watch that movie?" Because no one watched the movie! And he said, "I don't know, I was interested by the poster." And I said, "Yeah, but why were you interested?" He said, "I don't know, because of your face!" And I said, "Yeah, but why?" And he was like, "I don't know, I think I have seen you before." So I said, "But where? It's impossible!" And then we came to the realization that he had seen Philip Seymour Hoffman's last movie, which was *A Most Wanted Man.*

Of course. I play a very small role. What I remember from playing it was that my main goal for this part was to be seen through; I tried to not be recognizable. So Paul said, "Well, it must be this movie." And I'm like, "But it's not possible." Something that we laughed about was that maybe it was Philip Seymour Hoffman—who I liked a lot during the shoot—who put us together. Maybe it was his plan that Paul would see my next movie.

The first time I saw *Phantom Thread* I was thinking of all the women in *The Master*; they all sort of resemble each other. And when I saw *Phantom Thread,* I hadn't seen you in a film before, so all I had to go on was that you were this new actor, but part of me thought, "She looks a little bit like the women in *The Master.*" It's interesting. I think all things, I don't like to put too much importance on things, but obviously somehow everything is connected. Somehow going in circles, you know?

Something else about your performance that struck me is how changeable Alma is. I don't mean that she's adaptable, or that she's resourceful or a survivor, but physically she looks very different from scene to scene—it's a quality you have as an actor that in your own movie you seem to shape-shift a bit. What I can say from playing this character is: The only thing I gave her in the beginning and the moments when I was alone, which grew smaller and smaller as I grew more into the story, was a sort of openness. She was so open that I became dizzy. It felt like going to the edge of a window and then leaning out of it—just so far that you don't fall, but you have the feeling that you might fall. I think by entering it so empty I was changeable. I could change by a whisker. If a bit of wind went by, I would move like a leaf. Or if the light was changing, I could feel my emotions change, and I think my body too was always adapting to what there was. Especially to Reynolds.

Philip Seymour Hoffman was a shape-shifting actor, but when he showed up in a movie you know it's him and you know he's capable of being good. When you show up in *Phantom Thread*, two things which happen right in a row really struck me: The way you stumble, and the blush, which is not acting. Yeah, of course it's not acting.

You turn purple! I don't know how early in the shooting that was, but what an entrance. Since I started acting I kept saying, "Please, please can we get rid of makeup?" but not really knowing why. People looked at me like, "Who are you? Why do you want to do it differently?" Paul was the first person who listened to me. I said to him, "Please, at least for the beginning—I mean she's working in a restaurant, she has no money and it's obviously a working-class situation. Can you please have her without make-up?" So the way you see me in this scene is the way I woke up in the morning: There's no hair, no make-up. I didn't even have a mirror before being filmed. Most of the time you don't see an actor blushing because there's so much make-up. I always found it very sad, I never understood why we had to put on all this make-up.

It's unforgettable. I am a person who blushes! And the other thing is, I was absolutely ready to fail. I didn't come into the shoot ready to impress with my acting. I came in and I was really ready for everything to happen and I was ready to fail. And of course I stumbled, I stumbled very easily on these wooden plates they put down for the camera to move on. But the nice thing is that I didn't stop my acting, it was just part of the scene. And my blushing was not because of having stumbled in front of the crew, but because of Daniel. Him seeing me, that's why I blushed.

It feels like even in that moment, before anything else passes between these two characters, it's going to be this monumental duet and dance and relationship. Especially because, how I view the film, you palpably seem to become stronger. It's very unexpected because in a movie like *Rebecca*, which some people have compared *Phantom Thread* to, Joan Fontaine is quiet and cowed and confused for almost the whole thing. It's a great performance, but you're stronger. Yes, exactly. Paul told me that the only reference I had was Rebecca. And when I read the script for the first time, that's how I read it. She was a victim, and there were other things—there was a mean housekeeper who's not there in the final film. Played differently, I think it would have also been a great movie, but it would have been more like

a story of revenge. She would've been a victim, then out of her suffering she suddenly starts poisoning him. But because I was me, and Paul let me be me, I was stronger than expected, or what was written in the script. And that's what Paul is interested in—he doesn't want anything as it is in the script, he's more interested in what's going to happen now. The way I acted—it has to do with what you said, of my body being so changeable, because someone being changeable is unexpected and incalculable, and that can make you be afraid. I think Reynolds becomes afraid of Alma because she becomes so unreadable.

I love how often it's about who gets the last word, even in the beginning. When Reynolds says, "Stand normally," and you say, "You didn't say that, you said stand straight; that doesn't mean the same thing." There's so much in there about how rigid and controlling he is— but also, Alma's just met him, she's at his house in her underwear, his sister is sitting there and you still insist on getting the last word and it's hilarious. I know, and that's an exact mix of my interpretation and me being me. It was in me and so strong, I couldn't just stand there. So all these things that came out were just my way of trying to deal with it, because it was so hard for me. Even now, you can see sometimes that I try and have the last word, but in the end I do stand still. But for someone like me, with my kind of character, it was torture—I never would have expected that I managed to do this whole movie. It was very stressful, every evening I was completely exhausted because I had to stand and say yes and not reply, be nice. I could've just replied all the time, you know. This is, I think, what you can feel because sometimes it slipped out of me and I said a word, and he came with the next one and then I stayed quiet. Which is a lot for me. Usually, from where I come from, I'm very straightforward. I like to not be quiet.

What's interesting is that, even though we don't know a lot about Alma's backstory, it's so clear— in terms of class, money, nationality—where she might've been during the war; the possible suggestion that she's German-Jewish; that this is someone who may be very frustrated with being told what to do and saying yes, even in this relatively safe place. You must say yes a hundred times in this movie. But they're all different. Yes. And my decision was—and you can see this in the movie—every single yes I say with all of my heart. Whenever I was saying yes, I was opening the windows of the universe and saying, "Of course I'm going to say yes and give you my love, but what is this game? This is my heart, this is my "yes", this is who I am and who we all are." Every time I say yes my voice almost trembles. It went into a frequency that I usually don't use in my normal life. I could see it happen, and now when I see the movie I think it's so crazy. Every yes is a certain type of yes, almost like saying, "I love you."

You bring a lot of different feelings out of that word, and of course it has to do with context and how the relationship is formed. But in the scene when you make Reynolds dinner, the dialogue is so funny: "Do you have a gun?"

"Are you here to ruin my evening?" As you say, from the beginning I try and have the last word, and in this scene, for a split second, he gives me the last word. It's after I talk, he suddenly looks at me and I remember inside I was triumphant, like, "Oh yes, he's quiet." But then he goes on and he completely destroys me. And I didn't know what to say.

Alma seems so terrified at that moment. Because what Reynolds says to her is so scary: "Why don't you fuck off back to where you came from?" And he knew that. And eventually Paul knew. So in this scene, what I said to him was improvisational. Daniel is someone who is very open, but he would always stick to the text. If he changes it, he'll change it in the morning at the last moment. I'm the opposite; I like to use the script as loose material, I improvise and then I go back to it, and then I improvise again. Maybe it's because I have no big difficulties remembering lines, I have a photographic memory so it's easy for me.

In this scene, I couldn't take it anymore, I knew it would happen at some point and it's obvious it happened at this point. But then what I say to him, "You and your world and your people," that's me talking to him more than Alma to Reynolds. Which, at this stage of shooting, kind of became the thing, of her letting her say what she wants. So Daniel's reaction was one he had to adapt because what I had said was improvised. This is why he's suddenly quiet, before he then goes and— with all of his power of being an older actor with everything he's done—destroys me. When I asked Paul about it later, I said, "You must have known; the scene always felt like it had no ending to me." And he said, "You're right, I didn't give it an ending and I was kind of hoping for this." I think it's genius, it's why Paul is a genius.

These eruptive exchanges in his movies, they're so much more natural and organic than they were at the beginning of his career. It's something about the way he works with actors. I used to find myself thinking, "Oh, here is the big moment, how is he going to find his way out of it?" But in *The Master* or *Phantom Thread*, I'm not thinking about it as artifice anymore. It feels, within the context of the movie, so real. Even the way your language in that scene fails you a bit, you know? Yes, which is why it's so perfect. I'm so thankful for Paul writing it this way and being so brave and letting it have no ending even though it was a big scene. And then also for Daniel being such a good actor, to be able to do this. He created this space where I was able to do what I did—I might have done it with another actor, maybe, but what he does and what you see in his eyes as he's realizing, "She just improvised;" it's only half a second and then he's back on his track, like a master. And he hits back so precisely.

I love the idea that Alma doesn't actually want to take over anything. She doesn't want to take over the house, she doesn't want to run the business, she doesn't want to be the designer, she doesn't even want to punish him. It's like this radical submission, she wants to

be Mrs. Woodcock and be married to him and start a family. She needs to control him so that she can be his loving wife. In a different movie there would have to be something very politically correct about it. But her motives are so true to her, and her life and the period. She just wants to be safe and have a family. This is, for me, the most important part of the movie. Because I'm a woman and now everybody talks about it. What I'm most proud about is that I was crazy enough to do my own thing. I created something of a woman which is not a woman.

She's a woman—very feminine—but something in the way she moves and acts becomes so neutral that is out of the masculine and the feminine game. Which is what I think also moves people, especially women who watch the movie. You can watch her like a creature or like a human being; it's not watching a woman being seductive, or a woman being submissive or taking revenge. I tried to make her very human and true; this I took from Paul's writing and the way he wrote—it was like a poem, it moved me like Emily Dickinson, I don't know why. I tried to go to this place of pure love, you know. It sounds very cheesy, but that's what I tried.

The other thing was that I tried to understand who this woman is. Because I didn't get much from the script, I created a backstory for myself and tried to understand what it means to be a woman in the fifties. And then I understood that she was seventeen in the forties—okay, what does that mean? So she was seven in the thirties, etc. And then I thought of the war and my grandmothers and all the women I knew of this time. These women were just so simple in that all they wanted was to be married and to have a life, a husband. But, in the same way, they were stronger than anything I know. They were carrying the War, the victims, and they were still able to choose these little visions of hope and have fantasies about just having a life and a family, and a son and a daughter and making a nice meal. This is, I think, why it was important for Alma to be so conventional.

Which is why when her fantasies come at the end, the context is so outrageous. Because we've seen her poisoning him, and we've also seen some of her cruelty, but the things she wants sound so peaceful and so modest. Alma is the voice of the movie from the beginning, and it frames everything: Her love for him, and his demandingness. Completely. Her love is unconditional, and I think it's love that not many people are capable of. In a way she's in love with a monster—not a very bad monster, but I got close to it and it was pretty bad. In the same way though, I completely understand why she loves him. It's like loving Jesus: In one way it's so big and in another way it's so weird and so strange, and almost too much.

In the New Year's Eve party scene, I find Alma in the middle of this bizarre, grotesque party— with the costumes and the dancing and the bear and the rocket ship—the most moving thing in the world. The fact that Reynolds stays up on the balcony at first; he doesn't want to join in, he doesn't want to stay. But Alma goes home with him; it's enough that he came. I don't know how Paul did it. Reading it in the script, it seems like a small thing, and then suddenly I was standing in the middle of all these balloons and everything. Standing there, my feeling was, "Wow! This is like a portrayal of life itself." You are one thing in the middle of all these beings and things, like a huge carnival of birth, all the time. Then if you're very lucky, someone comes and is looking for you, and then you go home with this person—of course you do.

I found with *Phantom Thread*, writing about it, I respond very much to the funniness of it. But at that moment, it ceases being funny. Then during your last monologue there's the shot of you guys at the ball after. It's very hard to tell if that's real or not, or if it's just what Alma is thinking. Well, you never know—I never know. I don't know if the end of the movie is how she wishes it to be in the future, if it's something that truly happens. I must tell you, whenever I watch the movie I discover more. I go a layer deeper. And Paul keeps his secrets to himself, which I think is so great. Sometimes I even wonder, because he has the voice in the beginning, are we dreaming? Is it all a dream? I really lose the sense of what is real and what is not, and I love that about this movie.

The Chambermaid German
poster, Vicky Krieps, 2014

Joan Fontaine, Florence Bates,
Rebecca, 1940

Philip Seymour Hoffman,
Vicky Krieps, and Daniel Brühl,
A Most Wanted Man, 2014

Afterword
Adam Nayman

The running joke in *Phantom Thread* about who gets to have the last word in the Woodcock household is, like most of the film's motifs, about control, premised on the idea that ending a conversation represents some small, provisional victory. The film's voiceover belongs to Alma, and her point of view so clearly shapes the story. As such, the closing monologue in which she maps her marriage onto some larger, cosmic continuum of time and experience—imagining not only the continuation of their union through earthly means of reproduction and parenthood, but also Reynolds's death and reincarnation as her lover in another life—can be taken as the last word on *Phantom Thread's* meditation on obsession and codependency. Except that the final desirous lines are ceded to her husband and his appetites. Here, Alma's lack of a rejoinder is telling; hers is a silent smile of assent, of agreement to a set of rules that, as designed by and for the players, conflate pain and playfulness in perpetuity.

Of all of Paul Thomas Anderson's endings, *Phantom Thread* offers the surest sense of equilibrium, as opposed to the morally wobbly outros of *Hard Eight* and *There Will Be Blood*, with their lonely, blood-stained patriarchs, or the uncertain futures awaiting the lovers in *Punch-Drunk Love*, *The Master* and *Inherent Vice*. Leaving aside the cynical, satirically inevitable money-shot payoff of *Boogie Nights*, its closest corollary may be the rapturous view of Melora Walters at the end of *Magnolia*, smiling through tears to signify the end of a bad night and the beginning of a new day. In 1999, that shot contained only as much pathos as the film preceding it could generate; twenty years later, Walters's close-up is affecting not only as a time capsule of the actor and the era but also as an inflection point in Anderson's career—the last moment before a seemingly shaky sidestep away from the epic aspirations of his early phase doubled as a balletic leap forward.

It's a fair bet that twenty years from now, *Phantom Thread's* coda will still seem perfectly measured as a matter of cinematic latticework. The overall shape of Anderson's career, however—and *Phantom Thread's* prematurely summative and uniquely self-reflexive place within it—remains open. In December of 2019, it was announced that the director would collaborate with Focus Features on his ninth feature, vaguely outlined as a "1970s high school movie" set in Los Angeles. The script's reported focus on a child actor, meanwhile, recalls the celebrity status thrust upon Stanley Spector in *Magnolia*, as well as the director's youthful industry connections, while simultaneously providing a reminder that childhood and adolescence have rarely figured directly as subjects in Anderson's cinema, filled as it is with stunned and stunted strivers and outliers; an inventory of overgrown kids whose pasts aren't through with them even when viewed at a distance.

The coming-of-age film, a genre necessarily preoccupied with rituals and milestones, is itself a rite of passage for personally oriented American filmmakers: Think *American Graffiti* and *E.T.*; *Fast Times at Ridgemont High* and *Goodfellas*; *Dazed and Confused* and *Moonlight*. From a certain angle, *Boogie Nights* qualifies, yet it's more of a piece with the rise-and-fall showbiz epic. Thus by returning to the primal scene of filmmaking career—the San Fernando Valley circa the production of *The Dirk Diggler Story*—Anderson is potentially and paradoxically doing something new inside what might be referred to as his comfort zone.

That wistful, lived-in familiarity with Los Angeles—of knowing what's around every corner—informs Anderson's set of videos for the pop group Haim, most vividly 2019's "Summer Girl." With its opening lyric "LA on My Mind," and good-naturedly exhibitionist concept, which finds the group's members consistently stripping away superfluous layers of clothing (including, hilariously and incongruously, a fur-lined parka) as they traipse through neighborhoods with the easy confidence of lifelong West Coasters, the clip bristles with civic pride. (Their G-rated striptease fulfills the title's seasonal prophecy). "Summer Girl's" subtle connection to the Mamas and the Papas's classic "California Dreamin'" brings to mind that song's extraordinarily moving use—via Jose Feliciano's tender cover version—in Quentin Tarantino's LA-set *Once Upon a Time. . . in Hollywood* (2019), a film that, no less than *Phantom Thread*, was received as a show of maturity for its congenitally adolescent director.

While promoting *Once Upon a Time*, Tarantino took a good-natured swipe at *Boogie Nights*'s authenticity, restating an apparently long-standing complaint about the look and characterization of Burt Reynolds's Jack Horner; later that summer, the two filmmakers did an onstage Q&A following a Directors Guild of America screening of *Once Upon a Time. . . in Hollywood* during which Anderson went out of his way to praise Tarantino's evocations of LA—specifically the montage of neon signs flashing to life scored to the Rolling Stones's "Out of Time" that heralds the bittersweet final act: "[You] took care of the neon signs in LA. . . . you stopped a minute to take care of that. Living in this city,

it's such a beautiful moment when that happens, when the sun's just gone down and the lights come on. . . it breaks my fucking heart, because you feel the inevitable coming."

Anderson's appearance on equal footing with Tarantino here, almost a quarter century after he was billed—not necessarily according to his wishes or best interests—as the (slightly) older filmmaker's inheritor, can't help but bring us back to matters of boys-club auteurism and the canon, as well as the nostalgic allure for the "good old days." If *Boogie Nights* and *Once Upon a Time. . . in Hollywood* share anything, it's a tendency to romanticize their mutual setting through rose-colored glasses, and to view subsequent periods or avenues of transition with anxious skepticism. (The shoot-out at Rahad Jackson's in *Boogie Nights* is modeled on the Wonderland murders, which were themselves reminiscent of the Mansons' invasion of Sharon Tate's Hollywood Hills home; a scene Tarantino rewrites as a counter-mythological intervention.) That both Anderson and Tarantino should indulge in such transparent longing—such overt California dreamin'—for an idealized past even as they stand tall over the Hollywood of the present (while still dwarfed, industrially speaking, by massive franchises on all sides) is what places and sustains them inside a film-brat lineage whose members have always cannibalized and sanctified their predecessors.

Where Tarantino's exhaustively annotated fantasias ultimately turn critics into fanboys, Anderson's allusions aren't as easily reconciled. For the former, history is always subsumed by cinema. With Anderson, it eludes or exceeds the terms of its own recreation, no matter how or elaborate: His later films are masterworks that don't quite fill their own canvases, drawing power from the negative space. I return to that shot of H.W. and Mary Sunday descending from the porch in *There Will Be Blood*, lost and found in an instant, out of time and inside it, the future rushing up to meet them, and it encapsulates the most remarkable thing about these films—the way that their vividness resides in what they can't quite show, in how they oblige us to weave necessary connective tissues out of phantom threads, to participate in some way in their completion. I'm finished.

Production Details

There Will Be Blood   The Master

THERE WILL BE BLOOD

Release date
December 10, 2007
(September 27, 2007
Fantastic Fest)

Budget
$25m
(estimated per IMDb and
Box Office Mojo)

Production company
Ghoulardi Film Company

Distributor
Paramount Vantage
Miramax Films

Cast
Daniel Day-Lewis
Paul Dano
Kevin J. O'Connor
Ciarán Hinds
Dillon Freasier
Russell Harvard

Crew
Writer and director
   P.T. Anderson

Producers
   P.T. Anderson
   Daniel Lupi
   JoAnne Sellar
   David Williams
   Eric Schlosser exec
   Scott Rudin exec

Composer
   Jonny Greenwood

Cinematography
   Robert Elswit

Editing
   Dylan Tichenor

Costume design
   Mark Bridges

Casting
   Cassandra Kulukundis

Production design
   Jack Fisk

THE MASTER

Release date
September 11, 2012
(September 1, 2012 Venice)

Budget
$32m
(estimated per IMDb and
Deadline, $30m per IndieWire)

Production company
Ghoulardi Film Company
JoAnne Sellar Productions
Annapurna Pictures

Distributor
The Weinstein Company

Cast
Joaquin Phoenix
Philip Seymour Hoffman
Amy Adams
Laura Dern
Ambyr Childers
Rami Malek
Jesse Plemons

Crew
Writer and director
   P.T. Anderson

Producers
   P.T. Anderson
   Daniel Lupi
   JoAnne Sellar
   Will Weiske
   Megan Ellison
   Albert Chi
   Ted Schipper exec
   Adam Somner exec

Composer
   Jonny Greenwood

Cinematography
   Mihai Mălaimare Jr.

Editing
   Leslie Jones
   Peter McNulty

Costume design
   Mark Bridges

Casting
   Cassandra Kulukundis

Production design
   Jack Fisk
   David Crank

INHERENT VICE

Release date
December 12, 2014
(October 4, 2014 NYFF)

Budget
$20m
(estimated per IMDb and IndieWire)

Production company
IAC Films, Ghoulardi Film
Company, RatPac-Dune
Entertainment

Distributor
Warner Bros.

Cast
Joaquin Phoenix
Josh Brolin
Katherine Waterston
Owen Wilson
Reese Witherspoon
Benicio del Toro
Jena Malone
Maya Rudolph
Martin Short

Crew
Writer and director
   P.T. Anderson

Producers
   P.T. Anderson
   Daniel Lupi,
   JoAnne Sellar
   Eli Bush
   Albert Chi
   Steven Mnuchin exec
   Scott Rudin exec
   Adam Somner exec

Composer
   Jonny Greenwood

Cinematography
   Robert Elswit

Editing
   Leslie Jones

Costume design
   Mark Bridges

Casting
   Cassandra Kulukundis

Production design
   David Crank

BOOGIE NIGHTS

Release date
October 10, 1997
(September 11, 1997 TIFF)

Budget
$15m
(estimated per IMDb and BO Mojo)

Production company
Lawrence Gordon Productions
Ghoulardi Film Company

Distributor
New Line Cinema

Cast
Mark Wahlberg
Julianne Moore
Burt Reynolds
Don Cheadle
John C. Reilly
William H. Macy
Heather Graham
Philip Seymour Hoffman
Robert Ridgely
Luis Guzmán
Philip Baker Hall
Alfred Molina

Crew
Writer and director
   P.T. Anderson

Producers
   P.T. Anderson
   John Lyons
   Michael De Luca exec
   Lawrence Gordon exec
   Lynn Harris exec
   Lloyd Levin
   Daniel Lupi
   JoAnne Sellar

Composer
   Michael Penn

Cinematography
   Robert Elswit

Editing
   Dylan Tichenor

Costume design
   Mark Bridges

Casting
   Christine Sheaks

Production design
   Bob Ziembicki

Art direction
   Ted Berner

HARD EIGHT

PUNCH-DRUNK LOVE

HARD EIGHT

Release date
February 28, 1997
(January 20, 1996 Sundance)

Budget
$3m
(estimated per IMDb)

Production company
Rysher Entertainment

Distributor
The Samuel Goldwyn Company

Cast
Philip Baker Hall
John C. Reilly
Gwyneth Paltrow
Samuel L. Jackson

Crew
Writer & director
    P.T. Anderson

Producers
    Robert Jones
    John Lyons
    Hans Brockmann exec
    François Duplat exec
    Keith Samples exec

Composers
    Jon Brion
    Michael Penn

Cinematography
    Robert Elswit

Editing
    Barbara Tulliver

Costume design
    Mark Bridges

Casting
    Christine Sheaks

Production design
    Nancy Deren

Art direction
    Michael Krantz

MAGNOLIA

Release date
December 8, 1999

Budget
$37m
(estimated per IMDb and BO Mojo)

Production company
Ghoulardi Film Company
JoAnne Sellar Productions

Distributor
New Line Cinema

Cast
Tom Cruise
Julianne Moore
John C. Reilly
William H. Macy
Philip Baker Hall
Melora Walters
Melinda Dillon
Philip Seymour Hoffman
Jason Robards
Jeremy Blackman
Alfred Molina

Crew
Writer and director
    P.T. Anderson

Producers
    P.T. Anderson
    Michael De Luca exec
    Lynn Harris exec
    Daniel Lupi
    JoAnne Sellar
    Dylan Tichenor

Composer
    Jon Brion

Cinematography
    Robert Elswit

Editing
    Dylan Tichenor

Costume design
    Mark Bridges

Casting
    Cassandra Kulukundis

Production design
    Mark Bridges
    William Arnold

PUNCH-DRUNK LOVE

Release date
October 25, 2002 Canada
November 1, 2002 USA
(May 19, 2002 Cannes)

Budget
$25m
(estimated per IMDb and
'The Numbers')

Production company
Columbia Pictures
Revolution Studios
New Line Cinema

Distributor
Sony Pictures Releasing

Cast
Adam Sandler
Emily Watson
Philip Seymour Hoffman
Mary Lynn Rajskub
Luis Guzmán
Robert Smigel

Crew
Writer and director
    P.T. Anderson

Producers
    P.T. Anderson
    Daniel Lupi
    JoAnne Sellar
    Dan Collins

Composer
    Jon Brion

Cinematography
    Robert Elswit

Editing
    Leslie Jones

Costume design
    Mark Bridges

Casting
    Cassandra Kulukundis

Production design
    William Arnold

PHANTOM THREAD

Release date
December 11, 2017

Budget
$35m
(estimated per IMDb)

Production company
Annapurna Pictures
Ghoulardi Film Company
Perfect World Pictures

Distributor
Focus Features (US)
Universal Pictures (International)

Cast
Daniel Day-Lewis
Vicky Krieps
Lesley Manville

Crew
Writer and director
    P.T. Anderson

Producers
    P.T. Anderson
    Daniel Lupi
    JoAnne Sellar
    Adam Somner exec
    Peter Heslop exec

Composer
    Jonny Greenwood

Cinematography
    P.T. Anderson (uncredited)

Editing
    Dylan Tichenor

Costume design
    Mark Bridges

Casting
    Cassandra Kulukundis

Production design
    Mark Tildesley

Acknowledgements

FROM THE AUTHOR

I should start by thanking JoAnne Sellar for her time as an interview subject and for connecting me with some of her and Paul Thomas Anderson's most important collaborators. My sincerest thanks to Robert Elswit, Mark Bridges, Dylan Tichenor, Jonny Greenwood, Jack Fisk, and Vicky Krieps for their candour, humour and insight. Josh and Benny Safdie graciously took time out from becoming deservedly famous to write my foreword—a mitzvah.

Masterworks is the second book that I've written for Abrams, and I'm grateful to Executive Editor Eric Klopfer for his faith in me to follow up one long, complex auteur study with another. This was also my second time around being edited directly by David Jenkins, a longtime friend whose commitment to his job as well as the happiness and well-being of the people around him is total. He's never once let me down: Maybe in the next life.

David and I were grateful this time around for the indispensible contributons of Adam Woodward, who took on an expanded editorial role and also served as our point person with PTA's camp. I wouldn't have written this book without the behind-the-scenes efforts of Clive Wilson, and there'd be nothing to look at without the work of Little Whites Lies's gifted team of designers and illustrators. Extra-special thanks to my new pal Tertia Nash for her gorgeous, intuitive chapter layouts, and also to my old friend Sophie Mo for getting things started on the design front.

For me, writing a book inevitably means talking peoples' ears off, and thank yous are due to those who listened and occasionally got some helpful words in edgewise: Michael Koresky, Danelle Eliav, Jesse Cumming, Mallory Andrews, Becca Moss, Courtney Duckworth, Soraya Roberts, Chris Ryan, Alysia Urrutia, Eric Hynes, Violet Lucca, Charles Bramesco, Sean Fennessey, Haley Mlotek, Mark Peranson, SImran Hans, and Kameron Austin Collins. I cannot understate the importance of the close reading and feedback that I received from Manuela Lazic (the best of colleagues, whose work on *Phantom Thread* is quoted in the text), Brendan Boyle (who told me what didn't work and was largely correct) Sofia Majstorovic (watch this space) and Madeleine Wall, whose input was so substantive and supportive that I even spelled her name correctly in these acknowledgements.

No longer to be found haunting the halls of Innis College, Anna Swanson and Adara Reid did wonderful work as researchers in addition to being good friends and gifted toddler-whisperers. A shout-out also to Innis's librarian, the endlessly accomodating Kate Armstrong, who helped to secure some important material; additional thanks to the staff of the TIFF Reference Library, as well as Brad Deane and consummate pro and Interpol superfan Lydia Ogwang for arranging my lecture on *The Master* at TIFF Bell Lighbox.

I never get tired of thanking the people closest to me: Sandy, Vesa, Matt, Suzie, David, Evelyne and, of course, Tanya and Lea: Being in love with them makes life no great mystery.

Finally, this book is dedicated to the memory of Kevin Courrier, who to my surprise didn't hate *Phantom Thread*, and who I keep close to me whenever I'm writing anything.

FROM THE EDITOR

A massive opening thank you to Eric Klopfer at Abrams for being the kind of editor and guide (intellectual, emotional, other) with whom you dream about working. The time he takes to supply sage reasoning for every suggestion and decision is more than appreciated, and makes this process a learning one—the good type of learning. Thanks to Clive Wilson, behind whose avuncular exterior is a cool-headed operator and diplomat who speaks reasoned truth to over-reaching power. A shout out to our friend Sophie Mo, designer of our previous Abrams/Nayman joint, *The Coen Brothers: This Book Really Ties the Films Together*, whose page layout prowess forged a working template for future projects. Thanks to Fabrizio Festa, Tertia Nash and Simon Hayes for taking the design lead on the project you're now holding—I think the results of their envelope-pushing efforts speak for themselves. A big wave of gratitude to all the illustrators and collaborators who accepted our mad design briefs with nary a batted eyelid and delivered work that far exceeded expectations.

Thanks to Hendrik Faller and Zach Sebastian for directing an amazing promo video for the book, and to Jess Duffy for helping to organise it by sourcing lots of strange items off the internet. Thanks to Max Copeman for invaluable research assistance and to legal eagle Alex Wade. Thanks to everyone at TCO London for general support and positive vibes.

And finally, thanks to two Adams: Adam Woodward for shouldering the massive load of helping to sculpt the entire editorial drive of the book, setting up interviews and fine-tuning the text; and Adam Nayman, powerhouse critic, academic, deep thinker, raconteur, and, we understand, pretty tasty basketball player. I remember seeing a video of Adam conducting a round-table review of PTA's *The Master* from when it played at the Toronto International Film Festival, and just being bowled over by the level of wit and insight he displayed. With Adam, there's always a sense that a film is a box to be unlocked, and he takes immense pleasure in cutting the most ornate and robust key possible to open that box and reveal the contents to the world. Adam—we hope this book does justice to your words.

Design Details

THERE WILL BE BLOOD

1890–1920

Lino relief print
Ink on paper

Sophie Mo
sophiemo.com

THE MASTER

1943–1950

Letterpress
Heidelberg press, Ink on paper
Zerkall 7625 Smooth 145 gsm

Hand and Eye Letterpress
handandeye.co.uk

INHERENT VICE

1970

**Flatbed scanner, Collage,
Screenprint**
Ink on paper

Tertia Nash
Lucy Davidson, K2 Screen Ltd
k2screen.co.uk

BOOGIE NIGHTS

1970–1980

Screenprint
Ink on cotton

Lucy Davidson, K2 Screen Ltd
k2screen.co.uk

HARD EIGHT

1990

Screenprint
Ink on baize felt

Lucy Davidson, K2 Screen Ltd
k2screen.co.uk

MAGNOLIA

1999

iMac G3 (1999)
Adobe Photoshop v5

Fabrizio Festa

PUNCH-DRUNK LOVE

2002

Blue biro
Ink on lined office paper

Tertia Nash

PHANTOM THREAD

1950

Embroidery
DMC Thread #193 on white satin

Niamh Wimperis
wimperis.co.uk

Bibliography

Andersen, Thom. *Los Angeles Plays Itself.* Thom Andersen Productions, 2003.

Alilunas, Peter. "'Shot Live on Videotape': The Televisual Era of Adult Film, 1978-1982." *Post Script*; Commerce, vol. 35, no. 3, Summer 2016, pp. 6–I.

Baron, Zach. "Paul Thomas Anderson on 'Phantom Thread', Daniel Day-Lewis, and Writing Obsessive, Difficult Men." GQ, www.gq.com/story/the-dark-optimism-of-paul-thomas-anderson.

Benjamin, Tammi, and Marc Mangel. "The Ten Plagues and Statistical Science as a Way of Knowing." *Judaism; New York*, vol. 48, no. 1, Winter 1999, pp. 17–34.

Bess, Gabby. "What It's Like to Be Hit on By a Pick-Up Artist." *Vice*, 19 Jan. 2018, www.vice.com/en_us/article/bjy3q4/playing-the-game-the-game-a-haunting-pick-up-artist-dating-sim-angela-washko.

Biskind, Peter. *Easy Riders Raging Bulls: How the Sex-Drugs-And Rock 'N Roll Generation Saved Hollywood.* Simon & Schuster, 1999.

Bradburn, Jamie. "Historicist: On the Way Home to Massey Hall." *Torontoist*, 5 Mar. 2011, torontoist.com/2011/03/historicist_on_the_way_home_to_massey_hall/.

Bradshaw, Peter. "Magnolia." *The Guardian*, 17 Mar. 2000. www.theguardian.com, www.theguardian.com/film/2000/mar/17/culture.reviews.

—. "Punch-Drunk Love." *The Guardian*, 7 Feb. 2003. www.theguardian.com, www.theguardian.com/culture/2003/feb/07/artsfeaturesl.

Brody, Richard. *The Astonishing Power of "The Master"* | *The New Yorker.* www.newyorker.com/culture/richard-brody/the-astonishing-power-of-the-master.

Brown, Donald, and Postmodern Fiction. "Inherent Vice by Thomas Pynchon." *Quarterly Conversation*, quarterlyconversation.com/inherent-vice-by-thomas-pynchon-review.

Brown, Lane. "Jon Brion on the Music of Punch-Drunk Love." *Vulture*, www.vulture.com/2016/03/jon-brion-remembers-punch-drunk-love.html.

Bruno, Nick. "The Art of Reinvention: Paul Thomas Anderson & His Influences – SHOOT THE PIANO PLAYER!" *Newsroom*, 14 Aug. 2015, nwfilmnewsroom.wordpress.com/2015/08/14/the-art-of-reinvention-paul-thomas-anderson-his-influences-shoot-the-piano-player/.

Buchanan, Kyle. "Love, Death, and Control: Paul Thomas Anderson on Making Phantom Thread." *Vulture*, 13 Dec. 2017, www.vulture.com/2017/12/director-paul-thomas-anderson-on-phantom-thread-mortality.html.

Calhoun, Dave. "Paul Thomas Anderson Interview - The Master - Time Out Film." *Time Out London*, www.timeout.com/london/film/paul-thomas-anderson-interview.

California Derrick. San Francisco : Edward S. Eastman, 1908. Internet Archive, archive.org/details/calderricl2sanf.

Canby, Vincent. "'Let There Be Light,' John Huston Vs. the Army." The New York Times, 16 Jan. 1981. *NYTimes.com*, www.nytimes.com/1981/01/16/movies/let-there-be-light-john-huston-vs-the-army.html.

—. *Review/Film Festival: Short Cuts; Altman's Tumultuous Panorama - The New York Times.* www.nytimes.com/1993/10/01/movies/review-film-festival-short-cuts-altman-s-tumultuous-panorama.html.

—. "The Manchurian Candidate." *Variety*, 17 Oct. 1962, variety.com/1962/film/reviews/the-manchurian-candidate-1200420234/.

Carson, Tom. "A Golden State: Paul Thomas Anderson's Secret, Sprawling, Multi-Film History of California." *Grantland*, 9 Dec. 2014, grantland.com/hollywood-prospectus/paul-thomas-anderson-inherant-vice-magnolia-boogie-nights-california-history/.

Carswell, Sean. "Doc, the Dude, and Marlowe: Changing Masculinities from The Long Goodbye to Inherent Vice." *Orbit: A Journal of American Literature*, vol. 6, no. 1, 15:00. orbit.openlibhums.org, doi:10.16995/orbit.484.

Cavell, Stanley. *Pursuits of Happiness: The Hollywood Comedy of Remarriage.* Revised ed. edition, Harvard University Press, 1984.

Charlie Rose - Adam Sandler & Paul Thomas Anderson Part 1. YouTube, www.youtube.com/watch?v=2z6PmQD47FI.

Chen, Phoebe. "How to Read a Fire: On Hitchcock's REBECCA." *Bright Wall/Dark Room*, 20 July 2018, www.brightwalldarkroom.com/2018/07/20/how-to-read-a-fire-on-hitchcocks-rebecca/.

Comella, Lynn, and Shira Tarrant Ph.D. *New Views on Pornography: Sexuality, Politics, and the Law: Sexuality, Politics, and the Law.* ABC-CLIO, 2015.

Corliss, Mary, and Carlos Clarens. "Designed for Film: The Hollywood Art Director." *Film Comment*, vol. 14, no. 3, 1978, pp. 27–58. JSTOR.

Cullum-Swan, Betsy. "The Alcoholic in Films: Self or Other?" *Symbolic Interaction*, edited by Norman K. Denzin, vol. 15, no. 2, 1992, pp. 241–44. JSTOR, doi:10.1525/si.1992.15.2.241.

Cunningham, Todd. "'The Master' May Win Awards, But It's a Box Office Loser So Far." *TheWrap*, 15 Oct. 2012, www.thewrap.com/master-may-win-awards-box-office-loser-so-far-60791/.

Dancyger, Kenneth. "EDITING FOR SUBTEXT: Altering the Meaning of the Narrative." *Cinéaste*, vol. 34, no. 2, 2009, pp. 38–42. JSTOR.

D'Angelo, Mike. *Boogie Nights.* film.avclub.com/boogie-nights-1798217059.

Dargis, Manohla. "Noir Days of Sun, Los Angeles Smog and Marijuana Haze." *The New York Times*, 11 Dec. 2014. *NYTimes.com*, www.nytimes.com/2014/12/12/movies/inherent-vice-directed-by-paul-thomas-anderson.html.

Davis, Edward. "Paul Thomas Anderson's 'The Master' Has A $30 Million Dollar Budget, Production Mostly Stonewalls NYTimes Article." *IndieWire*, 18 Apr. 2012, www.indiewire.com/2012/04/paul-thomas-andersons-the-master-has-a-30-million-dollar-budget-production-mostly-stonewalls-nytimes-article-111518/.

Denby, David. "Hard Life." *The New Yorker*, www.newyorker.com/magazine/2007/12/17/hard-life-2-2.

Dixon, Wheeler Winston. "Punch-Drunk Love." *Senses of Cinema*, 27 Feb. 2015, sensesofcinema.com/2015/cteq/punch-drunk-love/.

Dugdale, John. "Inherent Vice: Why Thomas Pynchon Is Made for the Movies." *The Guardian*, 16 Jan. 2015. *www.theguardian.com*, www.theguardian.com/books/2015/jan/16/inherent-vice-why-thomas-pynchon-is-made-for-the-movies.

Ebert, Roger. *Magnolia Movie Review & Film Summary (1999) | Roger Ebert.* www.rogerebert.com/reviews/great-movie-magnolia-1999.

—. *Punch-Drunk Love Movie Review (2002) | Roger Ebert.* www.rogerebert.com/reviews/punch-drunk-love-2002.

—. *Short Cuts Movie Review & Film Summary (1993) | Roger Ebert.* www.rogerebert.com/reviews/short-cuts-1993.

—. *The Long Goodbye Movie Review (1973) | Roger Ebert.* www.rogerebert.com/reviews/great-movie-the-long-goodbye-1973.

—. *The Master Movie Review & Film Summary (2012) | Roger Ebert.* www.rogerebert.com/reviews/the-master-2012.

—. *Hard Eight Movie Review & Film Summary (1997) | Roger Ebert.* www.rogerebert.com/reviews/hard-eight-1997.

Ehrenstein, David. "Shoot the Piano Player." *The Criterion Collection*, www.criterion.com/current/posts/927-shoot-the-piano-player.

Elkind, Sarah S. "Oil in the City: The Fall and Rise of Oil Drilling in Los Angeles." *The Journal of American History*, vol. 99, no. 1, 2012, pp. 82–90. JSTOR.

Everett, Cory. "'Inherent Vice' From Page To Screen: The 6 Biggest Changes From The Book." *IndieWire*, 15 Dec. 2014, www.indiewire.com/2014/12/inherent-vice-from-page-to-screen-the-6-biggest-changes-from-the-book-269172/.

Fairfax, Daniel. "A Zoomorphic Performance: Joaquin Phoenix in P.T. Anderson's The Master." *Senses of Cinema*, 13 Mar. 2015, sensesofcinema.com/2015/feature-articles/a-zoomorphic-performance-joaquin-phoenix-in-p-t-andersons-the-master/.

Fear, David. "Jon Brion: How I Made the Soundtrack for 'Punch-Drunk Love.'" *Rolling Stone*, 21 Nov. 2016, www.rollingstone.com/movies/movie-features/jon-brion-how-i-made-the-soundtrack-for-punch-drunk-love-129143/.

—. "Paul Thomas Anderson on 'Phantom Thread,' Daniel Day-Lewis's Retirement." *Rolling Stone*, 19 Dec. 2017, www.rollingstone.com/movies/movie-features/paul-thomas-anderson-why-i-needed-to-make-phantom-thread-127368/.

—. "Paul Thomas Anderson Reveals the Secrets of 'Inherent Vice.'" *Rolling Stone*, 15 Jan. 2015, www.rollingstone.com/movies/movie-news/paul-thomas-anderson-reveals-secrets-of-stoner-odyssey-inherent-vice-65544/.

Fennessey, Sean. "'A Whole Ocean of Oil Under Our Feet': 'There Will Be Blood' at 10." *The Ringer*, 22 Dec. 2017, www.theringer.com/movies/2017/12/22/16809404/there-will-be-blood-paul-thomas-anderson-10-years-daniel-day-lewis.

Figueroa, Dariel. "Meet Pickup Artist Ross Jeffries, The Inspiration For Tom Cruise's Character In 'Magnolia.'" *UPROXX*, 6 Jan. 2015, uproxx.com/movies/meet-pick-up-artist-guru-ross-jeffries-the-inspiration-for-tom-cruises-character-in-magnolia/.

Foley, Jack. *Indielondon.Co.Uk - Film - Punch-Drunk Love, Paul Thomas Anderson Q&A.* www.indielondon.co.uk/film/punch_drunk_love_q&apta.html.

Fort, Charles. "The Book Of The Damned." *Project Gutenberg*, www.gutenberg.org/files/22472/22472-h/22472-h.htm.

Foundas, Scott. "There Will Be Blood Is Anderson's Citizen Kane." *LA Weekly*, 26 Dec. 2007, www.laweekly.com/there-will-be-blood-is-andersons-citizen-kane/.

Fuchs, Cynthia. "Cigarettes & Red Vines - The Definitive Paul Thomas Anderson Resource: Interview: 'Hanging Around With Director Paul Thomas Anderson.'" *Cigarettes & Red Vines - The Definitive Paul Thomas Anderson Resource*, 1 Feb. 1998, cigsandredvines.blogspot.com/1998/02/interview-hanging-around-with-director.html.

Gleiberman, Owen, and Owen Gleiberman. "The 10 Most Overrated Films of the Decade." *Variety*, 28 Dec. 2019, variety.com/2019/film/columns/the-10-most-overrated-films-of-the-decade-the-master-skyfall-1203452706/.

Gleiberman, Owen, and Lisa Schwarzbaum. "Toronto Film Festival Review." *EW.Com*, ew.com/article/1997/09/26/toronto-film-festival-review/.

Goodwin, Christopher. "Cinema's New Boogie Man." *Sunday Times*; London (UK), 28 Sept. 1997, p. Culture 7.

Grierson, Tim. "Revisiting Hours: 'Short Cuts,' Altman and the Anti-'Life Itself.'" *Rolling Stone*, 21 Sept. 2018, www.rollingstone.com/movies/movie-features/stream-this-movie-short-cuts-727004/.

Hampton, Howard. "WHATEVER YOU DESIRE." *Film Comment*, vol. 37, no. 4, 2001, pp. 36–45. JSTOR.

Hann, Michael. "My Favourite Hitchcock: Rebecca." *The Guardian*, 7 Aug. 2012. *www.theguardian.com*, www.theguardian.com/film/filmblog/2012/aug/07/my-favourite-alfred-hitchcock-rebecca

Hering, David. "The Quietus | Film | Film Features | Old Clothes, New Europe: Phantom Thread's Hidden Histories." *The Quietus*, thequietus.com/articles/23989-phantom-thread-review.

Hitchcock, Peter. "Oil in an American Imaginary." *New Formations*, no. 69, 2010, pp. 81–97,2.

Howard, Alan R. "'The Long Goodbye': THR's 1973 Review." *The Hollywood Reporter*, www.hollywoodreporter.com/review/long-goodbye-review-1973-movie-1089809.

Hubbard, L. Ron. *Dianetics: A New Science of the Mind (Article) by Hubbard, L Ron;: STREET & SMITH PUBLICATIONS, ELIZABETH, NJ PAPER BACK BLACK* - Princeton Antiques Bookshop. www.abebooks.com/Dianetics-new-science-mind-article-Hubbard/8335691824/bd.

—. *Dianetics: The Modern Science of Mental Health - By L. Ron Hubbard*. www.scientology.ca/store/item/dianetics-the-modern-science-of-mental-health-paperback.html.

James, Sasha. "For the Hungry Boys and Girls: Paul Thomas Anderson's Official Pre-*Phantom Thread* Playlist." *TIFF*, www.tiff.net/the-review/paul-thomas-anderson-phantom-thread-playlist.

Jon Brion on PUNCH-DRUNK LOVE and the Hollywood Musical. YouTube, www.youtube.com/watch?v=o-kVU3XbeGM&feature=emb_title.

Jones, Kent. "Paul Thomas Anderson's The Master." *Film Comment*, www.filmcomment.com/article/the-master-paul-thomas-anderson-review/.

—. "TRIUMPH OF THE WILL." *Film Comment*, vol. 44, no. 1, 2008, pp. 24–27. JSTOR.

—. "What's Up, Doc?" Film Comment, www.filmcomment.com/article/inherent-vice-paul-thomas-anderson-joaquin-phoenix/.

Kakutani, Michiko. *Thomas Pynchon's 'Inherent Vice': Another Doorway to the Paranoid Dimension - The New York Times*. www.nytimes.com/2009/08/04/books/04kaku.html.

Kenny, Glenn. "Underneath the Bottle: 'In A Lonely Place' and Alcoholism on Notebook." *MUBI*, mubi.com/notebook/posts/underneath-the-bottle-in-a-lonely-place-and-alcoholism.

Koul, Scaachi. "Pickup Artists Are Still A Thing. And They Want You To Know They've Evolved." *BuzzFeed News*, www.buzzfeednews.com/article/scaachikoul/pickup-artists-manosphere-incels-the-game-mras.

Kreider, Tim. "Introducing Sociology." *Tim Kreider*, 3 Dec. 2013, timkreider.com/introducing-sociology/.

Laing, Olivia. "Sex, Jealousy and Gender: Daphne Du Maurier's Rebecca 80 Years on." *The Guardian*, 23 Feb. 2018. *www.theguardian.com*, www.theguardian.com/books/2018/feb/23/olivia-laing-on-daphne-du-mauriers-rebecca-80-years-on.

Lambert, Molly. "The Valley Plays Itself." *Grantland*, 8 Dec. 2014, grantland.com/features/paul-thomas-anderson-los-angeles-movies-the-valley/.

Lane, Anthony. *The Claustrophobic Elegance of "Phantom Thread."* Dec. 2017. *www.newyorker.com*, www.newyorker.com/magazine/2018/01/08/the-claustrophobic-elegance-of-phantom-thread.

Lattanzio, Ryan, and Ryan Lattanzio. "Listen to Quentin Tarantino and Paul Thomas Anderson Talk 'Once Upon a Time in Hollywood.'" *IndieWire*, 24 Aug. 2019, www.indiewire.com/2019/08/quentin-tarantino-paul-thomas-anderson-once-upon-a-time-in-hollywood-podcast-1202168301/.

Lawson, Richard. "'The Master' Fails to Make Us Believers." *The Atlantic*, 12 Sept. 2012, www.theatlantic.com/entertainment/archive/2012/09/the-master-review/323554/.

Lazic, Manuela. *Alma Matters: Modelling and Being in Phantom Thread | Balder and Dash | Roger Ebert*. www.rogerebert.com/balder-and-dash/alma-matters-modelling-and-being-in-phantom-thread.

Lehman, Peter. "'Boogie Nights:' Will the Real Dirk Diggler Please Stand Up?" *Jump Cut*; Berkeley, Calif., Dec. 1998, pp. 32–38.

—. "'Boogie Nights:' Will the Real Dirk Diggler Please Stand Up?" *Jump Cut*; Berkeley, Calif., Dec. 1998, pp. 32–38.

Leigh, Danny. "Megan Ellison, the Most Powerful New Force in Hollywood." *The Guardian*, 18 Feb. 2013. *www.theguardian.com*, www.theguardian.com/theguardian/2013/feb/18/megan-ellison-producer-the-master.

LeMenager, Stephanie. "The Aesthetics of Petroleum, after Oil!" *American Literary History*, vol. 24, no. 1, 2012, pp. 59–86. JSTOR.

Levine, Jon. "The Fall of the Pickup Artist." *Mic*, www.mic.com/articles/135918/the-fall-of-the-pickup-artist-inside-the-world-of-the-world-s-most-misunderstood-men.

Lifset, Robert, and Brian C. Black. "Imaging the 'Devil's Excrement': Big Oil in Petroleum Cinema, 1940-

2007." *The Journal of American History*, vol. 99, no. 1, 2012, pp. 135–44. JSTOR.

Lim, Dennis. *A Director Continues His Quest*. www.nytimes.com/2012/12/30/movies/awardsseason/paul-thomas-anderson-on-preparing-for-and-following-up-the-master.html.

—. "Paul Thomas Anderson, on Preparing for and Following Up 'The Master.'" *The New York Times*, 27 Dec. 2012. *NYTimes.com*, www.nytimes.com/2012/12/30/movies/awardsseason/paul-thomas-anderson-on-preparing-for-and-following-up-the-master.html.

Linville, Interviewed by James. *Billy Wilder, The Art of Screenwriting No. 1*. no. 138, 1996. www.theparisreview.org, www.theparisreview.org/interviews/1432/billy-wilder-the-art-of-screenwriting-no-1-billy-wilder.

Loesser, Susan. *A Most Remarkable Fella: Frank Loesser and the Guys and Dolls in His Life: A Portrait by His Daughter*. 1 edition, Hal Leonard, 2000.

Lopez, John. "Good Disintegration: Paul Thomas Anderson and Robert Altman's Special Relationship." *Grantland*, 11 Dec. 2014, grantland.com/hollywood-prospectus/good-disintegration-paul-thomas-anderson-and-robert-altmans-special-relationship/.

Lozano, Kevin. "Jonny Greenwood: Phantom Thread Original Motion Picture Soundtrack." *Pitchfork*, pitchfork.com/reviews/albums/jonny-greenwood-phantom-thread-original-motion-picture-soundtrack/.

Malcolm, Derek. *Short Cuts | Reviews | Guardian.Co.Uk Film*. www.theguardian.com/film/News_Story/Critic_Review/Guardian_review/0,,544570,00.html.

Maslin, Janet. *'Magnolia': Twists of Fate in L.A. Lives*. archive.nytimes.com/www.nytimes.com/library/film/121799magnolia-film-review.html.

Masters, Nathan. "When Oil Derricks Ruled the L.A. Landscape." *KCET*, 11 Aug. 2011, www.kcet.org/shows/lost-la/when-oil-derricks-ruled-the-la-landscape.

May, Sam. "The Long Goodbye: Robert Altman's Hooray for Hollywood." *Little White Lies*, lwlies.com/articles/the-long-goodbye-robert-altmans-hooray-for-hollywood/.

McCarthy, Todd. "Punch-Drunk Love." *Variety*, 19 May 2002, variety.com/2002/film/markets-festivals/punch-drunk-love-2-1200549551/.

—. "'Phantom Thread': Film Review." *The Hollywood Reporter*, www.hollywoodreporter.com/review/phantom-thread-review-1063279. Accessed 1 Feb. 2020.

McKenna, Kristine. "Cigarettes & Red Vines - The Definitive Paul Thomas Anderson Resource: Interview: Creative Screenwriting, Paul Thomas Anderson." *Cigarettes & Red Vines - The Definitive Paul Thomas Anderson Resource*, 21 Nov. 1997, cigsandredvines.blogspot.com/1997/11/interview-creative-screenwriting-paul.html.

Mendelsohn, Jacob. "Flatland | Robert Altman's 'Short Cuts' (1993)." *Bright Wall/Dark Room*, 2 July 2019, www.brightwalldarkroom.com/2019/07/02/robert-altman-short-cuts-1993/.

Millar, Iain. "Television: Get Thee behind Me, Ginger! ; FILM OF THE WEEK; Follow the Fleet Tuesday, 1pm BBC2: [First Edition]." The Independent on Sunday; London (UK), 31 July 2005, p. 29.

Miller, Jim. "Journey Through the Past." *Rolling Stone*, 1 Mar. 1973, www.rollingstone.com/music/music-album-reviews/journey-through-the-past-192717/.

Miller, Russell. *Bare-Faced Messiah: The True Story of L. Ron Hubbard.* Silvertail Books, 2014, avalonlibrary. net/ebooks/Russell%20Miller%20-%20Bare-faced%20 Messiah.pdf.

Modell, Josh. "Paul Thomas Anderson AV Club Interview." *Film,* film.avclub.com/paul-thomas-anderson-1798213013.

Moores, JR. "An Attempt To Explain The 'Difficult' Neil Young Records." *Vinyl Me Please,* 17 June 2016, www. vinylmeplease.com/magazine/a-handy-guide-to-the-difficult-neil-young-records/.

Morgan, Kim. "Inherent Vice | New Beverly Cinema." *New Beverly Cinema - The Premier Revival Theater in Los Angeles,* thenewbev.com/blog/2017/05/inherent-vice/.

Mottram, James. *Sundance Kids: How the Mavericks Took Back Hollywood.* London : Faber, 2006. www. torontopubliclibrary.ca, www.torontopubliclibrary.ca/ detail.jsp?Entt=RDM379346&R=379346.

Murray, Noel. *Robert Altman.* film.avclub.com/robert-altman-1798226806.
—. "The Dovetailing Music and Film Careers of Neil Young." *The Dissolve,* thedissolve.com/features/ interdisciplinary/94-the-dovetailing-musical-and-directorial-careers-of/.
—. "The Long Goodbye." *The Dissolve,* thedissolve.com/ reviews/1271-the-long-goodbye/.

Murthi, Vikram. "New Classic: Paul Thomas Anderson's 'Inherent Vice.'" *IndieWire,* 24 Feb. 2016, www. indiewire.com/2016/02/new-classic-paul-thomas-andersons-inherent-vice-124830/.

Nicholson, Amy. "Fifteen Years Later: Tom Cruise and 'Magnolia.'" *Grantland,* 6 Aug. 2014, grantland.com/ features/tom-cruise-magnolia-amy-nicholson/.

O'Brien, Geoffrey. "Pynchon's Blue Shadow." *The New York Review of Books,* 3 Jan. 2015, www.nybooks.com/ daily/2015/01/03/pynchon-blue-shadow-inherent-vice/.

O'Hehir, Andrew. "'Inherent Vice': Pynchon Meets Anderson in an Absurd, Glorious Search for Meaning, circa 1970." *Salon,* 12 Dec. 2014, www.salon. com/2014/12/12/inherent_vice_pynchon_meets_ anderson_in_an_absurd_glorious_search_for_ meaning_circa_1970/.

"Oil! By Upton Sinclair (Book Review)." *The Spectator; London,* vol. 139, no. 5172, Aug. 1927, p. 261.

Olsen, Mark. "Paul Thomas Anderson and Collaborators Unravel the Mysteries of 'Phantom Thread.'" *Los Angeles Times,* 21 Dec. 2017, www.latimes.com/ entertainment/movies/la-ca-mn-phantom-thread-paul-thomas-anderson-20171221-story.html.
—. "Paul Thomas Anderson Reveals Unseen Scenes from 'The Master.'" *Los Angeles Times,* 5 Nov. 2012, www. latimes.com/entertainment/movies/la-xpm-2012-nov-05-la-et-mn-paul-thomas-anderson-the-master-unseen-scenes-20121103-story.html.

Ortega, Tony. Blogging Dianetics from Cover to Cover | The Underground Bunker. tonyortega.org/blogging-dianetics-from-cover-to-cover/.

Perez, Rodrigo. "Paul Thomas Anderson At NYFF: 5 Influences of 'Inherent Vice' Plus Curated Clips & Films You Should Know." IndieWire, 5 Oct. 2014, www.indiewire.com/2014/10/paul-thomas-anderson-at-nyff-5-influences-of-inherent-vice-plus-curated-clips-films-you-should-know-271616/.
—. "'I Don't Consider That We're Dealing With A Cult' – Paul Thomas Anderson Talks About 'The Master'

At TIFF." *IndieWire,* 9 Sept. 2012, www.indiewire. com/2012/09/i-dont-consider-that-were-dealing-with-a-cult-paul-thomas-anderson-talks-about-the-master-at-tiff-106295/.

Phipps, Gregory Alan. "Making the Milk into a Milkshake: Adapting Upton Sinclair's Oil! Into P. T. Anderson's There Will Be Blood." *Literature-Film Quarterly,* vol. 43, no. 1, Jan. 2015, pp. 34-. Canada In Context.

Pinkerton, Nick. "The Master?" The Point Magazine, 15 Dec. 2017, thepointmag.com/criticism/the-master-paul-thomas-anderson/.

Poland, David. "Cigarettes & Red Vines - The Definitive Paul Thomas Anderson Resource: Interview: 'Boogie Man: Roughcut Q&A.'" *Cigarettes & Red Vines - The Definitive Paul Thomas Anderson Resource,* 31 Oct. 1997, cigsandredvines.blogspot.com/1997/10/ interview-boogie-man-roughcut-q.html.

Pynchon, Thomas. *Inherent Vice.* New York : Penguin Press, 2009. www.torontopubliclibrary. ca, www.torontopubliclibrary.ca/detail. jsp?Entt=RDM2504727&R=2504727.
—. V. New York : Modern Library, 1966. *www. torontopubliclibrary.ca,* www.torontopubliclibrary.ca/ detail.jsp?Entt=RDM172108&R=172108.

Rabin, Nathan. "Keynote: The Shining." *The Dissolve,* thedissolve.com/features/movie-of-the-week/243-keynote-the-shining/.
—. "The Beautiful Imperfection of Magnolia." *The Dissolve,* thedissolve.com/features/encore/696-the-beautiful-imperfection-of-magnolia/.

Radish, Christina. "Paul Thomas Anderson on 'Phantom Thread' & Developing the Film with Daniel Day-Lewis." *Collider,* 9 Feb. 2018, collider.com/paul-thomas-anderson-interview-phantom-thread-daniel-day-lewis/.

"R/FanTheories - PT Anderson's PUNCH DRUNK LOVE Is about Superman." *Reddit,* www.reddit.com/r/ FanTheories/comments/1ws7g6/pt_andersons_ punch_drunk_love_is_about_superman/.

Richardson, John H. "The Secret History of Paul Thomas Anderson." *Esquire,* 22 Sept. 2008, www.esquire. com/features/75-most-influential/paul-thomas-anderson-1008.

Sauvage, Pierre, and Paul Thomas Anderson. "Beware the Golden Fang! An Interview with Paul Thomas Anderson." *Cinéaste,* vol. 40, no. 2, 2015, pp. 18–22. JSTOR.

Scott, A. O. "FILM FESTIVAL REVIEW; Love and the Single Misfit In a Topsy-Turvy World." *The New York Times,* 5 Oct. 2002. NYTimes.com, www.nytimes. com/2002/10/05/movies/film-festival-review-love-and-the-single-misfit-in-a-topsy-turvy-world.html.

Seitz, Matt Zoller. *Inherent Vice Movie Review & Film Summary (2014) | Roger Ebert.* www.rogerebert.com/ reviews/inherent-vice-2014.

Shoard, Catherine. "Paul Thomas Anderson: 'You Can Tell a Lot about a Person by What They Order for Breakfast'." *The Guardian,* 1 Feb. 2018. www. theguardian.com, www.theguardian.com/film/2018/ feb/01/paul-thomas-anderson-you-can-tell-a-lot-about-a-person-by-what-they-order-for-breakfast.

Sickels, Robert C. "1970s Disco Daze: Paul Thomas Anderson's 'Boogie Nights' and the Last Golden Age of Irresponsibility." *Journal of Popular Culture; Bowling Green, Ohio,* vol. 35, no. 4, Spring 2002, pp. 49–60.

Silman, Anna. "A Relationship Expert Psychoanalyzes Phantom Thread's Twisted Romance." *The Cut,* 15 Jan. 2018, www.thecut.com/2018/01/dissecting-the-twisted-relationship-in-phantom-thread.html.

Silverman, Jason M. "'We May Be Through with the Past ...': Magnolia, the Exodus Plague Narrative, and Tradition History." *Religion and the Arts,* vol. 20, no. 4, Jan. 2016, pp. 459–90. brill-com.myaccess.library. utoronto.ca, doi:10.1163/15685292-02004003.

Sinclair, Upton. *Oil!* New York : Penguin Books. www. torontopubliclibrary.ca, www.torontopubliclibrary.ca/ detail.jsp?Entt=RDM804670&R=804670.

Slowik, Michael. "Isolation and Connection: Unbounded Sound in the Films of Paul Thomas Anderson." *New Review of Film and Television Studies,* vol. 13, no. 2, 2015, pp. 149–69. Scholars Portal Journals, doi:10.1080 /17400309.2015.1005378.

Sparham, Laurie. *Phantom Thread Review: The Most Surprising Love Story of the Year | Vanity Fair.* www.vanityfair.com/ hollywood/2017/12/phantom-thread-review.

Sperb, Jason. B*lossoms & Blood : Postmodern Media Culture and the Films of Paul Thomas Anderson* Austin : University of Texas Press, 2013. www. torontopubliclibrary.ca, www.torontopubliclibrary.ca/ detail.jsp?Entt=RDM3199542&R=3199542.

Stephens, Chuck. "THE SWOLLEN BOY: Paul Thomas Anderson's BOOGIE NIGHTS and Diggler Days." *Film Comment,* vol. 33, no. 5, 1997, pp. 10–14. JSTOR.

Strauss, Bob. "Paul Thomas Anderson Talks 'Phantom Thread' and Why England Is 'Not the Valley.'" *East Bay Times,* 12 Jan. 2018, www.eastbaytimes. com/2018/01/11/movies-paul-thomas-anderson-talks-phantom-thread-and-why-england-is-not-the-valley/.

Strauss, Neil. *HE AIMS! HE SHOOTS! YES!! - The New York Times.* www.nytimes.com/2004/01/25/style/he-aims-he-shoots-yes.html?

Swanson, Dave. "When Neil Young Took an Odd 'Journey Through the Past.'" *Ultimate Classic Rock,* ultimateclassicrock.com/neil-young-journey-through-the-past-album-released/.

Tatsumi, Takayuki. "Planet of the Frogs: Thoreau, Anderson, and Murakami." *Project Muse,* muse-jhu-edu.myaccess.library.utoronto.ca/article/522146/pdf.

Toles, George E. *Paul Thomas Anderson.* Urbana : University of Illinois Press, 2016. www. torontopubliclibrary.ca, www.torontopubliclibrary.ca/ detail.jsp?Entt=RDM3524680&R=3524680.

Twain, Mark. *The American Claimant.* 1892, Print.

"UPTON SINCLAIR OFF TO FIGHT FOR BOOK: Novelist on Way to Boston With His Son to Defend 'Oil,' Accused of Indecency. YOUTH, 25, WILL AID HIM Sinclair Sees Political Motives and Present Charge as Ruse — Will Appeal If He Loses." *New York Times,* 1927, p. 16.

Vogel, Steve. "John Huston Film about WW II Soldiers That Army Suppressed Is Restored." Washington Post, 24 May 2012. *www.washingtonpost.com,* www.washingtonpost.com/politics/john-huston-film-about-ww-ii-soldiers-that-army-suppressed-is-restored/2012/05/23/gJQA7LS3lU_story.html.

Westbrook, Donald A. "Walking in Ron's Footsteps: 'Pilgrimage' Sites of the Church of Scientology." *Numen,* vol. 63, no. 1, Jan. 2016, pp. 71–94. *brill.com,* doi:10.1163/15685276-12341409.

White, Armond. "A Guilt-Soaked Epic." *www.nypress.com*, www.nypress.com/news/a-guilt-soaked-epic-AGNP1020080109301099957.

White, Armond. "The Magnolia Syndrome The Magnolia Syndrome Two ..." *www.nypress.com*, www.nypress.com/news/the-magnolia-syndrome-the-magnolia-syndrome-two-IVNP1020000125301259980.

Woods, Travis. "Does It Ever End? | Inherent Vice (2014)." *Bright Wall/Dark Room*, 26 Apr. 2019, www.brightwalldarkroom.com/2019/04/26/paul-thomas-anderson-inherent-vice-2014/.

Worden, Daniel. "Fossil-Fuel Futurity: Oil in 'Giant.'" *Journal of American Studies*, vol. 46, no. 2, 2012, pp. 441–60. JSTOR.

Zacharek, Stephanie. "Phantom Thread Works Hard at Being a Masterpiece. But Is It?" *Time*, time.com/5075162/phantom-thread-movie-review/.

—. "There Will Be Blood" | salon.com. www.salon.com/2007/12/26/blood/.

Illustration

34 *There Will Be Blood* © Celyn Brazier

62 *The Master* © Sarah Maycock

96 *Inherent Vice* © Tavan Maneetapho

118 *Boogie Nights* © Laura Callaghan

140 *Hard Eight* © Simon Hayes

162 *Magnolia* © Alice Tye

186 *Punch-Drunk Love* © Tim McDonagh

214 *Phantom Thread* © Jaxon Northon

End Papers © Shyama Golden

Fleurons, Endmarks & Embellishments © Simon Hayes

41; 75; 88; 124; 142; 170; 191; 223
    Infographics © George Wylesol

Image credits

2 PictureLux/The Hollywood Archive/Alamy Stock Photo

6 Collection Christophel/Alamy Stock Photo

12 MUBI/Shin Katan

15 Everett Collection Inc./Alamy Stock Photo

17 MUBI/Shin Katan

20 MUBI/Shin Katan

22 TCD/Prod.DB /Alamy Stock Photo

23 Everett Collection Inc/Alamy Stock Photo

25 PictureLux/The Hollywood Archive/Alamy Stock Photo

28 United Archives GmbH/Alamy Stock Photo

37 *(top)* cineclassico/Alamy Stock Photo
   (center) Everett Collection Inc./Alamy Stock Photo

44 World History Archive/Alamy Stock Photo

49 *(top)* AF archive/Alamy Stock Photo
   (left) Pictorial Press Ltd/Alamy Stock Photo
   (right) AF archive/Alamy Stock Photo
   (bottom) Entertainment Pictures/Alamy Stock Photo

52 Collection Christophel/Alamy Stock Photo

56 TCD/Prod.DB/Alamy Stock Photo

60 Entertainment Pictures/Alamy Stock Photo/Alamy Stock Photo

67 Archive PL/Alamy Stock Photo

70 Photo 12/Alamy Stock Photo

77 *(top)* Pictorial Press Ltd/Alamy Stock Photo
   (right) PictureLux/The Hollywood Archive/Alamy Stock Photo
   (bottom) Allstar Picture Library/Alamy Stock Photo

80 Photo 12/Alamy Stock Photo

84 AF archive/Alamy Stock Photo

86 Everett Collection Inc./Alamy Stock Photo

87 Everett Collection Historical/Alamy Stock Photo

99 *(top)* Everett Collection Inc./Alamy Stock Photo
   (left) Everett Collection Inc/Alamy Stock Photo
   (right) Contributor: Everett Collection Inc./Alamy Stock Photo

102 PictureLux/The Hollywood Archive/Alamy Stock Photo

106 Everett Collection Inc./Alamy Stock Photo

121 TCD/Prod.DB/Alamy Stock Photo

127 *(top)* Everett Collection Inc./Alamy Stock Photo
    (right) Everett Collection Inc./Alamy Stock Photo
    (bottom) Everett Collection, Inc./Alamy Stock Photo

130 TCD/Prod.DB/Alamy Stock Photo

134 Photo 12/Alamy Stock Photo

147 *(top)* Pictorial Press Ltd/Alamy Stock Photo
    (right) Pictorial Press Ltd/Alamy Stock Photo
    (left) Everett Collection, Inc./Alamy Stock Photo

150 Moviestore Collection Ltd/Alamy Stock Photo

154 Allstar Picture Library/Alamy Stock Photo

158 Moviestore Collection Ltd/Alamy Stock Photo

175 *(top)* Moviestore Collection Ltd/Alamy Stock Photo
    (right) Photo 12/Alamy Stock Photo
    (bottom) Moviestore Collection Ltd/Alamy Stock Photo

177 Lebrecht Music & Arts/Alamy Stock Photo

178 Everett Collection Inc./Alamy Stock Photo

182 Everett Collection Inc./Alamy Stock Photo

185 Pictorial Press Ltd/Alamy Stock Photo

195 Entertainment Pictures/Alamy Stock Photo

201 Everett Collection, Inc./Alamy Stock Photo

209 CD/Prod.DB/Alamy Stock Photo

210 Everett Collection Inc./Alamy Stock Photo

213 Everett Collection, Inc./Alamy Stock Photo

218 Entertainment Pictures/Alamy Stock Photo

230 *(top)* Everett Collection Inc./Alamy Stock Photo
    (left) TCD/Prod.DB /Alamy Stock Photo
    (right) Everett Collection, Inc./Alamy Stock Photo

232 Allstar Picture Library/Alamy Stock Photo

235 Collection Christophel/Alamy Stock Photo

245 *(top)* Photo 12/Alamy Stock Photo
    (bottom) Entertainment Pictures/Alamy Stock Photo

249 Everett Collection Inc/Alamy Stock Photo

253 trekandshoot/Alamy Stock Photo

256; 257; 258; 259 MUBI/Shin Katan

263 PictureLux/The Hollywood Archive/Alamy Stock Photo

267 *(top)* Everett Collection Inc/Alamy Stock Photo
    (bottom) Keystone Press/Alamy Stock Photo

270 Collection Christophel/Alamy Stock Photo

272 *(top)* Everett Collection Inc/Alamy Stock Photo
    (center) Everett Collection Inc/Alamy Stock Photo
    (bottom) TCD/Prod.DB/Alamy Stock Photo

273 MUBI/Shin Katan

274 PictureLux/The Hollywood Archive/Alamy Stock Photo

280 PictureLux/The Hollywood Archive/Alamy Stock Photo

288 Calvin Thomas

FOR LITTLE WHITE LIES

Editor *David Jenkins*
Editor *Adam Woodward*
Art Director *Fabrizio Festa*
Lead Designer *Tertia Nash*
Designer *Sophie Mo*
Head of Books *Clive Wilson*
Publisher *Vince Medeiros*

FOR ABRAMS

Executive Editor *Eric Klopfer*
Production Manager *Denise LaCongo*
Managing Editor *Mike Richards*
Researchers *Adara Reid and Anna Swanson*

ABOUT THE AUTHOR

Adam Nayman is a critic, author and lecturer. He teaches cinema studies at the University of Toronto and is a contributing editor to *Cinema Scope*; he reviews films for *The Ringer, Sight and Sound* and *Little White Lies.* His books include *It Doesn't Suck: Showgirls*, from ECW Press, and *The Coen Brothers: This Book Really Ties the Films Together*, from Abrams. He lives in Toronto with his wife Tanya and their daughter Lea.

Library of Congress Control Number: 2020931032

ISBN   978-1-4197-4467-9
eISBM   978-1-68335-916-6

Printed and bound in China
10 9 8 7 6 5 4 3 2

Abrams books are available at special discounts when purchased in quantity for premiums and promotions as well as fundraising or educational use. Special editions can also be created to specification. For details, contact specialsales@abramsbooks.com or the address below.

ABRAMS The Art of Books
195 Broadway, New York, NY 10007
abramsbooks.com